Black LGBT Health
in the United States

Black LGBT Health in the United States

The Intersection of Race, Gender, and Sexual Orientation

Edited by
Lourdes D. Follins and Jonathan M. Lassiter

LEXINGTON BOOKS
Lanham • Boulder • New York • London

Published by Lexington Books
An imprint of The Rowman & Littlefield Publishing Group, Inc.
4501 Forbes Boulevard, Suite 200, Lanham, Maryland 20706
www.rowman.com

Unit A, Whitacre Mews, 26-34 Stannary Street, London SE11 4AB

British Library Cataloguing in Publication Information Available

The hardback edition of this book was previously catalogued by the Library of Congress as follows:

Library of Congress Cataloging-in-Publication Data

Names: Follins, Lourdes Dolores, editor. | Lassiter, Jonathan, editor.
Title: Black LGBT health in the United States : the intersection of race, gender, and
    sexual orientation / edited by Lourdes D. Follins and Jonathan Lassiter.
Description: Lanham : Lexington Books, 2016. | Includes bibliographical references
    and index.
Identifiers: LCCN 2016041508 (print) | LCCN 2016047826 (ebook) |
    ISBN 9781498535762 (cloth : alk. paper) | ISBN 9781498535779 (Electronic)
Subjects: LCSH: Sexual minorities—Medical care—United States. | African American
    gays—United States. | Gays—Medical care—United States. | Bisexuals—
    Medical care—United States. | Transsexuals—Medical care—United States. |
    Homosexuality—United States.
Classification: LCC RA564.9.S49 B53 2016 (print) | LCC RA564.9.S49 (ebook) |
    DDC 362.1086/640973—dc23
LC record available at https://lccn.loc.gov/2016041508

ISBN 9781498535762 (cloth : alk. paper)
ISBN 9781498535786 (pbk. : alk. paper)
ISBN 9781498535779 (electronic)

∞™ The paper used in this publication meets the minimum requirements of American National Standard for Information Sciences—Permanence of Paper for Printed Library Materials, ANSI/NISO Z39.48-1992.

Printed in the United States of America

I dedicate this book to all of the power-filled, passionate, and steadfast young LGBTQ/SGL young people of color who I worked with as a psychotherapist and who I have had the honor of interviewing as a researcher. If it wasn't for them, I would not be the kind of woman I am today.

—Lourdes Dolores Follins

This book is dedicated to all us Black same-gender-loving and trans people who continue to live our lives with dignity in the face of constant oppression that seeks to destroy us. I will continue to tell our stories. This book is also dedicated to my mother, Joyce Annette Lassiter, and father, John Mathis Lassiter, Jr., whose strength, sacrifice, and love keeps me striving to make the world a better place.

—Jonathan Mathias Lassiter

Contents

Preface   ix

Acknowledgments   xv

Introduction: For Us, By Us: A Manifesto of Black SGL
and Trans Health   1
Jonathan Mathias Lassiter

1   The Forgotten Intersection: Black LGBTQ/GNC Youth
in Juvenile Detention in the United States   11
Amorie Robinson

2   Black Bisexual Women's Health in the United States:
A Systematic Literature Review   25
Jonathan Mathias Lassiter

3   Uses of the Interstitial as Power: Black, Bisexual
Men Building Maroon Health   39
H. Sharif "Herukhuti" Williams

4   Resistance as Resilience: How the Black Bisexual
Community Keeps One Another Healthy   55
Della V. Mosley, Roberto L. Abreu, and Candice Crowell

5   Narratives of Health among Black Trans Men:
An Exploratory Intersectional Analysis   73
Tonia C. Poteat and Lourdes Dolores Follins

6   Balancing Act: Identity Management and Mental Health
among Black LBT Women   87
Siobhan Brooks

 7 Rainbows or Ribbons? Queer Black Women Searching
    for a Place in the Cancer Sisterhood   103
    LaShaune P. Johnson and Jane A. McElroy

 8 Status Quo: Intersectionality Theory, Afrocentric
    Paradigms, and Meeting the Healthcare Needs of Gay
    and Bisexual African American Men   121
    Dante' D. Bryant

 9 Identity, Sexual Identity Disclosure, and HIV Risk
    in Black Sexual Minority Men: A Conceptual Overview   137
    Rahwa Haile, Mark B. Padilla, and Edith A. Parker

10 Shades of Black: A Psychotherapy Group for Black Men
    Who Have Sex with Men   151
    Tfawa T. Haynes and Sannisha K. Dale

11 Effective Strategies Used by African American Same Gender
    Loving Men in Promoting Health and Well-Being   169
    Lawrence O. Bryant

12 Perceptions of Health: Self-Rated Health among
    Black LGB People   185
    Kasim Ortiz, Angelique Harris,
    Kenneth Maurice Pass, and Devon Tyrone Wade

Conclusion   203

Index   209

About the Editors and Contributors   221

Preface

Although the social and legal environments for lesbian, gay, bisexual, and transgender (LGBT) individuals in the United States have changed rapidly in the last twenty years, these changes (e.g., increased social acceptability, the 2015 Supreme Court ruling legalizing same-sex marriage, the repeal of "Don't Ask, Don't Tell," and local laws that prohibit employment and housing discrimination) have not led to improved health outcomes for Black[1] LGBT individuals (Burwick, Gates, Baumgartner, & Friend, 2014). In fact, while some Black LGBT individuals benefit from these changes, many members of these communities still face disproportionate risks to their physical and mental health. Despite marriage equality, Black female same-sex couples report household median incomes $20,000 less than Black male same-sex couples and are less likely to have health insurance compared to their Black different-sex counterparts (Kastanis & Gates, 2013). When compared to LGBT individuals of other ethnoracial backgrounds or heterosexuals of any ethnoracial group, Black LGBT individuals rate higher on measures of psychological distress, perceived stress, and co-occurring disorders (Balsam, Molina, Beadnell, Simoni, & Walters, 2011; Hughes, Matthews, Razzano, & Aranda, 2003; O'Donnell, Meyer, & Schwartz, 2011); have fewer financial resources (Kastanis & Gates, 2013); suffer higher mortality rates from diseases such as breast cancer, heart disease, diabetes, and HIV/AIDS (Institute of Medicine [IOM], 2011; Millet, Peterson, Wolitski, & Stall, 2006); have higher rates of alcohol and substance use in response to stress, and report greater concurrent discrimination based on gender, race, and sexual orientation (Balsam et al., 2011; Fredriksen-Golden, Kim, Barkan, Balsam, & Mincer, 2010; Hughes, Johnson, & Matthews, 2008).

In spite of this, many Black LGBT individuals demonstrate resilience, which Luthar, Cicchetti, and Becker (2000) define as a "dynamic process encompassing positive adaptation within the context of significant adversity"

(p. 543). Much of the literature on Black LGBT individuals is largely focused on the mental health of these communities (e.g., anxiety, depression, and psychological distress) and the public health issues they face (i.e., HIV/AIDS, smoking tobacco cigarettes). However, there are still knowledge gaps about the cultural realities, strengths, and protective factors of Black LGBT populations. Understanding how Black LGBT individuals overcome various biopsychosocial and spiritual barriers and lead healthy lives can help community members, researchers, and providers develop interventions and strategies to promote the growth and development of Black LGBT individuals and their communities. Utilizing both a resilience paradigm and an intersectional perspective that look for the protective factors and strengths of a community that is simultaneously impacted by multiple systems of oppression (Bowleg, 2008; Wong, 2011) offers providers and researchers more options for how to work with Black LGBT individuals and their loved ones.

In order to expand the conversation about Black LGBT health in the United States, this book is the first published text that solely focuses on the health of Black LGBT people. What also makes this text unique is that the authors—either in their chapters or in conversation with other chapters—describe both the risk and protective factors of these communities. More often than not, the LGBT health empirical and theoretical literature either refers to the healthcare needs of Black LGBT populations as an aside, utilizes very small samples of Black LGBT individuals (<30 percent; Moradi, DeBlaere, & Huang, 2010), or examines the behaviors that place Black gay and bisexual men and Black transwomen at risk for contracting HIV (Huang et al., 2009). As a result, one could assume that the health and healthcare needs of these populations are the same as the larger LGBT population, or worse, that HIV is the primary healthcare concern facing Black LGBT communities. In order to address this myopic approach, each chapter of this book is written from the vantage point that the intersectionality of anti-Black racism, heterosexism, homonegativity, biphobia, transphobia, and social class significantly and simultaneously impacts the lives and hence, the health of Black LGBT people (Bowleg, 2008; Follins, Walker, & Lewis, 2014).

In addition, this book will provide readers with both empirical research and insightful analyses about the protective factors that enhance the health of Black LGBT people as well as the various risk factors that negatively impact the lives of Black LGBT people. This book also goes beyond a "Black LGBT 101" in that it is assumed that the audience already has some familiarity with theories related to intersectionality, LGBT identity development, racial socialization, racial identity, and gender identity. This book also attempts to fill in the gaps by providing information about the health of subpopulations about which we know the least: Black bisexual-identified women, Black bisexual-identified men, and Black transgender men. Another aspect of this book that makes it stand out is the commitment to including the work of Black LGBT researchers and providers who are up-and-coming alongside those who are known in their fields. It has increasingly become commonplace for edited volumes of LGBT health and governmental reports about LGBT health to be comprised of the originators of the field, who tend to be older White men and others who may or may not be LGBT (see IOM, 2011; Makadon, Mayer, Potter, & Goldhammer, 2015; Meyer & Northridge, 2007 for examples). The editors wanted to give readers an opportunity to discover the work of Black LGBT researchers and providers who are newer and lesser-known.

As mental health professionals and behavioral science researchers, the editors not only have thirty years of experience working with and on behalf of Black LGBT people between them, but they are also members of these communities. As such, both editors have a personal stake in ensuring that community members, clergy, providers, public health officials, and students in the fields of psychology, public health, and social work have more information about the health of Black LGBT individuals. As authors, activists, and academics, the editors of this contributed volume have lived, learned, and studied what it means to be Black and LGBT in the United States. Our work in our communities, our experiences as members of these communities, and a review of the literature led us to believe that this book must answer the following questions: Which health conditions, besides HIV, disproportionately affect Black LGBT individuals and why? What new information is there about the health status of Black LGBT individuals? What are the health-related behaviors and beliefs of Black LGBT individuals and communities? Are there indigenous meanings and understandings of health, barriers, and resilience among Black LGBT communities? What kind of healthcare access do Black LGBT individuals have? What are the healthcare utilization experiences of Black LGBT individuals? What effective strategies are Black LGBT people already using to promote and maintain their health? Given that there is still much to be learned about the health of Black LGBT individuals in the United States, this book is designed to fill in some of the gaps and move beyond the current foci of the literature.

Despite our efforts to ensure that this volume had contributors from across the country, there were some challenges getting *enough* Black academics, activists, and providers who were either openly LGBT-identified or identified as same gender loving. While we were optimistic that we would be able to find authors whose work describes the health and well-being of most communities within the larger Black LGBT population, in some instances, it was difficult to find authors who could do so. With that said, we sadly acknowledge that there are voices, experiences, and perspectives that are missing from this volume: Black LGBT individuals over the age of fifty and transwomen. It is important to share that there were authors who were prepared to a contribute a chapter about these members of these communities, but were prohibited from doing so because of life circumstances (e.g., illness, enrollment in a highly regimented, federally funded fellowship, and other life disruptions) or the arbitrary and unnecessarily punitive rules of academia (e.g., book chapters do not count toward tenure, one must be overly productive in order to be productive enough).

While there are several books about LGBT health in general, there are currently no books specifically about Black LGBT health. Our book diverges sharply from the limited and pathology-focused perspective of Black LGBT individuals and communities, which are often taken by authors in general LGBT health texts. This volume is more comprehensive in that it includes groundbreaking research and theory related to all aspects of Black LGBT health (i.e., mental, physical, spiritual) and takes a holistic, intersectional approach in including risk and resiliency factors. It is our hope that not only does this book provide some answers and insights into the various factors that impact the lives, the health, and the well-being of Black LGBT people in the United States, but that it also leads to more questions and inquiry that leads to more conversations, program development, and research. The lives of Black LGBT people depend on it.

NOTE

1. This volume purposefully uses the US Census Bureau's definition of Black, "having origins in any of the Black race groups of Africa" (McKinnon, 2003) to emphasize the shared experiences of members of these groups due to their race.

REFERENCES

Balsam, K. F., Molina, Y., Beadnell, B., Simoni, J., & Walters, K. (2011). Measuring multiple minority stress: The LGBT people of color microaggressions scale. *Cultural Diversity and Ethnic Minority Psychology, 17*, 163–174.

Bowleg, L. (2008). When Black + lesbian + woman ≠ Black lesbian woman: The methodological challenges of qualitative and quantitative intersectionality research. *Sex Roles, 59*, 312–325.

Burwick, A., Gates, G., Baumgartner, S., & Friend, D. (2014). *Human services for low-income and at-risk LGBT populations: An assessment of the knowledge base and research needs.* OPRE Report Number 2014–79. Washington, DC: U.S. Department of Health and Human Services.

Follins, L. D., Walker, J., & Lewis, M. K. (2014). Resilience in Black lesbian, gay, bisexual, and transgender individuals: A critical review of the literature. *Journal of Gay and Lesbian Mental Health, 18(2).* doi: 10.1080/19359705.2013.828343

Fredriksen-Golden, K. I., Kim, H. J., Barkan, S. E., Balsam, K. F., & Mincer, S. L. (2010). Disparities in health-related quality of life: A comparison of lesbians and bisexual women. *American Journal of Public Health, 100*, 2255–61.

Huang, Y., Brewster, M., Moradi, B., Goodman, M., Wiseman, M., & Martin, A. (2009). Content analysis of literature about LGB people of color: 1998–2007. *The Counseling Psychologist, 38*, 363–396. doi: 10.1177/0011000009335255

Hughes, T., Johnson, T., & Mathews, A. (2008). Sexual orientation and smoking: Results from a multisite women's health study. *Substance Use & Misuse, 43*, 1218–1239. doi: 10.1080/10826080801914170

Hughes, T. L., Matthews, A., Razzano, C., & Aranda, F. (2003). Psychological distress in African American lesbian and heterosexual women. *Journal of Lesbian Studies, 7*, 51–68.

Institute of Medicine. (2011). *The health of lesbian, gay, bisexual, and transgender people: Building a foundation for better understanding.* Washington, DC: The National Academies Press.

Kastanis, A. & Gates, G. (2013). *LGBT African-American individuals and African-American same-sex couples.* Retrieved from: http://williamsinstitute.law.ucla.edu/research/census-lgbt-demographics-studies/lgbt-african-american-oct-2013/

Lewis, M. K. & Marshall, Jr, I. (2012). *LGBT psychology: Research perspectives and people of African descent.* New York, NY: Springer.

Luthar, S. S, Cicchetti, D., & Becker, B. (2000). The construct of resilience: A critical evaluation and guidelines for future work. *Child Development, 71*, 543–562.

Makadon, H. J., Mayer, K. H., Potter, J., & Goldhammer, H. (2015). *The Fenway guide to lesbian, gay, bisexual, and transgender health.* Philadelphia, PA: American College of Physicians.

McKinnon, J. (2003). *The Black population in the United States: March 2002.* Current Population Reports, Series P20–541. Washington, DC: The United States Census Bureau.

Meyer, I. H. & Northridge, M. E. (2007). *The health of sexual minorities: Public health perspectives on lesbian, gay, bisexual and transgender population.* New York, NY: Springer.

Millett, G. A., Peterson, J. L., Wolitski, R. J., & Stall, R. (2006). Greater risk for HIV infection of Black men who have sex with men: A critical literature review. *American Journal of Public Health, 96*, 1007–1019.

Moradi, B., DeBlaere, C., & Huang, Y. (2010). Centralizing the experiences of LGB people of color in counseling psychology. *The Counseling Psychologist, 38*, 322–330. doi: 10.1177/0011000008330832

O'Donnell, S., Meyer, I. H., & Schwartz, S. (2011). Increased risk of suicide attempts among Black and Latino lesbians, gay men, and bisexuals. *American Journal of Public Health, 101*, 1055–1059.

Wong, P. T. P. (2011). Positive psychology 2.0: Towards a balanced interactive model of the good life. *Canadian Psychology, 52*, 69–81.

Acknowledgments

I need to first acknowledge *Olodumare* (God), my *egguns*, and my *orishas* for guiding and protecting me in a country that does everything in its power to deny the humanity of and kill Black people, Black women, and Black LGBTQ/same-gender loving (SGL) people. I also have to acknowledge my mother, Dolores Follins (*ibae*), who raised me to be independent, taught me how to think critically, and encouraged me to read as much as possible. I would also be terribly remiss if I did not acknowledge the life-affirming support and validation of my brilliant, remarkably gifted, sharp-tongued, and witty co-editor, Jonathan M. Lassiter. Jonathan, you took a leap of faith and asked to work with me and I am forever grateful for your insight, your candor, and your awesome copyediting skills.

—*Lourdes Dolores Follins*

I would like to acknowledge my creator, the guiding force in my life that is a light unto my path and a lamp unto my feet. I acknowledge the people who came before me and courageously spoke truth to power, letting me know by their examples that I also had a responsibility to speak for those whose voices are too often muted. This book would not have been possible without the contributors who dedicated so much effort to this volume. I would also like to acknowledge my co-editor, Lourdes Dolores Follins, for being an inspiring light in my life and voice of encouragement.

—*Jonathan Mathias Lassiter*

Introduction

For Us, By Us: A Manifesto of Black SGL and Trans Health

Jonathan Mathias Lassiter

We, Black same-gender-loving (SGL[1]) and trans people, continue to speak although our voices are often muted by others. Refusing silence is essential to maintaining our health. Our story is one of resilience. It is a story of surviving and thriving in the face of forces meant to disenfranchise, delegitimize, and destroy us. Yet our experiences of disease are disproportionately popularized. These images of illness limit our health in that they constrict us into categories (e.g., "high-risk" regarding Black SGL men and transwomen; "invisible" for Black SGL women) that deny us agency and access to health-inducing resources. In these categories, our humanity is obfuscated and we are sentenced to death. As Black SGL and trans people who work within the healthcare system and as lay people concerned about our personal health, we must control the narrative about our lives and thus expand the notions of health and ways of being healthy. This manifesto highlights the ways in which Black SGL and trans people are resilient, the mainstream narrative of disease to which we are subjected, and presents demands for action that center Black SGL and trans people's voices and health in healthcare policy, research, and service delivery.

We, Black SGL and trans people, actively call ourselves into existence via self-definition (Bowleg, Huang, Brooks, Black, & Burkholder, 2003; Singh, 2013) in the midst of marginalization. We use various resilience strategies—cognitive, interpersonal, behavioral, cultural, spiritual—to affirm ourselves in a world that attempts to invalidate us (Follins, Walker, & Lewis, 2014). We approach the world on our terms and confront prejudice and discrimination in our social environments (Bowleg, Brooks, & Ritz, 2008). We push ourselves and those around us to move beyond the status quo (Bowleg, 2013; Wilson & Miller, 2002). We upset gender norms (Singh, 2013) and challenge restrictive ways of being (Bowleg et al., 2008) through our very existence.

Black SGL and trans people's resilience stems from personality characteristics, social support networks, spirituality, and racial pride. We are creative and generative beings who use visual and performing arts to express ourselves and elevate our moods in times of distress (Buttram, 2015). We are optimistic, self-reflective, adaptive, and use our challenges as catalysts for growth (Bowleg, 2013; Bowleg et al., 2003; Singh 2013; Wilson et al., 2016). Black SGL and trans people seek out social support from both biological and fictive kin, peers who share similar identities, and various social media networks (Reed & Mill, 2016; Singh, 2013; Wilson et al., 2016). Spirituality and racial pride are foundational sources of strength (Follins et al., 2014; Walker, Longmire-Avital, & Golub, 2014). Our spiritual and religious connections not only foster internal fortitude (e.g., meaning-making, hope, spiritual growth), but also provide external communities which we can use to access resources such as food pantries, employment services, and others who will listen to our challenges (Buttram, 2015; Follins et al., 2014; Lassiter, 2014). Racial pride and connections to Black communities are distinctly helpful in that they foster our self-acceptance and provide examples of how to navigate discrimination (Follins et al., 2014; Walker et al., 2014). The process of integrating our Black, SGL, and trans identities is a particular source of power that allows us to operate as authentic, whole beings with role flexibility and autonomy (Bowleg, 2013; Lassiter, 2015). We, Black SGL and trans people, struggle toward health even in the face of oppression. However, that narrative is often absent or downplayed.

The mainstream narrative of what it means to be a Black SGL or trans person in the United States is one that focuses on pathology. In many mainstream communities (e.g., white heterosexual-led organizations; predominately heterosexual Black neighborhoods; white LGB[2] and trans spaces), media outlets, and academic discourses, to be Black SGL or trans means to be a problem, *something* to be fixed. Black SGL and trans people are rarely regarded as whole human beings, but often are dissected and addressed according to some singular aspect of our being that is thought to be outside of societal parameters or contributing to some form of disease. Our myriad identities (e.g., Black, working class, genderqueer) are stigmatized and we are made to feel subordinate (Purdie-Vaughns & Eibach, 2008). We often experience intersectional oppression (e.g., gay racism, misogynoir, patriarchal transphobia, religious homonegativity; Boykin, 1996; Lassiter, 2015; Ward, 2005). Prejudice and discrimination impact our lives at the structural, interpersonal, and individual levels.

This multilevel marginalization has contributed to some of us adopting a view of ourselves as problems (Bing, 2004; Greene, 2002; Quinn et al., 2015). This *conceptual incarceration*—internalization of false ideologies that do not affirm one's being-ness and results in learned helplessness and personal reenactment of oppressive trauma (Nobles, 1986)—contributes not only to negative self-views, but also physical and mental health disparities (e.g., gynecological cancers, HIV, suicide; Institute of Medicine, 2011). Indeed, Black SGL and trans people face risk and marginalization in several domains of our lives, but that is not our whole story; it does not end there. Yet, we are often cast as the "face" of disease in outlets such as *The New York Times* (McNeil, 2013) and overwhelmingly in research accounts (McGruder, 2009). This master narrative—official and de facto scripts and policies that define what and who are deemed valuable and thus worthy of acknowledgement (Stanley, 2007)—restricts the image of Black SGL and trans people that is projected out into the world. This is because overwhelmingly, our stories as Black SGL and trans people are not told by us.

Stories of Black SGL and trans people are often filtered through the culturally biased lens of gatekeepers of various arenas (e.g., policy makers, funding agencies, researchers, board members of organizations and corporations) who are often not Black SGL and trans people. A survey of social media (e.g., #GayMediaSoWhite and #Whitefeminism on Twitter), television shows (e.g., Will & Grace, Looking, Girls), scholarly literature reviews (Delgado-Romero, Galvan, Maschino, & Rowland, 2005; Shelton, Delgado-Romero, & Wells, 2009), and statistics related to federal funding (Ginther et al., 2011) all demonstrate that Black SGL and trans people are systematically and systemically prohibited from defining and disseminating their own experiences in mainstream spaces. This has serious implications for Black SGL and trans people's health. Most journals do not include us in their health-related studies (Arnett, 2008) and when they do, they tend to focus on our genitals (Huang, Brewster, Moradi, Goodman, Wiseman, & Martin, 2010).

We are also often kept from obtaining positions that will allow us to become gatekeepers due to institutional discrimination (Harley, 2008; Kameny et al., 2014). When we gain the skills and credentials that allow us to focus on and better our distinct experiences as Black SGL and trans people, we are often denied the financial resources to conduct the work in academic (Ginther et al., 2011) and community spaces. For those of us who are able to finance our work, the final products are often deemed to lack scholarly rigor and merit (Turner, Gonzalez, & Wood, 2008). When we are able to get our work to people in Black SGL and trans communities, we find that financial barriers in economically strained organizations (Wilson & Yoshikawa, 2007) and lack of culturally sensitive personnel make it difficult to establish and sustain culturally specific treatment, prevention, and resistance initiatives. There is a dire need for Black SGL and trans people to help formulate and implement strategies that will move us beyond *conceptual incarceration* and focusing solely on narratives of risk. We need people who are not only Black, SGL, or trans by phenotype and identity, but who also possess deep cultural worldviews (Myers, 1987) that esteem Blackness and sexual and gender diversity. Such worldviews center non-binary thinking, collective ideology, non-material orientation, improvisational modes of being, and Black cultural expressions (Jones, 2003). Only then can we begin to craft holistic ways of being that is conducive to good health. Thus, I propose the following actions:

HEALTH POLICY

1. Modify current federal, state, and local anti-discrimination laws so that they not only focus on LGBT people in general, but also specifically address the discriminatory experiences of Black SGL and trans people who live at the intersection of racial and sexual oppression.
2. Craft and pass new federal, state, and local anti-discrimination laws to address not only discriminatory policies based on race and sexual orientation, but also economic discrimination such as unfair lending policies that exploit low-income people (who are more likely to be Black and SGL).
3. Craft and pass federal, state, and local environmental and trade laws that prevent organizations from outsourcing jobs and overburdening communities of color with toxins.
4. Create national pipeline educational programs that target and recruit Black students in elementary school to promote an interest in healthcare and health research careers.
5. Develop more targeted grant, scholarship, and culturally matched mentorship programs for Black SGL and trans undergraduate and graduate students pursuing healthcare and health research careers.
6. Make more systematic and systemic efforts to recruit, hire, promote, and retain Black SGL and trans people on federal, state, and local governmental agency boards, programmatic planning panels, and budgeting committees.
7. Allocate more long-term federal, state, and municipal financial resources to culturally specific health prevention programs and indigenous health organizations that are created and implemented in Black SGL and trans communities.
8. Finance calls for proposals at the federal, state, and local level that preference innovative approaches to culturally specific health treatment for Black SGL and trans people.
9. Provide federal, state, and municipal tax benefits and sustainability grants for health organizations and indigenous healers who provide holistic healthcare for Black SGL and trans clients.

HEALTH RESEARCH AND DISSEMINATION

1. Make more systematic and systemic efforts to recruit, hire, promote, and retain Black SGL and trans people on federal, state, and municipal governmental agency boards, programmatic planning panels, faculties, editorial review boards, and grant review committees.
2. Make university administrators' raises and promotions contingent on creating affirming work environments and career advancement opportunities for Black SGL and trans faculty at public and private institutions.
3. Create and require mandatory ongoing sensitivity trainings and evaluative programs for university faculty and administrators related to racial, sexual, class, (dis)ability, and other multicultural issues.
4. Educate administrators and faculty on a broad array of scholarly and non-scholarly research dissemination outlets and their importance to community work.
5. Modify tenure and promotion guidelines at public and private universities so that Black SGL and trans scholars' research is not penalized because it does not conform to mainstream academic topic and methodology preferences.
6. Administrators and faculty will place more value on research dissemination outside of mainstream academic journals to include books, book chapters, newsletters, and community presentations.
7. Federal, state, and local educational accrediting agencies and foundations will provide funding to promote development and sustainability of research training programs for Black SGL and trans students and junior faculty.
8. Federal, state, and local educational accrediting agencies and foundations will allocate funds to foster the creation of spaces for Black SGL and trans scholars to gather, collaborate with, and affirm each other.
9. Federal, state, and local educational accrediting agencies and foundations will finance Calls for Proposals that preference culturally specific research that utilizes resilience frameworks for Black SGL and trans people's health.

HEALTHCARE SERVICE DELIVERY

1. Federal, state, and local educational and health departments and funding agencies will provide funding for Black SGL health providers to build holistic healthcare facilities in Black communities that focus on the medical, psychological, economic, spiritual, and sociopolitical welfare of Black SGL and trans people.

2. Federal, state, and local health organizations will make more systematic and systemic efforts to recruit, hire, promote, and retain Black SGL and trans healthcare providers and administrators.
3. Public and private university administrators will make faculty raises and promotions in healthcare training programs contingent on creating affirming classrooms, educational experiences, and training opportunities for Black SGL and trans students.
4. Make healthcare administrators' raises and promotions contingent on creating affirming work environments and career opportunities for Black SGL and trans providers.
5. Create educational and health-related collaborations between healthcare organizations and Black-centered spiritual, religious, and other cultural institutions (e.g., Black sororities and fraternities) to provide services for Black SGL and trans people.
6. Healthcare organizations will hire and retain culturally sensitive consultants to train and consistently evaluate healthcare providers and administrators' cultural competency for working with Black SGL and trans people.
7. Healthcare providers will conduct holistic assessments with Black SGL and trans clients to determine the interplay of various sociocultural, economic, and other structural factors and their health.
8. Deliberately and comprehensively integrate cultural resources (e.g., racial, spiritual, gender, and sexual orientation-specific information and affirmation) into routine healthcare practices.
9. Encourage, center, and honor Black SGL and trans people's healthcare preferences in governmental and public healthcare agencies.
10. Integrate Black-centered indigenous forms of healing into the healthcare system.
11. Provide funding for to promote and sustain Black indigenous healers and healing centers.

Black SGL and trans people are not one-note people who only sing songs of oppression and disease. We are multifaceted, self-determined, and resilient in the context of environments that undermine us. Healthcare policy, research, and practice should center us as holistic, intersectional beings. When Black SGL and trans people are centered in healthcare policy, research, and services, we feel affirmed and are more likely to participate in indigenous and mainstream healthcare as providers and clients. This increased participation will lead to significant gains in our collective and individual holistic well-being. Healthcare policy, research, and practice should explicitly acknowledge our complexities and use resilience frameworks to work with us in maintaining our health (Herrick, Stall, Goldhammer, Egan, & Mayer, 2014). Black SGL and trans people should be at the head of the table when it comes to crafting policy, allocating funds, and disseminating work related to our health and lived realities. We must demand to speak for ourselves and cultivate spaces for us, by us. We must continue to recognize and support ourselves as people comfortably outside the status quo while countering the master narrative and shifting mainstream notions of who and what is valued. This manifesto is not suggesting that we turn a blind eye to the ailments of Black SGL and trans people. To the contrary, it is demanding that we focus on whole, intersectional Black SGL and trans individuals. Our humanity and health depend on it.

NOTES

1. "Same gender loving" was originally coined by Dr. Cleo Manago, the founder of AmASSI Health and Cultural Centers and Black Men's Xchange, to describe people with same-sex attractions and sexual behaviors in the Black American community. It is a culturally affirming alternative that Black Americans can use to describe their sexual orientation in a way that acknowledges the uniqueness of Black American life and culture instead of oft white-identified terms such as gay and lesbian or LGBT.

2. LGB is used here to note that the author is referring to white American lesbians, gays, and bisexuals. The author purposely did not use the term SGL because he is not referring to Black Americans—of which SGL is a specific cultural signifier.

REFERENCES

Arnett, J. (2008). The neglected 95%: Why American psychology needs to become less American. *American Psychologist, 63*, 602–614. doi: 10.1037/0003–066X.63.7.602

Bing, V. (2004). Out of the closet but still hiding. *Women & Therapy, 27*, 185–201. doi: 10.1300/J015v27n01_13

Boykin, K. (1996). *One more river to cross: Black and gay in America*. New York, NY: Anchor Books.

Bowleg, L. (2013). "Once you've blended the cake, you can't take the parts back to main ingredients': Black gay and bisexual men's descriptions and experiences of intersectionality." *Sex Roles, 68*, 754–767. doi: 10.1007/s11199–012–0152–4

Bowleg, L., Brooks, K., & Ritz, S. F. (2008). "Bringing home more than a paycheck:" An exploratory analysis of Black lesbians' experiences of stress and coping in the workplace." *Journal of Lesbian Studies, 12*, 69–84. doi: 10.1300/1089416080 2174342

Bowleg, L., Huang, J., Brooks, K., Black, A., & Burkholder, G. (2003). Triple jeopardy and beyond: Multiple minority stress and resilience among Black lesbians. *Journal of Lesbian Studies, 7*, 87–108. doi:10.1300/J155v07n04_06

Buttram, M. (2015). The social environmental elements of resilience among vulnerable African American/Black men who have sex with men. *Journal of Human Behavior in the Social Environment, 25*, 923–933. doi: 10.1080/10911359.2015.1040908

Delgado-Romero, E., Galván, N., Maschino, P., & Rowland, M. (2005). Race and ethnicity in empirical counseling and counseling psychology research: A 10-year review. *The Counseling Psychologist, 33*, 419–448. doi: 10.1177/0011000004268637

Follins, L., Walker, J., & Lewis, M. K. (2014). Resilience in Black lesbian, gay, bisexual, and transgender individuals: A critical review of the literature. *Journal of Gay & Lesbian Mental Health, 18*, 190–212. doi: 10.1080/19359705.2013.828343

Ginther, D., Schaffer, W., Schnell, J., Masimore, B., Liu, F.... & Kington, R. (2011). Race, ethnicity, and NIH research awards. *Science, 33*, 1015–1019. doi: 10.1126/science.1196783

Greene, B. (2002, Summer). Heterosexism and internalized racism among African Americans: The connections and considerations for African American lesbians and bisexual women: A clinical psychological perspective. *Rutgers University Law Review, 54*(4), 931–957.

Harley, D. (2008). Maids of academe: African American women faculty at predominately White institutions. *Journal of African American Studies, 12*, 19–36. doi: 10.1007/s12111-007-9030-5

Herrick, A., Stall, R., Goldhammer, H., Egan, J., & Mayer, K. (2014). Resilience as a research framework and as a cornerstone of prevention research for gay and bisexual men: Theory and evidence. *AIDS & Behavior, 18*, 1–9. doi: 10.1007/s10461-012-0384-x

Huang, Y., Brewster, M., Moradi, B., Goodman, M., Wiseman, M., & Martin, A. (2010). Content analysis of literature about LGB people of color: 1998–2007. *The Counseling Psychologist, 38*, 363–396. doi: 10.1177/0011000009335255

Institute of Medicine. (2011). *The health of lesbian, gay, bisexual, and transgender people: Building a foundation for better understanding.* Washington, DC: The National Academies Press.

Jones, J. (2003). TRIOS: A psychological theory of the African legacy in American culture. *Journal of Social Issues, 59*, 217–242. doi: 10.1111/1540-4560. t01-1-00014

Kameny, R., DeRosier, M., Taylor, L., McMillen, J., Knowles, M., & Pifer, K. (2014). Barriers to career success for minority researchers in the behavioral sciences. *Journal of Career Development, 41*, 43–61. doi: 10.1177/0894845312472254.

Lassiter, J. (2014). Extracting dirt from water: A strengths-based approach to religion for African American same-gender-loving men. *Journal of Religion & Health, 53*, 178–189. doi: 10.1007/s10943-012-9668-8

———. (2015). Reconciling sexual orientation and Christianity: Black same-gender loving men's experiences. *Mental Health, Religion & Culture, 18*, 342–353. doi: 10.1080/13674676.2015.1056121

McGruder, K. (2009). Black sexuality in the U.S.: Presentations as non-normative. *Journal of African American Studies, 13*, 251–262. doi: 10.1007/s12111-008-9070-5

McNeil, D. (2013, December 4). Poor Black and Hispanic men are the face of H.I.V. *The New York Times.* Retrieved from http://www.nytimes.com/2013/12/05/us/poor-black-and-hispanic-men-are-face-of-hiv.html?_r=0

Myers, L. (1987). The deep structure of culture: Relevance of traditional African culture in contemporary life. *Journal of Black Studies, 18,* 72–85. doi: 10.1177/002193478701800105

Nobles, W. (1986). *African psychology: Toward its reclamation, reascension and revitalization.* Oakland, CA: Black Family Institute.

Purdie-Vaughns V., & Eibach, R. (2008). Intersectional invisibility: The distinctive advantages and disadvantages of multiple subordinate-group identities. *Sex Roles, 59,* 377–391. doi: 10.1007/s11199–008–9424–4

Quinn, K., Dickson-Gomez, J., DiFranceisco, W., Kelly, J., St. Lawrence, J., ... Broaddus, M. (2015). Correlates of internalized homonegativity among Black men who have sex with men. *AIDS Education and Prevention, 27,* 212–226. doi: 10.1521/aeap.2015.27.3.212

Reed, S., & Mill, R. (2016). Thriving and adapting: Resilience, sense of community, and syndemics among young Black gay and bisexual men. *American Journal of Community Psychology, 57,* 129–143. doi: 10.1002/ajcp.12028

Shelton, K., Delgado-Romero, E., & Wells, E. (2009). Race and ethnicity in empirical research: An 18-year review. *Journal of Multicultural Counseling and Development, 37,* 130–140. doi: 10.1002/j.2161–1912.2009.tb00097.x

Singh, A. (2013). Transgender youth of color and resilience: Negotiating oppression and finding support. *Sex Roles, 68,* 690–702. doi: 10.1007/s11199–012–0149-z

Stanley, C. A. (2007). When counter narratives meet master narratives in the journal editorial-review process. *Educational Researcher, 36*(1), 14–24. doi: 10.3102/0013189X06298008

Turner, C., Gonzalez, J., & Wood, J. (2008). Faculty of color in academe: What 20 years of literature tells us. *Journal of Diversity in Higher Education, 1,* 39–168. doi: 10.1037/a0012837

Walker, J., Longmire-Avital, B., & Golub, S. (2014). Racial and sexual identities as potential buffers to risky sexual behavior for Black gay and bisexual emerging adult men. *Health Psychology, 34,* 841–846. doi: 10.1037/hea0000187

Ward, E. (2005). Homophobia, hypermasculinity and the US Black church. *Culture, Health & Sexuality, 7,* 493–504. doi:10.1080/13691050500151248.

Wilson, D. B. M., & Miller, R. (2002). Strategies for managing heterosexism used among African American gay and bisexual men. *Journal of Black Psychology, 28,* 371–391. doi: 10.1177/009579802237543

Wilson, P., Meyer, I., Antebi-Gruszka, N., Boone, M., Cook, S., & Cherenack, E. (2016). Profiles of resilience and psychosocial outcomes among young Black gay and bisexual men. *American Journal of Community Psychology, 57,* 144–157. doi: 10.1002/ajcp.12018

Wilson, P., & Yoshikawa, H. (2007). Improving access to quality health care among African American, Asian and Pacific Islander, and Latino lesbian, gay, and bisexual populations. In I. H. Meyer & M. E. Northridge (Eds.), *The health of sexual minorities: Public health perspectives on lesbian, gay, bisexual, and transgender populations* (pp. 607–637). New York, NY: Springer.

Chapter 1

The Forgotten Intersection

Black LGBTQ/GNC Youth in Juvenile Detention in the United States

Amorie Robinson

The humanity of Black lesbian, gay, biattractional, transgender, questioning, and gender nonconforming (LGBTQ/GNC) youth is under constant scrutiny because of the myths and stereotypes that cast them as deficient and criminal. Consequently, many of these youth (eighteen years and under) are engaged in an unrelenting struggle to maintain their personal dignity in the face of inhospitable and hostile environments. Although they essentially face all the conventional challenges of adolescence, they also encounter some which are unique to their status as multiply marginalized individuals in society (Pritchard, 2013). One such challenge that disproportionately plagues Black LGBTQ/GNC youth is the threat of detention and incarceration within the juvenile justice system. Black LGBTQ/GNC youth are overrepresented in this system (Majd, Marksamer, & Reyes, 2009; Osher, Woodruff, & Sims, 2002).

This chapter will highlight the detention and incarceration disparities faced by Black LGBTQ/GNC youth, factors that contribute to their placement in the juvenile justice system, and their experiences within that system. In addition, examples of resilience among Black LGBTQ/GNC youth in the juvenile justice system are provided. These examples are important because they will help us understand how these youths continue to survive and thrive in the face of incredible disenfranchisement. Finally, this chapter concludes with recommendations—at the individual, institutional, and structural levels—for preventing Black LGBTQ/GNC youth detention and incarceration and promoting resilience among those adolescents already in the juvenile justice system.

BLACK LGBTQ/GNC YOUTH IN THE
JUVENILE JUSTICE SYSTEM

Large-scale surveys have not collected specific data on the numbers and experiences of Black LGBTQ/GNC youth in the juvenile justice system. Therefore, our knowledge of the number of these youth under detention or incarceration is speculative, based on estimates from data about both LGBTQ/GNC youth and Black youth, in general. It is estimated that 300,000 LGBTQ/GNC youth are arrested and detained every year, and more than 60 percent of them are Black or Latino (Hunt & Moodie-Mills, 2012). In a survey of 1400 detained youth across seven jurisdictions, 20 percent self-identified as LGBT, and 85 percent of them identified as youth of color (Irvine, 2010).

Black youth are unfairly overrepresented in the US juvenile justice system (Farmer, 2010; Nanda, 2011). In 2010, Black youth comprised 17 percent of all juveniles in the United States, but comprised 31 percent of all juvenile arrests, 40 percent of detentions, 34 percent of adjudications (guilty determinations), and 45 percent of cases transferred to adult criminal court (Chiu, 2014). Black youth are more likely to be arrested for status offenses,[1] referred to juvenile court, and processed rather than offered remedial social and health services, in comparison to their White counterparts (Chiu, 2014; Huizinga et al., 2007). For example, Black youth were 269 percent more likely to be arrested for violating curfew laws than White youth (Huizinga et al., 2007). Although White youth are more likely to report using drugs and 30 percent more likely to report selling drugs, Black youth are more than twice as likely to be arrested and detained for drug offenses (Arya & Augarten, 2008). Black youth are more frequently transferred to adult court than White youth and are seven times more likely to receive prison sentences from adult courts than White youth arrested for similar offenses (Arya & Augarten, 2008).

We do not yet have a concrete count of the number of Black LGBTQ/GNC youth in the juvenile justice system. More research in this area is direly needed. However, what we can deduce from these data is that LGBTQ/GNC youth of color are overrepresented in the juvenile justice system (Feinstein, Greenblatt, Hass, Kohn, & Rana, 2001; Mallon & DeCrescenzo, 2006; Mountz, 2011) and that many of these youth are Black (Hunt & Moodie-Mills, 2012).

FACTORS ASSOCIATED WITH BEING PLACED
IN THE JUVENILE JUSTICE SYSTEM

There are three major pathways which lead to LGBTQ/GNC youth's juvenile court involvement: family rejection (Ryan, Huebner, Diaz, & Sanchez, 2009), homelessness (Keuroghlian, Shtasel, & Bassuk, 2014; Ray & Berger, 2007), and a hostile school climate (Burdge, Licona, & Hyemingway, 2014; Kosciw, Greytak, Bartkiewicz, Boesen, & Palmer, 2012). Many Black LGBTQ/ GNC youth are stigmatized by their families of origin due to their same-sex attractions or gender expression (Bennett & Battle, 2001). They may be subject to neglect, ridicule, or abuse at the hands of caregivers who do not understand, condone, or accept non-heteroattractional or non-gender binary identities (Clements & Rosenwald, 2008; Mallon & DeCrescenzo, 2006). Homonegative attitudes and behaviors of Black family members often stem from religious (LaSala & Frierson, 2012), cultural (Greene, 1997), and communal (Rosario, Schrimshaw, & Hunter, 2004) norms that deem same-sex attractionality and GNC behavior as sinful or antagonistic to Black cultural values and norms (Parks, Hughes, & Matthews, 2004; Pew Research Center, 2016). Family rejection alienates Black LGBTQ/GNC youth from familial, community, and religious resources, making them more vulnerable to depression, trauma, and other mental health disorders (Battle & Crum, 2007; Meyer, 2010), academic problems (Mitchum & Moodie-Mills, 2014; Toomey, Ryan, Diaz, Card, & Russell, 2010), economic strain (Mountz, 2011), and future abuse by others (Roberts, Rosario, Corliss, Koenen, & Austin, 2012).

Family rejection often is associated with the detention and incarceration of Black LGBTQ/GNC youth in the juvenile justice system via homelessness. Research (Rosario, Schrimshaw, & Hunter, 2012) has demonstrated that family rejection is the major contributor to homelessness among LGBTQ/GNC youth. Out of despair or to flee hostility and abuse at home, some youth run away and resort to illegal behaviors such as theft, "survival sex," violating youth curfew laws, and sleeping in public spaces to survive (Irvine, 2010; Katz, 2014). Homelessness leaves youth vulnerable to commercial sexual exploitation by predators and sex trafficking (Institute of Medicine, 2011). Black LGBTQ/GNC youth go from a bad situation at home to a worse one on the streets. In an effort to help Black LGBTQ/GNC homeless youth, some of them are placed in the child welfare system by well-intentioned adults (Fedders, 2013; Mountz, 2011; Wilson, Cooper, Kastanis, & Nezhad, 2014). Yet, many Black LGBTQ/GNC youth experience the same types of stigma and abuse in these placements that originally led to homelessness. Compared to heterosexual youth, more than twice as many LGBTQ/GNC youth reported being treated poorly in group and foster care homes (Mallon & DeCrescenzo, 2006). The child welfare system largely fails in its mission to ensure safety, permanency, and well-being of LGBTQ/GNC youth (Wilson et al., 2014). As a result, many Black LGBTQ/GNC youth find themselves either homeless again or ushered into the juvenile justice system.

The school-to-prison pipeline is another contributing factor to the detention and incarceration of Black LGBTQ/GNC youth. These youths are often stereotyped and administrators, teachers, and peers tend to treat them as if they are hyper-aggressive (Graziano & Wagner, 2011; Holsinger & Hodge, 2016) and sexually deviant (Snapp, Hoenig, Fields, & Russell, 2015). These perceptions contribute to harsh and disproportionate punishments in school (Kosciw et al., 2012). LGBTQ/GNC youth are often reprimanded for public displays of affection and violating gender norms, and their identities are misread as defiance (Snapp et al., 2015). Many LGBTQ/GNC youth who experience a hostile school climate may fight to protect themselves. Their push back against mistreatment is sometimes is viewed as aggressive (Russell, Ryan, Toomey, Diaz, & Sanchez, 2011) and they are frequently blamed for their own victimization (Pritchard, 2013) which leaves them vulnerable to being disciplined instead of the perpetrator. A hostile school climate can contribute to higher rates of truancy, absenteeism, dropout rate, suspensions, lower grades, and psychological trauma (Mitchum & Moodie-Mills, 2014). Further stress develops when LGBTQ/GNC youth are given harsher school sanctions for minor disciplinary infractions, and when school officials rely on the juvenile justice system to assist. This unduly criminalizes Black LGBTQ/GNC youth (Kosciw et al., 2012).

Black transgender and GNC youth are at higher risk for involvement in the juvenile justice system than are cisgender youth (Katz, 2014). Their involvement in the system is frequently associated with petty crimes related to attempts to live out their authentically felt gender (e.g., shoplifting clothing that matches their gender identity, engaging in survival sex in order to afford hormones) or is a result of the discrimination and abuse that they experience within their families, schools, foster care placements, and homeless shelters (Garnette, Irvine, Reyes, & Wilber, 2011). Black transgender and GNC youth are often penalized for attempting to survive and live authentically in a society that does not value them.

Black LGBTQ/GNC youth are often the victims of the anti-Black implicit bias of the judicial system's gatekeepers coupled with *adultification*. Adultification is the act of perceiving Black youth not as children and adolescents, but as adults with full cognitive capacity and thus worthy of the same punishments that are typically administered to adults (Ferguson, 2001). Adultification often operates at a preconscious level or implicitly. Henning (2013) contends that contemporary narratives portraying Black youth as dangerous and irredeemable lead prosecutors to disproportionately reject age or developmental stage as mitigating factors for their behavior. Furthermore, as a result of implicit bias and adultification, probation officers often attribute Black youths' crimes as stemming from deviance and characterological criminality, whereas White adolescents' crimes are seen as aberrations stemming from environmental circumstances (Dancy, 2014). These differences in attribution contribute significantly to differential assessments of the risk of re-offending and to sentence recommendations. Regardless of actual individual offenses, Black LGBTQ/GNC youth experience several biased interpersonal exchanges and structural challenges that place them at greater risk for coming in contact with the juvenile justice system.

EXPERIENCES OF BLACK LGBTQ/GNC YOUTH IN THE JUVENILE JUSTICE SYSTEM

Once in juvenile detention placement, Black LGBTQ/GNC youth are highly likely to face brutal physical, emotional, and sexual harassment and assaults, along with prolonged periods of segregated isolation (Majd, Marksamer, & Reyes, 2009). In the first case in the United States to address the treatment of LGBTQ/GNC youth in juvenile facilities, a federal judge deemed the conditions at the Hawaii Youth Correctional Facility as dangerous, after the ACLU filed a lawsuit on behalf of three youth who were constantly brutalized and harassed because of their attractional orientation and gender identity. Incidents at the facility included singling out these youths for physical assaults in the living quarters and shower area by fellow inmates (ACLU, 2006). Staff routinely used slurs such as "fag" and "fruitcake," unnecessarily placed one of the youth in solitary confinement, and smeared semen on the face of one of the other youth (ACLU, 2006). During interviews by Daniel Redman (2010), one fifteen-year-old gay male ward at the Louisiana Swanson Center for Youth shared that he revealed to staff that he was sexually assaulted and whipped with a clothes hanger by peers, but was told he was too late to issue a report. A case in Los Angeles revealed that a staff member arranged for a biattractional male youth to get beaten up by a group of "straight" male youth (Redman, 2010). One feminine gay male youth was sent to lockdown for wearing his hair up. When a male-to-female transgender youth wished to use a female name and pronouns, the counselors refused and advised staff to force her to wear male clothing (Redman, 2010).

Black LGBTQ/GNC youth experience sexual violence from both peers and staff inside correctional facilities. In general, LGBTQ/GNC youth reported a significantly higher (ten to twelve times higher) rate of youth-on-youth sexual victimization (10.3 percent), compared with hetero-attractional youth (1.5 percent; Beck, Cantor, Hartge, & Smith, 2013). Some reports (Hunt & Moodie-Mills, 2012; Majd et al., 2009) suggest that staff turn a blind eye to incidents of sexual assault and abuse against LGBTQ/GNC youth due to a belief that having same-sex attraction and a GNC identity are invitations for sex. Physical, emotional, and sexual assaults that take place in juvenile detention against any child is reprehensible and damaging to a child's health outcomes.

Also worth mentioning is the likelihood of an LGBTQ/GNC youth being unfairly labeled a "sex offender," regardless of whether he or she actually committed a sexual crime. This pathologization of same-sex sexuality makes these youths more likely to be prosecuted for age-appropriate consensual sexual activity than their hetero-attractional and gender-conforming peers (Hunt & Moodie-Mills, 2012; Mountz, 2011). A devastating consequence for these youth is the requirement to register as a sex offender which could haunt them for the rest of their lives, and negatively impact their chances for employment and other opportunities (Majd et al., 2009). Overall, Black LGBTQ/GNC youth are mistreated in the juvenile justice system and face systemic and systematic barriers to achieving vindication, health, and well-being upon release.

RESILIENCE AMONG BLACK LGBTQ/GNC YOUTH IN THE JUVENILE JUSTICE SYSTEM

Black LGBTQ/GNC youth have demonstrated unique and often unrecognized survival tactics and areas of unbridled creativity in the face of injustice. For over a decade, I have had the pleasure of working with many of these youths and witnessing their determination. For example, I have seen Black gay male adolescents at the Ruth Ellis Center in Highland Park, Michigan—which serves primarily Black LGBTQ/GNC homeless youth, many who have entered into the juvenile justice system—use dance to express themselves. Some of these adolescents practice forms of stylish dance moves called "voguing" and "J-setting" which helps channel their energies in a productive way (Ruth Ellis Center, 2010). These art forms, which originated during the 1960s Harlem ballroom culture by Black gay men and the J-Settes cheering team at Jackson State University, were adopted by these youngsters as a way to not only express their creativity and athleticism, but also their emotions. Youth who I have seen in psychotherapy at the juvenile court clinic have disclosed how much voguing and J-Setting have allowed them to release stress and manage their anger around the atrocities of their lives. It has developed opportunities to participate in competition, to bond, to form "houses" or chosen families, and to form dance groups that compete during Black Gay Pride events. Already alienated or rejected by their biological families, this outlet has served as a source of an alternative family, as well as housing opportunities. Within this subculture, youth learn how to communicate effectively, social assertiveness, decision-making, interpersonal skills, and survival skills, not to mention receive emotional support (Graham, Crissman, Tocco, Hughes, Snow, & Padilla, 2014).

Social support is a big component of resiliency for Black LGBTQ/GNC youth in the juvenile justice system. I have been told by staff at the local juvenile detention facility in Detroit where I administer psychological assessments and conduct LGBTQ/GNC cultural competency trainings that these youths come together to avoid feeling isolated and unsafe. Clients I have spoken to who have been placed at the facility, for mostly status offenses, report the need to band together for protection against staff and peer bullying and harassment. The groups give themselves names and create their own signals to communicate with each other indirectly. They convey to me that this provides them with a sense of feeling powerful. Three of my clients at the juvenile court clinic, who identified as Black lesbians (ages of fifteen to seventeen years), were placed on probation for running away from home. Listening to their stories it became clear that their only crime was escaping the trauma of their parents' calling them a "dyke," forcing them to "dress like a lady," preventing them to have friendships with their LGBTQ/GNC friends, or to date anyone of the same sex. They each found a safe place to stay with a friend or sweetheart whose parents were welcoming and accepting. Rather than being praised for having made healthy decisions for themselves, they were criminalized for being incorrigible, oppositional, and defiant without regard to why their decisions were made. Had there been earlier intervention, such as family therapy, perhaps these situations could have been averted. Luckily, some of these clients were able to join the clinic's Rainbow Teens support group which gave them a safe space in which to have their voices and feelings validated, offer and receive emotional support, learn effective coping strategies for addressing microaggressions, and developing a renewed sense of confidence in communicating with peers and adults. Their testimonies describe their talents, skills, creativity, and determination to complete their probationary requirements.

BEST PRACTICE RECOMMENDATIONS

Individual, institutional, and structural practices and policies are needed to prevent Black LGBTQ/GNC youth's detention and incarceration and to enhance their resiliency when they do encounter the juvenile justice system. The following recommendations are strategies that can be prove helpful in preventing Black LGBTQ/GNC youth incarceration, promoting protective factors among those youths already incarcerated, and help formerly detained youth maintain their freedom.

Individual Level Recommendations

- Decrease family rejection by developing programs that promote awareness, understanding, and acceptance of same-sex attractions and non-binary gender presentations. An example of such a program is the Family Acceptance

Project (Ryan, Russell, Huebner, Diaz, & Sanchez, 2010) which was designed to assist families in providing supportive and nurturing home environments for LGB youth.

- Develop and promote culturally appropriate support groups and mentors for parents with LGBTQ/GNC children and adolescents.
- Create mentorship programs for Black LGBTQ/GNC youth that pair them with Black LGBTQ/GNC supportive adults who can provide guidance related to developmental milestones and navigating stigma and oppression.

Institutional Level Recommendations

- Create culturally sensitive training programs for law enforcement and correctional facility staff to help them develop empathy and skills to better serve the needs of Black LGBTQ/GNC youth.
- Develop and implement training programs for new and continuing teachers and juvenile justice system workers that enhance explicit and implicit bias awareness, and also provide evidence-based strategies to neutralize those biases.
- Train youth care and juvenile justice professionals (e.g., judges, attorneys, mental health providers, teachers) to engage in assessment of one's own personal beliefs and attitudes related to Black LGBTQ/GNC youth and how those beliefs may potentially affect clients.
- Intentional and sustained recruitment and retention of "out" LGBTQ/GNC individuals across all races and ethnicities on the board of directors and other gatekeeping positions in governmental and nonprofit organizations.
- Hire cultural competency trainers who are familiar with Black LGBTQ/GNC youth and committed to engaging in social justice initiatives on their behalf.
- Create and enforce school policies that are attuned to and punish bullying, harassment, and microaggressions toward Black LGBTQ/GNC students. Audit and recommend Black LGBTQ/GNC-affirming revisions to school discipline policies.
- Create safe-spaces including gender neutral bathrooms in schools and correctional facilities.
- Mental health professionals should screen for trauma among all youth at their earliest point of contact with the juvenile justice system.
- Create programming for treating trauma disorders among youth Black LGBTQ/GNC youth.

Structural Level Recommendations

- Develop comprehensive nondiscrimination policies in juvenile justice agencies, including detention facilities, that specifically address attractional

orientation and gender identity. Such policies should include guidelines about confidentiality, disclosure about one's identity, use of affirming gender pronouns and sexual attraction labels, as well as how youth may emotionally and physically respond to harassment.
- Create new and enforce existing laws for that prohibit conversion therapies, use of gendered spaces, and unwarranted searches of transgender youth.
- Develop and enforce policies that require correctional facilities to provide medically necessary transition-related health care to transgender youth, as determined by qualified medical professionals familiar with the evidence-based standards of care developed by the World Professional Association for Transgender Health (Coleman, 2012).
- Correctional facilities should consistently enforce the Prison Rape Elimination Act regulations and guidelines on standards of care for Black LGBTQ/GNC youth (Shay, 2013; Wilber, 2015) in order to maintain safety and culturally competent care for transgender and GNC youth.

CONCLUSION

Black LGBTQ/GNC youth are increasingly present within the juvenile justice system and deserve the same type of services, care, protections, rights, safety, and respect rendered to their peers. The social and cultural climate in which Black LGBTQ/GNC youth are raised needs serious evaluation in order to prevent them from entering the juvenile justice system. This chapter presented statistics and information about the lived experiences of Black LGBTQ/GNC youth who are at-risk for, already experiencing, or now recovering from contact with the juvenile justice system. It is hoped that the information and data that was provided in this chapter help foster equity of services and familial and community change in order to eliminate juvenile justice disparities and unfair treatment among Black LGBTQ/GNC youth.

NOTE

1. A status offense is a non-criminal act that is considered a law violation only because of a youth's status as a minor. Examples include school truancy, running away from home, violating curfew, underage use of alcohol, and loitering.

REFERENCES

ACLU (2006, February 8). Judge blasts Hawai'i juvenile detention facility for pervasive harassment of gay and transgender youth. Retrieved from https://www.aclu.

org/news/judge-blasts-hawaii-juvenile-detention-facility-pervasive-harassment-gay-and-transgender-youth

Arya, N., & Augarten, I. (2008). *Critical condition: African-American youth in the justice system.* Washington, DC: Campaign for Youth Justice. Retrieved from http://www.campaignforyouthjustice.org/research/cfyj-reports/item/critical-condition-african-american-youth-in-the-justice-system

Battle, J., & Crum, M. (2007). Black LGB health and well-being. In I. H. Meyer & M. E. Northridge (Eds.), *The health of sexual minorities: Public health perspectives on lesbian, gay, bisexual, and transgender populations* (pp. 320–352). Springer US.

Beck, A. J., Cantor, D., Hartge, J., & Smith, T. (2013, June). *Sexual victimization in juvenile facilities report by youth.* Retrieved from http//:www.bjs.gov/content/pub/pdf/svjfry12.pdf

Bennett, M., & Battle, J. (2001). We can see them, but we can't hear them": LGBT members of African American families. In M. B. Bernstein & R. Reimann (Eds.), *Queer families, queer politics: Challenging culture and the state* (pp. 53–67). New York, NY: Columbia University Press.

Burdge, H., Licona, A. C., & Hyemingway, Z. T. (2014). *LGBTQ youth of color: Discipline disparities, school push-out, and the school-to-prison pipeline.* San Francisco, CA: Gay-Straight Alliance Network and Tucson, AZ: Crossroads Collaborative at the University of Arizona. Retrieved from https://gsanetwork.org/files/aboutus/LGBTQ_brief_FINAL-web.pdf

Chiu, L. (2014, February 26). *After decades of spending, minority youth still overrepresented in system. Youth of color in the juvenile justice system.* Retrieved from http://jjie.org/after-decades-of-spending-minority-youth-still-overrepresented-in-system/106398/

Clements, J. A., & Rosenwald, M. (2008). Foster parents' perspectives on LGB youth in the child welfare system. *Journal of Gay & Lesbian Social Services, 19*(1), 57–69.

Coleman, E. (2012). *Standards of care for the health of transsexual, transgender, and gender nonconforming people (version 7).* World Professional Association for Transgender Health. Retrieved from http://www.wpath.org

Dancy, T. E. (2014). The adultification of Black boys. In K. J. Fasching-Varner, R. E. Reynolds, K. A. Albert, & L. L. Martin (Eds.), *Trayvon Martin, race, and American justice* (pp. 49–55). Boston, MA: Sense Publishers.

Farmer, S. (2010). Criminality of Black youth in inner-city schools: 'Moral panic', moral imagination, and moral formation. *Race Ethnicity & Education, 13*(3), 367–381.

Fedders, B. (2013). LGBT youth in the child welfare and juvenile justice systems: Charting a way forward. *Temple Political & Civil Rights Law Review, 23,* 431–449.

Feinstein, R., Greenblatt, A., Hass, L., Kohn, S., & Rana, J. (2001). *Justice for all? A report on lesbian, gay, bisexual and transgendered youth in the New York juvenile justice system.* New York, NY: Urban Justice Center.

Ferguson, A. A. (2001). *Bad boys: Public schools in the making of Black masculinity.* Ann Arbor, MI: University of Michigan Press.

Garnette, L., Irvine, A., Reyes, C., & Wilber, S. (2011). Lesbian, gay, bisexual, and transgender (LGBT) youth and the juvenile justice system. In F. T. Sherman &

F. H. Jacobs (Eds.), *Juvenile justice: Advancing research, policy, and practice* (pp. 156–173). Hoboken, NJ: John Wiley.

Graham, L. F., Crissman, H. P., Tocco, J., Hughes, L. A., Snow, R. C., & Padilla, M. B. (2014). Interpersonal relationships and social support in transitioning narratives of Black transgender women in Detroit. *International Journal of Transgenderism, 15*(2), 100–113.

Graziano, J. N., & Wagner, E. F. (2011). Trauma among lesbians and bisexual girls in the juvenile justice system. *Traumatology, 17*(2), 45–55.

Greene, B. (1997). Ethnic minority lesbians and gay men: Mental health and treatment issues. In B. Greene (Ed.), *Ethnic and cultural diversity among lesbians and gay men: Psychological perspectives on lesbian and gay issues, Vol. 3* (pp. 216–239). Thousand Oaks, CA: Sage.

Henning, K. N. (2013). Criminalizing normal adolescent behavior in communities of color: The role of prosecutors in juvenile justice reform. *Cornell Law Review, 98*, 383–462.

Holsinger, K., & Hodge, J. P. (2016). The experiences of lesbian, gay, bisexual, and transgender girls in juvenile justice systems. *Feminist Criminology, 11*(1), 23–47.

Hunt, J., & Moodie-Mills, A. (2012, June 29). *The unfair criminalization of gay and transgender youth.* Retrieved from http://www.americanprogress.org/issues/lgbt/report/2012/06/29

Huizinga, D., Thornberry, T., Knight, K., Lovegrove, P., Loeber, R., Hill, K., & Farrington, D. P. (2007, July). *Disproportionate minority contact in the juvenile justice system: A study of differential minority arrest/referral to court in three cities.* Washington, DC: Office of Juvenile Justice and Delinquency Prevention.

Institute of Medicine. (2011). *The health of lesbian, gay, bisexual, and transgender people: Building a foundation for better understanding.* Washington, DC: National Academies Press.

Irvine, A. (2010). "We've had three of them": Addressing the invisibility of lesbian, gay, bisexual, and gender nonconforming youths in the juvenile justice system. *Columbia Journal of Gender and Law, 19*(3), 675–701.

Katz, A. B. (2014). LGBT youth in the juvenile justice system: Overrepresented yet unheard. *Law School Student Scholarship.* Retrieved from http://scholarship.shu.edu/student_scholarship/503

Keuroghlian, A. S., Shtasel, D., & Bassuk, E. L. (2014). Out on the street: A public health and policy agenda for lesbian, gay, bisexual, and transgender youth who are homeless. *American Journal of Orthopsychiatry, 84*(1), 66.

Kosciw, J. G., Greytak, E. A., Bartkiewicz, M. J., Boesen, M. J., & Palmer, N. A. (2012). *The 2011 national school climate survey: The experiences of lesbian, gay, bisexual and transgender youth in our nation's schools.* New York, NY: Gay, Lesbian and Straight Education Network.

LaSala, M. C., & Frierson, D. T. (2012). African American gay youth and their families: Redefining masculinity, coping with racism and homophobia. *Journal of GLBT Family Studies, 8*(5), 428–445.

Majd, K., Marksamer, J., & Reyes, C. (2009). *Hidden injustice: Lesbian, gay, bisexual, and transgender youth in juvenile courts.* Legal Services for Children, National

Juvenile Defender Center, & National Center for Lesbian Rights. Retrieved from http://www.ncjrs.gov/App/publications/abstract.aspx?ID=257742

Mallon, G. P., & DeCrescenzo, T. (2006). Transgender children and youth: A child welfare practice perspective. *Child Welfare, 85*(2), 215–241.

Meyer, I. H. (2010). Identity, stress, and resilience in lesbians, gay men, and bisexuals of color. *The Counseling Psychologist, 38*(3), 442–454.

Mitchum, P., & Moodie-Mills, A. C. (2014). *Beyond bullying: How hostile school climate perpetuates the school-to-prison pipeline for lgbt youth.* Washington, DC: Center for American Progress.

Mountz, S. (2011). Revolving doors: LGBTQ youth at the interface of the child welfare and juvenile justice systems. *LGBTQ Policy Journal at the Harvard Kennedy School, 1,* 29–45.

Nanda, J. (2011). Blind discretion: Girls of color and delinquency in the juvenile justice system. *UCLA Law Review, 59,* 1502–1539.

Osher, D., Woodruff, D., & Sims, A. E. (2002). Schools make a difference: The over-representation of African American youth in special education and the juvenile justice system. In D. Losen & G. Orfield (Eds.), *Racial inequity in special education* (pp. 93–116). Boston, MA: Harvard Education Press.

Parks, C. A., Hughes, T. L., & Matthews, A. K. (2004). Race/ethnicity and sexual orientation: Intersecting identities. *Cultural Diversity and Ethnic Minority Psychology, 10*(3), 241–254.

Pew Research Center. (2016, May 12). *Changing attitudes on gay marriage.* Washington, DC: Author. Retrieved from http//:www.pewforum.org/2016/05/12/changing-attitudes-on-gay-marriage/

Pritchard, E. D. (2013). For colored kids who committed suicide, our outrage isn't enough: Queer youth of color, bullying, and the discursive limits of identity and safety. *Harvard Educational Review, 83*(2), 320–345.

Ray, N., & Berger, C. (2007). *Lesbian, gay, bisexual and transgender youth: An epidemic of homelessness.* Washington, DC: National Gay and Lesbian Task Force Policy Institute.

Redman, D. (2010). "I was scared to sleep": LGBT youth face violence behind bars. *The Nation.* Retrieved from https://www.thenation.com/article/i-was-scared-sleep-lgbt-youth-face-violence-behind-bars/

Roberts, A. L., Rosario, M., Corliss, H. L., Koenen, K. C., & Austin, S. B. (2012). Childhood gender nonconformity: A risk indicator for childhood abuse and post-traumatic stress in youth. *Pediatrics, 129*(3), 410–417.

Rosario, M., Schrimshaw, E. W., & Hunter, J. (2004). Ethnic/racial differences in the coming-out process of lesbian, gay, and bisexual youths: A comparison of sexual identity development over time. *Cultural Diversity and Ethnic Minority Psychology, 10*(3), 215.

———. (2012). Risk factors for homelessness among lesbian, gay, and bisexual youths: A developmental milestone approach. *Children and Youth Services Review, 34*(1), 186–193.

Russell, S. T., Ryan, C., Toomey, R. B., Diaz, R. M., & Sanchez, J. (2011). Lesbian, gay, bisexual, and transgender adolescent school victimization: Implications for young adult health and adjustment. *Journal of School Health, 81*(5), 223–230. doi: 10.1111/j.1746–1561.2011.00583.x

Ruth Ellis Center. (Producer). (2010). *Youth produced voguing documentary*. [Online video clip]. Available from https://www.youtube.com/watch?v=BJWQRa1bibc

Ryan, C., Huebner, D., Diaz, R. M., & Sanchez, J. (2009). Family rejection as a predictor of negative health outcomes in White and Latino lesbian, gay, and bisexual young adults. *Pediatrics, 123*, 346–352.

Ryan, C., Russell, S. T., Huebner, D., Diaz, R., & Sanchez, J. (2010). Family acceptance in adolescence and the health of LGBT young adults. *Journal of Child and Adolescent Psychiatric Nursing, 23*(4), 205–213. doi: 10.1111/j.1744–6171.2010.00246.x

Shay, G. (2013). PREA's elusive promise: Can DOJ regulations protect LGBT incarcerated people. *Loyola Journal of Public Interest Law 15*, 343.

Snapp, S. D., Hoenig, J. M., Fields, A., & Russell, S. T. (2015). Messy, butch, and queer LGBTQ youth and the school-to-prison pipeline. *Journal of Adolescent Research, 30*(1), 57–82.

Toomey, R. B., Ryan, C., Diaz, R. M., Card, N. A., & Russell, S. T. (2010). Gender-nonconforming lesbian, gay, bisexual, and transgender youth: School victimization and young adult psychosocial adjustment. *Developmental Psychology, 46*(6), 1580–1589.

Wilber, S. (2015). *Lesbian, gay, bisexual and transgender youth in the juvenile justice system: A guide to juvenile detention reform*. Baltimore, MD: Annie E. Casey Foundation. Retrieved from http://www.calcasa.org/wp/2015/12/NCLR-LGBT-youth-in-jj-systems.pdf

Wilson, B. D., Cooper, K., Kastanis, A., & Nezhad, S. (2014). *Sexual and gender minority youth in foster care: Assessing disproportionality and disparities in Los Angeles*. Los Angeles, CA: The Williams Institute, UCLA School of Law.

Chapter 2

Black Bisexual Women's Health in the United States

A Systematic Literature Review

Jonathan Mathias Lassiter

In the United States, Black bisexual women's experiences are mostly invisible in the mainstream heterosexual and same-gender-loving health research. These women's voices are often excluded from study findings or subsumed under the umbrella of lesbian, gay, bisexual, and transgender (LGBT) identities. Thus, there is very little scholarly information about who these women are and how they manage their health. A systematic review was conducted to assess and summarize the US public health and social science literature about Black bisexual women's health. This chapter provides a brief overview of the US literature about Black sexual minority women's health (i.e., lesbian and bisexual women) as these two populations are often studied together in research, and then moves into a detailed account of the systematic review specifically related to Black bisexual women's health in the United States. The chapter concludes with a discussion of knowledge gaps related to Black bisexual women's health, the implications of those knowledge gaps, and suggestions about how to further the literature.

BLACK SEXUAL MINORITY WOMEN'S HEALTH

Black sexual minority women (SMW) occupy a unique space in society. They are women at the intersection of racial, gender, and sexual orientation identities that are often maligned in the United States (Bowleg, Burkholder, Teti, & Craig, 2008; Greene, 2000; Szymanski & Meyer, 2008). They may also be subjected to other forms of oppression depending on their class, religious, and ability statuses. One such manifestation of intersectional gender, racial, and sexual orientation oppression is the existence of ethnosexual mythologies. Ethnosexual mythologies are myths that render Black SMW defective and contribute to their social marginalization (Greene, 2000). Such myths categorize Black SMW as sexually irresponsible, uninhibited, and insatiable as well as (too) strong women who emasculate Black men (Greene, 2000). These depictions at the structural level contribute to Black SMW experiencing prejudice and discrimination both within and outside of Black communities. These experiences of oppression, like gender-based and race-based discrimination, are often greater than those experienced by Black sexual minority men and white SMW (Calabrese, Meyer, Overstreet, Haile, & Hansen, 2015).

Black SMW's roles in Black communities are varied. They are mothers, sisters, aunts, grandmothers, wives, girlfriends, coworkers, and congregants. Many have strong family ties and rely on relatives for support in resisting racism, sexism, misogynoir, and economic difficulties (Balsam, Molina, Blayney, Dillworth, Zimmerman, & Kaysen, 2015; Bowleg et al., 2008; Greene, 2000). In fact, one study found that Black SMW receive most of their major social support from family and partners (Frost, Meyer, & Schwartz, 2016). Many women engage in religious and spiritual practices and possess beliefs that help them cope with hardships. Due to the importance of family, religion, and the Black community at large, some Black SMW may choose not to disclose their sexual orientation to others who are not also sexual minorities (Balsam et al., 2015; Bowleg et al., 2008). Indeed, some women may view their sexual orientation as less important than their racial identity and believe that it is better to maintain relationships with family and community members than risk being ostracized (Bowleg et al., 2008). Other women may adopt a "don't ask, don't tell" policy with their family members in which their sexual orientation is implicitly known but never explicitly confirmed.

Some Black women find that they have to terminate relationships with some non-affirming family members. This can have both positive and negative effects on Black SMW's well-being. Some Black SMW find support within families that they create with friends and by having their own children (Greene, 2000). Black SMW women are more likely to be raising their children without help from a man and are less likely to have their custody threatened than white SMW women (Morris, Balsam, & Rothblum, 2002). These factors likely contribute to Black SMW having more autonomy in their personally created families of choice. However, they are also more likely to experience financial strain. Black SMW are more likely to have shorter work histories than white SMW and periods of homelessness (Balsam et al., 2015).

In addition, Black SMW endure a range of physical and mental health conditions. They have been found to have a higher likelihood of surviving childhood sexual abuse than white SMW (Calabrese et al., 2015). Black SMW have been found to have higher levels of substance abuse than Black sexual minority men (MacCarthy et al., 2015) but lower levels than white SMW (Calabrese et al., 2015). Furthermore, Black SMW have been found to engage in cigarette smoking less than and indicate a desire to stop smoking more than Latina SMW (Sanchez, Meacher, & Beil, 2005). Obesity and being overweight are also significant problems for some Black bisexual women (Matthews, Li, McConnell, Aranda, & Smith, 2016). Obesity is associated with arthritis, adult-onset diabetes, and heart disease for these women (Guh, Zhang, Bansback, Amarsi, Birmingham, & Anis, 2009). Furthermore, having a high BMI has been found to be associated with being discriminated against due to body size, which can contribute to depressive symptoms and poorer perceived physical health for Black SMW (Wilson, Okwu, & Mills, 2011). However, although some Black SMW may struggle with their weight, no eating disorder disparities have been found compared to heterosexual women or across gender and racial groups (Feldman & Meyer, 2007). Unfortunately, when Black SMW seek treatment for these health conditions, they experience negative interactions with their providers due to insensitivity related to their racial and sexual identities. These experiences can result in less healthcare usage (Li, Matthews, Aranda, Patel, & Maharshi, 2015). The scholarly literature about Black SMW provides detailed information about the lived experiences and health of this understudied population. However, the stories of Black bisexual women are often not highlighted in these reports. This systematic literature review attempts to address that omission.

METHODS

This systematic review was conducted in accordance with the PRIMSA guidelines. EBSCO Host and PubMed were searched on June 29, 2016, for all articles related to Black bisexual women. The following search terms were used: "African American 'bisexual women'" AND "black 'bisexual women.'" The MeSH terms were used for searches conducted in the PubMed database. Reference lists of retrieved publications were also examined for any additional relevant publications. No limitations or exclusions were made based on publication date.

Article Selection

All records were reviewed for duplicates. Duplicate and irrelevant records were removed, then abstracts were reviewed for relevance. They were deemed relevant if they mentioned focused on Black bisexual cisgender women separately or in conjunction with Black lesbian cisgender women. Next, full articles were reviewed to assess their eligibility criteria. The eligibility criteria were (1) published studies; (2) scholarly (peer-reviewed); and (3) the sample or a subsample had to be comprised of US-residing Black bisexual cisgender women. These inclusion criteria were chosen due to the author's desire to examine the lived experiences and health of Black bisexual women. Editorials, letters, technical reports, dissertations, and commentaries were excluded.

Data Collection Process

The total sample or subsample size of Black bisexual women included in each study was recorded. Age, geographic region of residence at time of study, and ethnicity were assessed for each study sample. In addition, information about study design (cross-sectional, longitudinal) and data analyses (qualitative, quantitative, mixed-method) was also collected. Finally, the main topics covered were recorded.

RESULTS

Overview

A summary of the article selection process is presented in Figure 2.1.

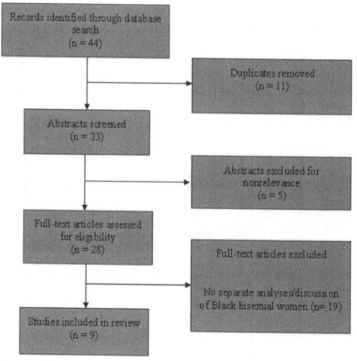

Figure 2.1   Article Selection Process for Systematic Literature Review.

A total of nine studies conducted from 1998 to 2016 were included in this review (see Table 2.1). Most of these studies (N = 8) were conducted with small sample sizes typically surveying less than 100 women. Black bisexual women included in these studies tended to be under the age of fifty and ethnically identified as African American. However, it should be noted that for the majority of the studies (N = 6) reported only race, not ethnicity. The Black bisexual women surveyed resided in geographical regions throughout the United States. However, no women from the Mountain region (Arizona, Colorado, Idaho, Montana, Nevada, New Mexico, Utah, and Wyoming) and only a very few from the Pacific region (Alaska, California, Hawaii, Oregon, and Washington) were included. All of the studies utilized a cross-sectional design. Data analysis methods used were either qualitative (N = 3) or quantitative (N = 6), but no studies utilized mixed-methods. Topics covered included: intimate partner violence, reproductive coercion, mental health, sexual risk behaviors, bisexual identity development, sexual protective behaviors, sexual assault, religious faith, internalized homonegativity, and resilience.

Major Themes from the Systematic Literature Review

Sex-negative, homonegative, bi-negative, and gender constrictive messages. Black bisexual women in the reviewed studies reported, that as children, they received negative messages about sexuality in general, and about same-sex attraction in particular (Bates, 2012; Comeau, 2012). Such messages indicated that having both heterosexual sexual relationships and same-sex attractions and sexual behaviors were bad, taboo, and could ruin one's future (Bates, 2012; Comeau, 2012). As children, some women's non-gender conforming behavior (i.e., being boyish) was harshly criticized and sometimes resulted in being physically punished by their caregivers (Bates, 2012; Comeau, 2012). When women do begin to identify as bisexual, they may also receive biphobic messages from monosexuals (heterosexual and exclusively same-sex attracted people) that bisexuality is illegitimate (Henderson, 2009).

Bisexual identity development. Some Black bisexual women have same-sex attractions and experiences (e.g., kissing girls) at a young age, but due to homonegative and bi-negative messages, they do not pursue those feelings until later in life (Bates, 2012; Comeau, 2012). Black bisexual women are often discouraged by family, peers, and religious congregants from pursuing their same-sex attractions (Bates, 2012; Comeau, 2012). Some are even subjected to conversion therapy in religious settings (Comeau, 2012). Yet, many women are able to explore their bisexuality when they leave their families and communities of origin (Comeau, 2012). Some women have identified college and prison as less restrictive environments that either affirmed or required same-sex behaviors and attractions (Comeau, 2012). Yet, for some

Table 2.1 Characteristics of Studies about Black Bisexual Women (N = 10)

Study	N	Mean Age	Ethnicity	US Geographic Region[a]	Study Design	Data Analysis Method	Topic(s) Covered
Alexander, Volpe, Abboud, & Campbell, 2016	42	21.3	African American	Not reported	Cross-sectional	Quantitative	Intimate partner violence, reproductive coercion, mental health, sexual risk behaviors
Bates, 2012	2	38	African American	South Atlantic	Cross-sectional	Qualitative	Bisexual identity development
Champion, Wilford, Shain, & Piper, 2005	23	Range given: 22–45	African American	West South Central	Cross-sectional	Qualitative	Sexual risk and protective behaviors
Cochran & Mays, 1998	65	31.7	Not reported	US national sample	Cross-sectional	Quantitative	Sexual orientation disclosure to physicians
Comeau, 2012	1	27	African American	South Atlantic	Cross-sectional	Qualitative	Bisexual identity formation in the absence of same-sex behavior
Henderson, 2009	886[b]	Not reported	Not reported	9 US cities[c]	Cross-sectional	Quantitative	Associations between sociodemographic factors and bisexual identity
Muzny, Rivers, Parker, Mena, Austin, & Schwebke, 2014	80	Not reported	Not reported	East South Central	Cross-sectional	Quantitative	Sexually transmitted infection and sexual behaviors
Sigurvinsdottir & Ullman, 2015	Not reported	Not reported	Not reported	East North Central	Cross-sectional	Quantitative	Sexual assault
Walker & Longmire-Avital, 2013	26	Not reported	Not reported	Not reported	Cross-sectional	Quantitative	Religious faith, internalized homonegativity, resilience

Note: [a]US geographic region designations based on US census categories. Guidelines can be found at: http://www.census.gov/econ/census/help/geography/regions_and_divisions.html. [b]The authors did not report the total sample size for the Black bisexual female subsample. The number presented here is based on calculating 33.5% of 2645 (total sample size). [c]The nine US cities included in this study are Philadelphia, Houston, District of Columbia, Oakland, Chicago, Los Angeles, Detroit, New York City, and Atlanta.

Black women, bisexual identity tends to decrease with age (Henderson, 2009). This may be due to the fact that some bisexual women marry men and exclusively engage in sexual relationships with men in an attempt to adhere to gender norms and the expectations of their families. Furthermore, sexual identity may fluctuate for some women along a continuum of heterosexual to bisexual to exclusively same-sex attracted (Cochran & Mays, 1998; Comeau, 2012; Henderson, 2009). Still, some Black women may identity as bisexual but may have sexual relationships with either men or women only (Bates, 2012; Henderson, 2009). Contextual factors such as attending same-sex affirming churches and having children have been found to influence bisexual identity, decreasing and increasing it respectively (Bates, 2012; Comeau, 2012). Black bisexual women who do marry male partners may find that they are able to explore their same-sex attraction more when they divorce (Bates, 2012). Yet, some women view a bisexual label as constrictive (Bates, 2012).

Mental health. Many Black bisexual women experience various forms of trauma as children and adults and subsequently suffer from negative mental health outcomes. They have reported experiencing physical and sexual violence more than their heterosexual counterparts who have reported it (Alexander, Volpe, Abboud, & Campbell, 2016). In addition, they have higher rates of reproductive coercion (being told not to use birth control by a male sexual partner) and trading sex for material resources than Black heterosexual women (Alexander et al., 2016). They also have reported more problems with alcohol than Black heterosexual women (Sigurvinsdottir & Ullman, 2015). Black bisexual women also experience depressive and post-traumatic stress symptoms more than heterosexual Black women and anxiety symptoms more than Black bisexual men, strictly same-sex attracted men, and lesbian-identified women (Sigurvinsdottir & Ullman, 2015).

Physical health. All of the research related to Black bisexual women's physical health has focused on their genitals via exploration of their sexual behaviors and health outcomes. Black bisexual women report in engaging in a varied repertoire of sexual behaviors including but not limited to touching, kissing, digital-vaginal sex, oral-vaginal sex, anal sex, and sex toy use (Champion, Wildford, Shain, & Piper, 2005). Alexander and colleagues (2016) found that Black bisexual women use condoms for vaginal sex less than heterosexual women. However, this study did not make a distinction between vaginal sex with male or female partners. This distinction may be important because bisexual women perceive that sex with male partners and female partners who also have sex with men as putting them at risk for sexually transmitted infections (STIs) more than sex with women who only have sex with women (Champion et al., 2005). Some Black bisexual women have reported that they are more likely to engage in vaginal sex with other women without a barrier than they are to let a man penetrate them without a condom (Champion et al., 2005). They have also reported that they use some type of protection (condom, dental dam) for anal sex with other women and when sharing sex toys (Champion et al., 2005). STI testing and suggesting using a barrier during sex are sometimes considered as evidence of infidelity and thus, some Black bisexual women abstain from these behaviors. Furthermore, when women do contract an STI, many assume it was due to sex with a male partner and do not disclose this information to their female partners (Champion et al., 2005). Black bisexual women have also been found to be more likely to be diagnosed with a yeast infection than lesbian-identified women (Muzny, Rivers, Parker, Mena, Austin, & Schwebke, 2014). Although Black bisexual women experience higher levels of negative mental and physical health outcomes than their Black heterosexual counterparts, a significant portion do not discuss their sexuality with their medical providers (Cochran & Mays, 1998). This lack of disclosure may be due to believing that their providers already know their sexual orientations or attempting to avoid insensitivity due to homonegative prejudice.

Protective factors. Researchers have examined some protective factors among this population. Such protective factors include advocating for bisexuals by educating members of the Black community about sexual orientation and gender diversity (Bates, 2012) and ending non-affirming relationships (Henderson, 2009). They also have high rates of healthcare involvement as 87–89 percent of women were found to have a personal physician (Cochran & Mays, 1998).

DISCUSSION

This systematic literature review is the first review of public health and social science scholarly literature focused solely on Black bisexual women in the United States. Nine articles were found and most of these studies were conducted with small samples of predominately young women throughout the United States. However, women in the Mountain and Pacific regions were either not represented or grossly underrepresented. All of the studies were cross-sectional (used data collected at one time-point) and covered topics ranging from bisexual identity development to mental and physical health. Overall, this small, underdeveloped body of literature focused heavily on risk factors, neglecting modes of resilience and resistance that Black bisexual women utilize in their everyday lives.

Implications and Future Directions

The findings of this study have significant implications for healthcare provision and research with Black bisexual women. Healthcare providers (e.g., physicians, psychologists, nurse practitioners, social workers) and health professional training organizations are encouraged to increase cultural sensitivity training related to Black bisexual women and their health. These women are not monosexual-identified and thus their health needs and experiences are likely to differ from exclusively heterosexual or lesbian-identified women. They should not be grouped together with those groups, for doing so erases their uniqueness. Healthcare providers may find it useful to incorporate culturally appropriate questions about sexuality into their intake forms and educate themselves about Black bisexual-specific resources that may be helpful to these women. A combination of the aforementioned actions is likely to help providers offer more tailored, affirming service to their clients.

While two of the studies explored the unique experiences of Black bisexual women and their bisexual identity development, more of this inquiry is needed. Experiences of communal and individual oppression were highlighted, yet the positive experiences and health protective factors in Black bisexual women's lives remain largely unexamined in the published literature. How do Black bisexual women resist systems of oppression? What are the methods of reconciliation that they use to become racially and sexually integrated beings? The health concerns of Black bisexual women are also understudied. Beyond psychological distress and sexual health, what are the health concerns of Black bisexual women? Black women, in general, have higher rates of cardiovascular disease, diabetes, hypertension, sickle cell anemia, and obesity compared to heterosexual white women (Russell, 2010). Yet, to the author's knowledge, no nuanced analyses that specifically examine the rates of these conditions among Black bisexual women have been undertaken. What structural, communal, and individual factors put them at risk for these conditions? In what ways do their health behaviors and life circumstances protect them from these disparities?

Efforts to recruit larger, more geographically and developmentally diverse samples of Black bisexual women need to be undertaken. What is the health trajectory of Black bisexual women throughout their lifespan? Do older women develop and accumulate enough resilience strategies so that oppressive systems impact their health less as they age or are they at greater risk the older they become? Also, what are the normative developmental milestones for Black bisexual women? How are geography, neighborhood composition, and social networks associated with their health?

Finally, but not least, how do Black bisexual women thrive? As the findings of this review demonstrate, health research with Black bisexual women tends to be pathology-focused. However, Black bisexual women's lives do not solely consist of disease and trauma or risk of disease and trauma. Many of these women lead fulfilling lives in the face of adversity, learning to grow from oppressive and non-affirming experiences. Researchers should closely examine protective factors such as social support, income, and spirituality. When research moves beyond a pathological lens, science can begin to understand more nuanced, holistic representations of Black bisexual women.

Integrating theoretical frameworks that are centered in intersectionality, feminist, and Afrocentric theory will help broaden the scope of scholarship about Black bisexual women. Intersectionality theory is inherently holistic and queries people's lives at the intersection of their identities and experiences of overlapping oppression (Bowleg, 2008). Feminist theory centers itself explicitly around women's experiences and interrogates inequality in their lives and imagines ways of being that are not male-centered or reactive to oppression (Collins, 2008). Afrocentric theory focuses on the integration of the spiritual and physical worlds within a cultural paradigm that preferences Black norms (Karenga, 1995). These frameworks depart from the Western medical model of pathology that is too often used to formulate and interpret research. Progressing beyond risk and oppression-focused work with Black bisexual women will further expand the public health and social science literature.

Diverse research design and methods will benefit this underdeveloped area of study. All of the studies in this review were cross-sectional and thus only provide a snapshot of Black bisexual women and their health experiences at one moment in time. Longitudinal methods that collect data about Black bisexual women's experiences and attitudes across time will help researchers understand the influence of time and developmental milestones on these women's lives. Furthermore, questions about causation can be studied when temporal aspects are incorporated into research projects. All of the studies either used a qualitative or quantitative data analysis strategy. None used mixed-methods which could provide information about both the prevalence of health conditions and the lived experiences of Black bisexual women with those conditions. Arrays of data collection methods that incorporate biological markers in addition to self-report measures are also needed.

Limitations

There were some limitations to this study. The review exclusively focused on peer-reviewed scholarly literature and did not include editorials, letters, technical reports, theses, dissertations, or commentaries. These excluded publications, while not necessarily scholarly (i.e., peer-reviewed), may have presented more in-depth discourse about Black bisexual women. Also, only two databases using specific search terms were used to identify publications for inclusion in this review. The review is most likely to be exhaustive; however, it is possible more publications could have been identified if more databases were searched. Readers are encouraged to use caution in generalizing the findings of this review. Black bisexual women residing in the United States were the target population for this review; therefore, it may be inappropriate to generalize these findings to Black bisexual women outside of the United States. Furthermore, given that the studies did not include women of different Black ethnicities, middle-aged and older Black women, or women from the Mountain and Pacific regions of the United States, the findings of this review may not apply to them. In addition, most of these studies were conducted with women who openly (at least for the purposes of being included in the studies) identified as bisexual. The life experiences and health of these women may differ from those of women who do not disclose their sexual orientations or identify as bisexual but are, nonetheless, engaged in romantic relationships with men and women.

CONCLUSION

This systematic literature review has interrogated the public health and social science literature related to Black bisexual women. It found that only nine studies exist that focus exclusively on this population. This research tends to be pathology-focused and conducted with small, young samples which in turn, create a narrow view of these women. Exploring research questions that focus on resilience, resistance, and thriving in addition to risk will create a more robust literature. This complex literature will help healthcare professionals provide more individually tailored, inclusive, and affirming services to their clients. Overall, a more holistic literature will help healthcare workers and researchers develop and implement strategies that assist Black bisexual women in creating healthier and more fulfilling lives.

REFERENCES

Alexander, K., Volpe, E., Abboud, S., & Campbell, J. (2016). Reproductive coercion, sexual risk behaviours and mental health symptoms among young low-income behaviourally bisexual women: Implications for nursing practice. *Journal of Clinical Nursing*. Advance online publication. doi: 10.1111/jocn.13238.

Balsam, K., Molina, Y., Blayney, J., Dillworth, T., Zimmerman, L., & Kaysen, D. (2015). Racial/ethnic differences in identity and mental health outcomes among young sexual minority women. *Cultural Diversity and Ethnic Minority Psychology, 21*, 380–390. doi: 10.1037/a0038680

Bates, D. (2012). Beyond expectations: The experiences of two African American bisexual women. *Journal of Bisexuality, 12*, 404–416. doi: 10.1080/15299716. 2012.702622

Bowleg, L. (2008). When Black + lesbian + woman ≠ Black lesbian woman: The methodological challenges of qualitative and quantitative intersectionality research. *Sex Roles, 59,* 312–325. doi: 10.1007/s11199–008–9400-z

Bowleg, L., Burkholder, G., Teti, M., & Craig, M. (2008). The complexities of outness: Psychosocial predictors of coming out to others among Black lesbian and bisexual women. *Journal of LGBT Health Research, 4,* 153–166. doi: 10.1080/15574090903167422

Calabrese, S., Meyer, I., Overstreet, N., Haile, R., & Hansen, N. (2015). Exploring discrimination and mental health disparities faced by Black sexual minority women using a minority stress framework. *Psychology of Women Quarterly, 39,* 287–304. doi: 10.1177/0361684314560730

Champion, J., Wilford, L., Shain, R., & Piper, J. (2005). Risk and protective behaviors of bisexual minority women: A qualitative analysis. *International Nursing Review, 52,* 115–122. doi: 10.1111/j.1466–2435.2005.00246.x

Cochran, S., & Mays, V. (1998). Disclosure of sexual preference to physicians by Black lesbian and bisexual women. *Western Journal of Medicine, 149*(5), 616–619.

Collins, P. (2008). *Black feminist thought: Knowledge, consciousness, and the politics of empowerment.* New York, NY: Routledge.

Comeau, D. (2012). Label-first sexual identity development: An in-depth case study of women who identify as bisexual before having sex with more than one gender. *Journal of Bisexuality, 12,* 321–346. doi: 10.1080/15299716.2012.702611

Feldman, M., & Meyer, I. (2007). Eating disorders in diverse lesbian, gay, and bisexual populations. *International Journal of Eating Disorders, 40,* 218–226. doi: 10.1002/eat.20360

Frost, D., Meyer, I., & Schwartz, S. (2016). Social support networks among diverse sexual minority populations. *American Journal of Orthopsychiatry, 86,* 91–102. doi: 10.1037/ort0000117

Greene, B. (2000). African American lesbian and bisexual women. *Journal of Social Issues, 56,* 239–249. doi: 10.1111/0022–4537.00163

Guh, D., Zhang, W., Bansback, N., Amarsi, Z., Birmingham, L., & Anis, A. (2009). The incidence of co-morbidities related to obesity and overweight: A systematic review and meta-analysis. *BMC Public Health, 9,* 1–20. doi: 10.1186/1471–2458–9–88

Henderson, L. (2009). Between the two: Bisexual identity among African Americans. *Journal of African American Studies, 13,* 263–282. doi: 10.1007/s12111–008–9072–3

Karenga, M. (1995). Black psychology. In K. Monteiro (Ed.), *Ethnicity and psychology: African, Asian-, Latino-, and Native-American psychologies* (Revised Printing, pp. 21–39). Retrieved from http://www.radford.edu/jaspelme/minority-groups/past_courses/Karenga_Black_Psychology.pdf

Li, C., Matthews, A., Aranda, F., Patel, C., & Patel, M. (2015). Predictors and consequences of negative patient-provider interactions among a sample of African American sexual minority women. *LGBT Health, 2,* 140–146. doi: 10.1089/lgbt.2014.0127

MacCarthy, S., Mena, L., Chan, P., Rose, J., Simmons, D.,...Nunn, A. (2015). Sexual network profiles and risk factors for STIs among African-American sexual minorities in Mississippi: A cross-sectional analysis. *LGBT Health, 2,* 276–281. doi: 10.1089/lgbt.2014.0019

Matthews, A., Li, C., McConnell, E., Aranda, F., & Smith, C. (2016). Rates and predictors of obesity among African American sexual minority women. *LGBT Health.* Advance online publication. doi: 10.1089/lgbt.2015.0026

Morris, J., Balsam, K., & Rothblum, E. (2002). Lesbian and bisexual mothers and nonmothers: Demographics and the coming-out process. *Journal of Family Psychology, 16,* 144–156. doi: 10.1037//0893–3200.16.2.144

Muzny, C., Rivers, C., Parker, C., Mena, L., Austin, E., & Schwebke, J. (2014). Lack of evidence for sexual transmission of genital candida species among women who have sex with women: A mixed methods study. *Sexually Transmitted Infections, 90,* 165–170. doi:10.1136/sextrans-2013–051361

Russell, L. (2010). *Fact sheet: Health disparities by race and ethnicity.* Retrieved from: https://www.americanprogress.org/issues/healthcare/news/2010/12/16/8762/fact-sheet-health-disparities-by-race-and-ethnicity/

Sanchez, J., Meacher, P., & Beil, R. (2005). Cigarette smoking and lesbian and bisexual women in the Bronx. *Journal of Community Health, 30,* 23–37. doi: 10.1007/s10900–004–6093–2

Sigurvinsdottir, R., & Ullman, S. (2015). The role of sexual orientation in the victimization and recovery of sexual assault survivors. *Violence and Victims, 30,* 636–648. doi: 10.1891/0886–6708.VV-D-13–00066

Szymanski, D., & Meyer, D. (2008). Racism and heterosexism as correlates of psychological distress in African American sexual minority women. *Journal of LGBT Issues in Counseling, 2,* 94–108. doi: 10.1080/15538600802125423

Walker, J., & Longmire-Avital, B. (2013). The impact of religious faith and internalized homonegativity on resiliency for Black lesbian, gay, and bisexual emerging adults. *Developmental Psychology, 49,* 1723–1731. doi: 10.1037/a0031059

Wilson, B., Okwu, C., & Mills, S. (2011). Brief report: The relationship between multiple forms of oppression and subjective health among Black lesbian and bisexual women. *Journal of Lesbian Studies, 15,* 15–24. doi: 10.1080/10894160.2010.50839

Chapter 3

Uses of the Interstitial as Power

Black, Bisexual Men Building Maroon Health

H. Sharif "Herukhuti" Williams

In the age of Al Qaeda, ISIS/ISIL, and Boko Haram, this is not an insignificant declaration to make: it is terrifying to be intentionally at odds with the status quo. To resist the colonizing impact of imperialist white supremacist capitalist heteropatriarchy upon the body, mind and spirit is to live in an ongoing relationship to and tension with terror. It is the knowledge that at any moment the daily brutality of oppression—be it state violence or microaggressions—could come barreling through the barricades we put into place to protect us. We know that there are structures in place to absorb, contain, or crush counterhegemonic praxis. Yet for those of us who have made the decision to resist, the option to not do so came at too high a price of our souls to be viable. So we live a maroon existence at the interstitial borderlands of the world created by and for our oppression and the worlds we've created to sustain ourselves while we gather support to dismantle the world that would be our undoing.

What, therefore, is health in this context? It has to be more than what can be achieved in partnership with one's medical doctor—whether allopath, naturopath or homeopath. And still, health outside of those strictures is rarely, if ever, addressed in the health literature. I mean a *sociocultural health* that considers the health of the immediate social and cultural environment within which persons live, love, fuck, function, work, relate, play, practice, participate, etc. The recognition of the role of social forces (e.g., oppression, discrimination, intergenerational exposure to structural violence, liberatory struggle, social justice movements) and culture including arts, aesthetics, rituals, and sacred spaces in the well-being of a person, group, or community is what I am calling sociocultural health. Sociocultural health is the quality of the relationship between the person and the social forces and cultural production around them. Sociocultural health is the ways in which community and culture support the health and wellness of the metaphysical bodies of people in a given environment. By metaphysical, I mean the social body, cultural body, spiritual body, and all of those bodies that participate in the production of life with the physical body, but yet are not constitutive of that body.

In this chapter, I use autoethnography and case study to examine the social determinants of sociocultural health for Black bisexual men (that is, Black men who share sexual, erotic, sensual, and/or intimacy resources with more than one gender of persons[1]) as we live at the interstitial spaces between community and colonialism as well as the intersection of race, ethnicity, gender, and sexuality. In so doing, I explore the potential for the development of a *maroon health paradigm* for/by/within Black bisexual men that relies upon our resources and serves as a counterhegemonic practice. As for the social determinants of health, I'm specifically thinking about imperialist white supremacist capitalist heteropatriarchy and the role it plays in sociocultural health.

Autoethnography is a research process that requires the researcher to become the research (Boylorn & Orbe, 2014; Jones, Adams, & Ellis, 2013). Whereas in ethnographic inquiry, an ethnographer embeds themselves in a community and observes the social activities of its members for the purpose of understanding the culture and social dynamics of that community, in autoethnographic inquiry, the ethnographer observes their phenomenological experience of home, community, society, etc. within a given moment, circumstance, or experience for the purpose of understanding larger social forces. What emerges is a story that reveals truth through meaning, texture, and tone. Like ethnography inquiry, autoethnography is a conversation between lived experiences, existing theories, and conceptual frameworks—informing and speaking to each other.

One major difference between ethnography and autoethnography is the exercise of power. Ethnography has historically been the tool of colonial interests imposing ethnocentric values and culturally laden assumptions on the *Other* (Mountz, 2009). Autoethnography, however, requires a practice of critical self-reflection and reflexivity (Jones, Adams, & Ellis, 2013). Being the researcher and the researched, the autoethnographer practices vulnerability as an epistemological tool through disclosure, authenticity, and revelation. Through the story, personal and social, the autoethnographer brings the nature of social life into focus for analysis and critical reflection.

The concept of a *maroon health paradigm* is based upon maroon societies that were created by Africans in the colonial era who liberated themselves from enslavement and established communities independent of the imperialist/colonial/slaving regime. Given that we are still living within imperialist white supremacist capitalist heteropatriarchy, a maroon health paradigm is one in which African[2] people form systems that nourish, nurture, and sustain them in ways that are resistant and counterhegemonic. I'm interested in exploring what that looks like in relation to sociocultural health, specifically, the quality of wellness, sustainability, and revitalization of Black bisexual men as social and cultural beings. This includes spiritual and existential well-being, the sense that one is empowered and possesses agency and subjectivity (one's awareness of oneself as a subject in the world, both producing social reality and produced by social structures).

BEYOND RESILIENCE: MAROON RESISTANCE

Resilience has become an important concept in theorizing the adaptive tools and abilities used by members of oppressed people (people of color, LGBT people, etc.) in response to the structural inequalities they encounter (Colpitts & Gahagan, 2016; Follins, Walker, & Lewis, 2014). Although there is no consistent definition of resilience in the social science and public health literature, researchers believe that both intrapersonal (e.g., strong sense of racial group membership, integration of multiple identities such as ethno-racial, sexual, and religious identity, a sense of self, and positive or active coping skills) and social factors (e.g., supportive community and protective interpersonal relationships) contribute to the degree to which members of these groups can live and function within a society that undermines their well-being (Colpitts & Gahagan, 2016; Follins, Walker, & Lewis, 2014). Resilience, the ability to recover after experiencing trauma, assault, injury, or the impact of an undermining force, has been attractive to researchers who wish to adopt a strengths-based alternative to prevailing pathological models for understanding oppressed people (Follins, Walker, & Lewis, 2014). However, as Colpitts and Gahagan (2016) observed, "resilience as a conceptual framework in understanding and measuring LGBTQ health . . . has traditionally been framed and conceptualized from an ethnocentric, white, Western perspective, as the emphasis on individualism demonstrates" (p. 6).

On a practical level and to borrow from boxing terminology, resilience measures how well you can take a punch. As a tool, it does not help anyone interested in understanding how to prevent the initiation of the punch or counter the punch to disarm the opponent and defend oneself. Resilience doesn't provide a language for analyzing the circumstances that brought one into the ring in the first place, recognizing who is benefiting from the staging of the fight, or determining if the deal made on the purse is exploitative or beneficial. Resilience just helps you make claims about how well someone can be a punching bag without falling out.

Conceptually, resilience is ideologically tied to interests that seek to maintain the status quo—a product of neoliberalism. It treats oppression as given/

constant that does not warrant critique, change, or challenge. Consequently, it is ideologically and ethically inadequate for work with oppressed people. The inadequacy of resilience theory makes a counterhegemonic framework necessary for those of us who approach health equity in the Black radical tradition—the ongoing project of liberatory, revolutionary struggle. Kelly (2002) defined the Black radical tradition as a, "political space where the energies of love and imagination are understood and respected as powerful social forces" (p. 4) with aims that focus on "total transformation of society, not just granting aggrieved populations greater political and economic power . . . . new social relationships, new ways of living and interacting, new attitudes toward work and leisure and community" (p. 5).

Black radical traditions are not satisfied with the prevalence of Black folks who have learned to be adaptive or habituated to oppression. That's not what it means to be healthy within a radical imagination. Black people who are maladaptive are preferable to those who are adaptive within imperialist white supremacist capitalist heteropatriarchy. A Black radical imagining of health embraces counterhegemonic and resistance praxis—a paradigm of what I call, maroon health. Maroon health is an example of what Sandoval (2000) described as *oppositional consciousness:* "a rhetoric of resistance, an apparatus for countering neocolonizing postmodern global formations" (p. 1). According to Kars (2015), maroons and marronage are described in the following ways:

> The term "maroons" refers to people who escaped slavery to create independent groups and communities on the outskirts of slave societies. Scholars generally distinguish two kinds of marronage, though there is overlap between them. "Petit marronage," or running away, refers to a strategy of resistance in which individuals or small groups, for a variety of reasons, escaped their plantations for a short period of days or weeks and then returned. "Grand marronage," much less prevalent, and the topic here, refers to people who removed themselves from their plantations permanently (n.p.).

Maroons practiced freedom in opposition to the white supremacist, slaving society and offered alternative ways of existing to Africans who remained hostage while state-sanctioned chattel slavery was maintained. St-Hilaire (2000) described the maroon societies of Jamaica thusly:

> Marronage was a common response of enslaved Africans throughout the Americas to the inhumanity of plantation life. In the early 1600s, under the Spanish, there already existed Maroon communities in the mountains of Jamaica. However, it was not until the British captured and colonized the island from 1652 onward that marronage grew to large-scale proportions. Plantation masters, with the backing of colonial authorities and their own private military forces,

expended considerable resources to subdue the early Maroons. Nevertheless, by the 1680s and 1690, formidable bands of Maroons were well established in the Blue Mountains of eastern Jamaica and in the Cockpit Country of northwestern Jamaica. Efforts to destroy the Maroon communities bore little fruit. By the 1720s, the Maroons' numbers and organizational capacity had grown to such strength that the Jamaican plantocracy and colonial authorities lived in a state of continual anxiety and fear. (p. 107)

The imperialist white supremacist capitalist heteropatriarchal state defined maroons as enemies of the state, terrorists, outlaws, and criminals. The combination of mainstream stigma, criminalization, and counterhegemonic resistance praxis makes marronage particularly useful in conceptualizing Black bisexual men and sociocultural health.

BLACK BISEXUAL MASCULINITIES AND MARRONAGE

For many reasons, Black bisexual men are disruptions to the status quo. Being Black, bisexual, and male puts one at odds with the mainstream of Black life, LGBT politics, and the larger society in ways that terrify the enemies of complexity. This is in part, due to what Black bisexual theologian, Shaykh Dr. Ibrahim Abdurrahman Farajajé, called the society's "fictions of purity," the title of his experimental essay (Farajajé, 2014). In this contribution to the anthology *Recognize: The Voices of Bisexual Men*, Farajajé (2014) wrote:

In cultures that prioritize either/or thinking, either/or monolithic/oppositional definitions of sexualities/genders, in an either/or world, anything that occupies a liminal, an intersectional, an interstitial location is seen as a threat . . . . those who inhabit interstitial spaces, those who move between worlds, those who are literally fringe-dwellers, are seen as the ultimate threat. (p. 147)

Black feminist thought has provided us with a powerful way to understand intersectional locations. We carry multiple social identities (e.g., race, ethnicity, gender, socioeconomic class, sexuality, generation, (dis)ability, nationality) that the societies and cultures into which we were born place upon us (Combahee River Collective, 1977; Crenshaw, 1989). There is a matrix of domination—structural inequality—that distributes power, privilege, status, and access to individuals and groups based upon their social identities (Collins, 2000). People receive advantages or disadvantages of power, privilege, status, and access for each of their social identities through the matrix of domination. The magnitude and direction of (dis)advantage for each social identity culminates at an intersection that is our (unique) social location in the society and culture. The matrix of domination that currently operates in the United States, the Westernized World, and most other parts of the globe is imperialist white supremacist capitalist heteropatriarchy.

Blackness is threatening to and within white supremacy. Although the racial classification "Black" was forged within the crucible of white supremacy, the cultural milieu—started on the continent of Africa and spread across the Diaspora—which we call Blackness shakes, shivers, troubles, and confounds white supremacy with each unbound, unbossed, and unbothered expression. By virtue of their multivalent nature, Black bisexualities challenge the integrity of heterosexism in Black communities and homonormativity, that is, the policing of narrowly defined ways to be LGBTQ in so-called LGBT communities as well as the monosexism[3] in these communities. We live, love, and fuck outside the confines of binary notions of gender and monosexual restrictions of single-gender love or same-gender love. Black bisexual masculinities contribute to competition between men who have sex with women within the sexual economy of heterosexuality and challenge the heterosexist male privilege that protects heterosexual men from objectification or being the objects of sexual pursuit by other men. For heterosexist men, we simultaneously threaten his hold on his woman and his booty. Consequently, Black bisexual masculinities are a threat to heteropatriarchy.

The phenomenon of gay identity politics emerged in the Westernized world with the uprising at the Stonewall Bar in New York City ("the Stonewall Riots") and colonized the lives of various people of the Global South and people of color in the West and affected ways of forming relationships (Cruz-Malavé & Manalansan, 2002; Hawley, 2001). The rainbow flag imperialism of gay identity politics privileges middle class, able-bodied, white gay cismen's interests and values as normative queerness and universal truths. Within these politics, the rhetoric of *coming out* says that to be a good queer, one must *come out of the closet* in proclaiming one's sexual identity—a sexual identity that is fixed, immutable, and genetic. Many Black bisexual men resist these politics and do not practice coming out politics as their Black gay and same-gender loving brothers do (Malebranche, Arriola, Jenkins, Dauria, & Patel, 2010). Using the term "down low," mainstream media and some researchers lacking cultural competence regarding Black bisexuality have mischaracterized these practices as acts of dishonesty, self-hate, and low levels of sexual identity development, but more rigorous inquiry has not supported these fallacies (Han, Rutledge, Bond, Lauby & LaPollo, 2014; Malebranche, 2008). This disidentification[4] with gay identity politics is Black bisexual men's practice of resistance—a sexual marronage. Many bisexual men practice sexual marronage to the extent that they disidentify with any label or classification—even bisexual as a label. The practices of secrecy, hiding, masking, and being covert are all important maroon tactics of protection, defense, and guerilla warfare. As a child of members of the Black Panther Party (BPP) and the grandchild of members of the American Labor Party, I learned to value these tactics as valuable skills for Black people, particularly revolutionaries.

Black bisexual men have been practicing various forms of marronage for quite some time. Kuwasi Balagoon, a Black radical anarchist revolutionary, was a bisexual man whose code name in the Black Liberation Army was, appropriately, "Maroon" (Umoja, 2015). Umoja (2015) described Balagoon's commitment to "win national liberation for New Afrikan people and to elimi-nate capitalism, imperialism, and ultimately authoritarian forms of govern-ment" (p. 216). Balagoon (2003) expressed the ethos of marronage:

> Where we live and work . . . We must organize on the ground level. The land-lords must be contested through rent strikes and rather than develop strategies to pay rent, we should develop strategies to take the buildings. . . . Set up com-munes in abandoned buildings. . . . Turn vacant lots into gardens. When our children grow out of clothes, we should have places we can take them, clearly marked anarchist clothing exchanges. . . . We must learn construction and ways to take back our lives . . . (in Umoja, 2015, p. 216)

A maroon and prisoner of war who had been diagnosed HIV-positive, Balagoon died while serving a life sentence in prison, on December 13, 1986, from pneumocystis pneumonia. Balagoon was not merely an *armchair revo-lutionary* maroon who only theorized what it meant to be counterhegemonic. He put his body on the line to practice his politics. He was a tenants' rights organizer, BPP member, and Revolutionary Armed Task Force member. He helped liberate Assata Shakur from the Clinton Correctional Institution for Women in New Jersey on November 2, 1979. His maroon sensibilities set the stage for my discussion of maroonage and sociocultural health.

SOCIOCULTURAL HEALTH

In westernized discussions of health, we discuss the health of the individual (e.g., medical health and mental health) and the health of groups of individu-als (e.g., public health). If we are being expansive in our thinking, we might also consider the capacities of the physical environment to positively or nega-tively impact the health of individuals such as environmental racism, food deserts, allergens, and lead exposure. Rarely, do we discuss the relationship between the health of a person and the social forces and cultural production around them.

As I think about sociocultural health, I am asking the question: In what ways do the social dynamics and the production of culture provide the sociocultural resources that address the needs of the person or Black bisexual men as a community? Farajajé-Jones (2000) described the conditions of Black queer men that inform my understanding of our sociocultural needs when he said, "our bodies have been colonized and treated as though they were someone's occupied territories, with all sorts of projections and fears mapped out across them" (p. 328).

To be a colonized body, have a body that is occupied territory is to live in a state of dispossession from one's feelings, desires, urges, and sense of pleasure and ecstasy. It is to not be at home regardless of where you are because the body within which one cannot escape until death is a prison. Therefore, sociocultural health practices for Black bisexual men will sometimes be as transgressive in form and function as the prison break Kuwasi Balagoon helped to organize. But they will necessarily be counterhegemonic and designed to decolonize. Farajajé-Jones (2000) argued that the "decolonization of Black queer male bodies begins with the physical/spiritual/psychological process of making our bodies and our desire our own" (p. 330).

How does one, therefore, create social forces and cultural products that fosters the decolonization process? One way of doing this is through sex. Not just any kind of sex, but sex as a physical, spiritual, and psychological process that is intentionally crafted to decolonize bodies and desires. Not just sex but experiences of the Erotic,[5] sensuality, and sexual pleasure that help people own their desires. But this is dangerous work due to the political economy of sexuality and erotophobia, particularly in westernized societies. As Farajajé-Jones (2000) pointed out, "part of our colonized mentality has made us queers think that if we deny and trivialize the centrality of sex in our lives, in our (s) experiences, in our creativity, in our thoughts, in our dreams, in our interactions, then we will be more acceptable to the dominating culture" (p. 331).

Through the creation of sexual maroon spaces and communities, there is a possibility of cultivating sociocultural health for Black bisexual men. Such erotic interventions provide "a measure between the beginnings of our sense of self and the chaos of our strongest feelings . . . . For having experienced the fullness of this depth of feeling and recognizing its power, in honor and self-respect we can require no less of ourselves" (Lorde, 1999, p. 79), our communities, and the societies within which we live.

BLACK FUNK: AN AUTOETHNOGRAPHY

By the end of the 1990s, I had come to the realization that I needed to integrate the various forms of activism with which I had been engaged over the course of a decade. I had seen the limitations of racial justice organizing. I had marched through Howard Beach with Al Sharpton and marched to Mayor Ed

Koch's midtown condo with Lisa Williamson and National Youth/Student Alliance to protest racist violence against Black people. I had marched on campus at the University of Southern California to protest the maltreatment of Black students by campus security.

I also spent four years running a support and advocacy group for men—the Brotherhood of African Men. The time cultivating a community of men that were capable of being vulnerable with each other, supporting each other across differences, and challenging each other to become better human beings was exhausting and rewarding. We held several weekly discussion groups, offered tai chi and yoga classes, organized Black history teach-ins, hosted a Friday night Black comedy show, and mentored young boys in the Nickerson Housing Project in Los Angeles. This kind of internal work reflected my shift in understanding the importance of decolonizing the mind and fostering critical consciousness that I read in Paulo Freire's *Pedagogy of the Oppressed* and Frantz Fanon's *The Wretched of the Earth*.

As I reflected on these experiences, however, I felt something was still missing. Whether we achieved our goals or not, there were limitations to our work. I was also going through my own self-inventory as a bisexual man. In a polyamorous relationship with a ciswoman for several years, I noticed that the sexual relationships I had with men tended to be less intimate than the non-sexual relationships I had with men. The sexual relationships seemed fraught with emotional challenges; the men seemed unable to feel their feelings and experience male-male emotional intimacy with a man with whom they were having sex. Having had an emotionally engaging relationship with my partner, I knew it was possible for me to have a sexual relationship in which the participants were emotionally present. Having had emotionally engaging relationships with men in my organization, I knew it was possible for me to have non-sexual relationships with men in which we were emotionally present. I couldn't understand what was happening or even a way to get answers.

Then I took a Theatre of the Oppressed (TO) workshop at a theatre education conference. TO is a decolonizing theatre methodology that uses the body's ability to know, tell stories, and be a resource in strategizing social change (Boal, 1979, 1992, 1995, 1998). Having practiced tai chi chuan, yoga, meditation, and Kemetic spirituality since I was fourteen years old, I was immediately attracted to TO's use of embodiment and the trickster motif—an energy that facilitates transformative learning through guile, subterfuge and trickery (Williams, 2006, 2009).

Soon after learning how to work with people using TO and the Joker/trickster motif, I designed and facilitated a workshop for men who experience same-sex desire called *Erotic Play for Men*. The workshop combined TO and meditation in a 90-minute space of intimate touch, conversation, and play.

I was invited to offer the workshop at DC Black Pride, an annual Black LGBT gathering in Washington, DC. But with the provocative title, I attracted about 20 men to the session. That first session was transformative for me as I watched the men take physical and emotional risks to be intimate with men who were strangers to them and, for a few, in the presence of men who were their friends. The feedback was also moving as the men shared how unique the experience of intimacy was for them outside of sex. Some of the men expressed that they had never experienced that level of intimacy with their sexual partners. Their expressions of the value of the experience confirmed for me the necessity of this work.

From 1999 to the early 2000s, I was invited to offer the workshop at Black Pride gatherings in Washington, DC, New York City, and Philadelphia. Each year in Washington DC, the attendance grew. At the height, there were approximately sixty men who participated in the workshop. Year after year, men would tell their friends about the workshop and the following year, their friends would attend. The ways in which the workshop informed the participant's embodied vocabulary—the sensual and erotic concepts their bodies were able to communicate—suggested to me that I had unearthed an area of knowing that should be pursued.

But the process was also transforming me. I began to see my role as an activist differently. My practice of activism shifted from the direct action mobilization of people to the streets to the direct action mobilization of people to the sheets. And I wanted more of it. My partner purchased a three-family home in the Fort Greene neighborhood of Brooklyn, New York, and rented one of the floors to me so that I could continue my work. At first, I used the space to host sex parties for men of color. There were several existing sex parties in New York City for men. They were places of ill repute that everyone knew of, but few admitted patronizing. Their legality was an open question in the community. Most people assumed they were illegal or at least a strain on the laws against prostitution because people were paying to have sex even if they weren't paying each other to have it. I visited a couple of them and had problems with their design.

All of the sex parties I visited had a basic layout, which I won't disclose here to protect these spaces from the intrusion of state agents such as law enforcement agencies and public health departments and outsiders. One common element of the design was what I call *the dark room*—the space in which sex occurs. These rooms were usually designed to be pitch black or very dark. If the rooms had windows, the windows were blacked out. All lights were turned off in the rooms. When entering the dark room, one had to allow one's eyes to adjust to the absence of light, oftentimes only perceiving shadows in the dark. While it could be hot to feel one's way through the mass of bodies to find someone whose body felt pleasing to the touch, I also felt that the pitch black environment of dark rooms contributed to a disassociation from one's desires and pleasures. Personally, the dark room wasn't the optimal sexual environment for me. I liked to look into the eyes of my lovers, gaze upon the changes in blood flow along their necks, arms, and legs, watch the muscle spasms that erupt throughout their bodies while I am touching, kissing, licking, sucking, or fucking them. None of those visual indicators were accessible to me in those spaces.

So I created a sex party design that diverged from the others. My dark room had a strobe light at times that provided a dramatic effect on the bodies as they moved on, around, between, and in each other. Other times, I used candles and an essential oil diffuser to create a sacred sexual ambience. While the other sex party venues were in shabby, and often, dirty environments, my venue, *The Workshop*, had newly installed hardwood floors, elaborately painted walls, and hanging fabrics. Through speakers in all the rooms, we played Neo-soul music: D'Angelo's "Brown Sugar" album, Tweet's "Hummingbird" album, Maxwell's "Urban Hang Suite" and "Unplugged" albums, etc.

The energy of the space was very different from what I experienced in the other sex parties. One night, a young man in his twenties visited the party. He and I had sex in the dark room. Later, we reconnected in the lounge area. Stretched out on the couch, him in my arms I listened as he told me about his life. It was moving to be present for his exercise of vulnerability. The intimacy—not forced or clumsy—was merely an extension of the environment that we—hosts, volunteers, organizers, and patrons—created. As deep and meaningful as the intimacy was, it did not compel us to seek any relationship outside of that moment. When the party was over and all everyone had left, I closed the door, returned home, showered, and went to my bed with my partner.

After several months, I became bored with only hosting sex parties as a form of decolonizing sex. By that time, I had finished a graduate degree of education in curriculum and instruction and started my doctoral studies in human development, organization sciences, and systems theory. I started to create different offerings that I thought would decolonize the ways Black people thought about their bodies, desires, sex, and relationships. I drew upon my childhood memories of going to The Muse, the children's museum up the street from our apartment. I remembered the wonder I experienced going to it, feeling a sense of play while I learned. From all of these various sources of inspiration, I came up with the idea of a sexual cultural center that would create programming designed for decolonization. Black Funk was born.

I started an online discussion group for members of Black Funk where those who were local and those who weren't could connect, share their experiences, and discuss whatever emerged in current events related to Black sexuality. The online discussion group was also a great way to promote the new programming. Black Funk offered a nude yoga class, a massage group, an erotic game night, The Workshop sex parties, and an erotic wrestling club called Erotic Fight Club.

To many people who were members of the professional class of Black LGBT service providers, I was disreputable as a purveyor of sex. Although HIV prevention education was considered a necessary community service, to provide opportunities for people to feel pleasure, explore their desires, and be sexual bodies was too decadent for some. The fact that I was bisexual and involved in a polyamorous relationship with a ciswoman was also a source of marginality for me in environments dominated by gay men. I didn't shy away from these controversies nor did I covet it (Herukhuti, 2003). Despite those challenges, I maintained relationships with people who were willing to do the same. One local, community-based AIDS service organization provided free condoms and lube for The Workshop. I became a member of the Black Gay Research Group and helped organize its first summit. I hosted one of the subgroup meetings in the same room at Black Funk where I held the young man as he lay nude in my arms sharing his life story with me.

When my partner and I ended our relationship, I moved Black Funk to the Clinton Hill neighborhood of Brooklyn, New York, which was not too far from where we originally began. I turned my loft into both living space and a space for Black Funk. I kept much of the programming from our earlier venue, but upgraded the web presence from the discussion group to a website. I also hosted community events and rented the space to other groups. An interfaith minister, community activist, and artist rented the space to hold a communal music event he created called *The Sound Circle*. A fraternal organization of Black men into leather, kink, and BDSM held a night of demonstrations for the community in the space. I conducted my doctoral dissertation project, *Our Bodies, Our Wisdom*, in the space (Williams, 2006). When Rashawn Brazell, a young Black queer man, was murdered, dismembered, and scattered around parts of Brooklyn, I held a community-healing forum in the space.

REFLECTION

While Black Funk was my home, it also became a home for others at different times (Williams, 2010). The physical space provided opportunities for people to find home in their bodies and security in their desires. The virtual space provided opportunities for people to recognize the existence of other people seeking to decolonize their sexualities. Black Funk was a maroon community amid an environment of imperialist, white supremacist capitalist heteropatriarchy. Whether through attending the early workshops before the center opened or events at Black Funk, participating in the online discussion group, using the first website, reading my book *Conjuring Black Funk: Notes on Culture, Sexuality, and Spirituality, Volume 1*, or reading my scholarship based upon doing decolonizing sex work, the people who have been touched by the work continue to find inspiration in it to move the project of decolonization forward for themselves and others (Clark, 2015). Stalling (2015) offered:

> I end this study with Herukhuti's explanation of why he founded the Black Funk Center (sic) because it recaps that black people can and do create revolutionary sexual cultures that can become the foundation for centers of sexual health, well-being, and decolonization. Such centers are as important as churches, community centers, libraries, theatres, and museums. Black communities need more sexual cultural centers like Black Funk, but since sexuality and eroticism tend to be ignored, there are few political ideologies or organizations that see such centers as a part of black revolutionary movements. (p. 235)

Sexual marronage is necessary and dangerous work. It is one among a number of important interventions in the development of sociocultural health for Black people. In the case of Black Funk, the interstitial and intersectional space of Black bisexual manhood provided the necessary ingredients that gave it birth and nurtured it. During each stage of its development, Black Funk benefited from knowledge gained in the crucible of life in the margins and holding, what Patricia Hill Collins called, *the outsider-within status* (Collins, 2000) that Black bisexual men have within monosexist, heteronormative and homonormative spaces. Maris-Wolf (2015) described existential realities of maroons in Virginia's Dismal Swamp by saying,

> maroons were set apart from others in the swamp not solely by space (a buffer of impenetrable wilderness), as scholars have suggested, but by the legal status they renounced, the fugitive status they embraced, and the bonds they forged with one another. (p. 453)

While there can be much hardship, trauma, and marginality that Black bisexual men experience as sexual maroons, the interstitiality and intersectionality that we experience can be a source of power if we choose to embrace it (Williams, 2010). The story of Black Funk and its development of sociocultural health is just one such example of how this possible.

NOTES

1. The term "bisexual" has been used and understood to mean different things over time including meaning intersex or genderqueer identity (Prosser & Storr, 1998,

p. 76). The definition of bisexuality I am using in this chapter is consistent with definitions used within the modern bisexual movement as articulated in the 1990 *Bisexual Manifesto* (BiNet USA, 2014).

2. I use the term "African" to refer to Black people living in Africa or the African Diaspora.

3. Monosexism is the structural violence and system of oppression that punishes people who do not limit their sexuality to one gender and rewards people who do, that is, heterosexual, gay, and lesbian people.

4. Muñoz coined the term "disindentification" in his book, *Disidentification: Queers of Color and the Performance of Politics* to conceptualize the actions and strategies of oppressed people to resist and/or subvert dominant and mainstream narratives of their subjectivities and identities.

5. My use of this term is informed by Lorde's conceptualization of the Erotic (1992) as "those physical, emotional, and psychic expressions of what is deepest and strongest and richest within each of us, being shared: the passion of love, in its deepest meanings" (p. 80).

REFERENCES

BiNet USA (2014). 1990 anything that moves bisexual manifesto. Retrieved from http://binetusa.blogspot.com/2014/01/1990-bi-manifesto.html

Boal, A. (1979). *Theatre of the oppressed*. New York, NY: Theatre Communications.

———. (1992). *Games for actors and non-actors*. New York, NY: Routledge.

———. (1995). *The rainbow of desire: The Boal method of theatre and therapy*. New York, NY: Routledge.

———. (1998). *Legislative theatre: Using performance to make politics*. New York, NY: Routledge.

Boylorn, R. M., & Orbe, M. P. (2014). *Critical autoethnography: Intersecting cultural identities in everyday life*. Walnut Creek, CA: Left Coast Press.

Clarke, Z. S. H. (2015). *Coming to my senses: A decolonizing autoethnographic exploration of Ọ̀ṣunality*. (Doctoral Dissertation). Available from ProQuest Dissertations and Theses database. (UMI No. 10014780)

Colpitts, E., & Gahagan, J. (2016). The utility of resilience as a conceptual framework for understanding and measuring LGBTQ health. *International Journal for Equity in Health, 15*(60), 1–8.

Combahee River Collective. (1977). *Combahee river collective statement*. Retrieved April 27, 2016, from http://circuitous.org/scraps/combahee.html

Collins, P. H. (2000). *Black feminist thought: Knowledge, consciousness, and the politics of empowerment, 2nd edition*. New York, NY: Routledge.

Crenshaw, K. (1989). Mapping the margins: Intersectionality, identity politics, and violence against women of color. *Stanford Law Review, 43*(6), 1241–1299.

Cruz-Malavé, A., & Manalansan, M. F. (2002). *Queer globalizations: Citizenship and the afterlife of colonialism*. New York, NY: New York University Press.

Farajajé, I. A. (2014). Fictions of purity. In R. Ochs & H. Williams (Eds.). *Recognize: The voices of bisexual men* (pp. 146–151), Boston, MA: Bisexual Resource Center.

Farajajé-Jones, E. (2000). Holy fuck. In K. Kay, J. Nagle, & B. Gould (Eds.), *Male lust: Pleasure, power, and transformation* (pp. 327–335). New York, NY: Harrington Park Press.

Follins, L. D., Walker, J. J., & Lewis, M. K. (2014). Resilience in Black lesbian, gay, bisexual, and transgender individuals: A critical review of the literature. *Journal of Gay & Lesbian Mental Health, 18*(2), 190–212.

Han, C., Rutledge, S. E., Bond, L., Lauby, J., & LaPollo, A. B. (2014). You're better respected when you carry yourself as a man: Black men's personal accounts of the down low "lifestyle." *Sexuality & Culture, 18*, 89–102.

Hawley, J. C. (2001). *Post-colonial queer: Theoretical intersections*. Albany, NY: State University of New York Press.

Herukhuti (2003). To inhabit my desires: Finding meaning in the face of HIV education. In S. G. Fullwood & C. Robinson (Eds.), *Think again* (pp. 39–41). New York State Black Gay Network and AIDS Project Los Angeles.

Jones, S. H., Adams, T. E., & Ellis, C. (2013). *Handbook of autoethnography*. Walnut Creek, CA: Left Coast Press.

Kars, M. (2015). *Maroons and marronage*. Retrieved April 27, 2016, from http://www.oxfordbibliographies.com/view/document/obo-9780199730414/obo-9780199730414-0229.xml

Kelly, R. D. G. (2002). *Freedom dreams: The Black radical imagination*. Boston, MA: Beacon Press.

Lorde, A. (1992). Use of the erotic: The erotic as power. In M. Decosta-Willis, R. Martin, & R. P. Bell (Eds.), *Erotique noire: Black erotica* (pp. 78–83). New York, NY: Anchor Books.

Malebranche, D. (2008). Bisexually active Black men in the United States and HIV: Acknowledging more than the "down low." *Archive of Sex Behavior, 37*, 810–816.

Malebranche, D., Arriola, K. J., Jenkins, T. R., Dauria, E., & Patel, S. N. (2010). Exploring the "bisexual bridge": A qualitative study of risk behavior and disclosure of same-sex behavior among Black bisexual men. *American Journal of Public Health, 100*(1), 159–164.

Maris-Wolf, T. (2013). Hidden in plain sight: Maroon life and labor in Virginia's Dismal Swamp. *Slavery & Abolition, 34*(3), 446–464.

Mountz, A. (2009). The other. In C. Gallaher, C. T. Dahlman, M. Gilmartin, A. Mountz, & P. Shirlow (Eds.), *Key concepts of political geography* (pp. 328–338). Thousand Oaks, CA: Sage.

Muñoz, J. E. (1999). *Disidentification: Queers of color and the performance of politics*. Minneapolis, MN: University of Minnesota Press.

Newman, S. J. (2013). Prevention, not prejudice: The role of federal guidelines in HIV-criminalization reform. *Northwestern University Law Review, 107*(3), 1403–1436. Retrieved from https://fgul.idm.oclc.org/login?url=http://search.proquest.com/docview/1445177437?accountid=10868

Prosser, J., & Storr, M. (1998). Introduction. In L. Bland & L. Doan (Eds.), *Sexology uncensored: The documents of sexual science* (pp. 75–77). Chicago, IL: University of Chicago Press.

Sandoval, C. (2000). *Methodology of the oppressed*. Minneapolis, MN: University of Minnesota Press.

St-Hilaire, A. (2000). Global incorporation and cultural survival: The Surinamese maroons at the margins of the world-system. *Journal of World-Systems Research, 6*(1), 101–131.

Stallings, L. H. (2015). *Funk the erotic: Transaesthetics and Black sexual cultures.* Urbana, IL: University of Illinois Press.

Umoja, A. K. (2015). Maroon: Kuwasi Balagoon and the evolution of revolutionary new Afrikan anarchism. *Science & Society, 79*(2), 196–220.

Williams, H. S. (2006). Our bodies, our wisdom: Engaging Black men who experience same-sex desire in Afrocentric ritual, embodied epistemology, and collaborative inquiry. *Dissertation Abstracts International, 67*(02), 618A.

———. (2009). Black mama sauce: Embodied transformative education. In S. Schapiro, K. Geller, & B. Fisher-Yoshida (Eds.), *Innovations in transformative learning: Space, culture, and the arts* (pp. 269–286). New York, NY: Peter Lang.

———. (2010). Bodeme in Harlem: An African diasporic autoethnography. *Journal of Bisexuality, 10*, 64–78.

Chapter 4

Resistance as Resilience

How the Black Bisexual Community Keeps One Another Healthy

Della V. Mosley, Roberto L. Abreu,
and Candice Crowell

In the United States, Black bisexuals[1] are a diverse group that is comprised of individuals with multiple identities (gender, religious, ethnicity, ability, etc.) who live in areas that provide variable consequences and rewards for possessing those identities (Greene, 1996; Phillips & Stewart, 2010). In a social hierarchy where Blacks and bisexuals rank low independent of one another (Greene, 2000; Scott, 2007), the very existence of Black bisexuals is a position of resistance. This chapter will make the case that resistance is an important component of resilience for Black bisexuals in the United States. Psychopolitical wellness will be introduced as a frame for reviewing the literature on oppression among Black bisexuals. Then, the extant literature on resilience for Black bisexuals will be highlighted. Recognizing resistance as a strengths-focused, preventative, and empowering component of resilience, key themes associated with Black bisexual resistance will also be reviewed. Finally, because Black bisexual individuals and groups are often rendered invisible in psychological texts, this chapter will weave in concrete examples of Black bisexuals who embody resistance as resilience in personally and culturally salient ways.

PSYCHOPOLITICAL WELLNESS: A FRAMEWORK FOR EXPLORING BLACK BISEXUAL RESILIENCE

The ecological perspective of psychopolitical wellness (Prilleltensky, 2003, 2008) provides a helpful framework for understanding how the Black bisexual community experiences and responds to oppression. Prilleltensky (2003) defined oppression as "a state of asymmetric power relations characterized by domination, subordination, and resistance, whereby the controlling person or group exercise its power by processes of political exclusion and violence and by psychological dynamics of deprecation" (p. 195). This definition recognizes that political oppression (e.g., historical and structural exclusion) is inextricably linked to psychological oppression (e.g., internalizing negative views of self and group), influencing one's ability to work toward liberation (Prilleltensky, 2003, 2008). In this psychopolitical framework, liberation is defined as "the process of resisting oppressive forces and striving toward psychological and political well-being" (Prilleltensky, 2003, p. 195). As a process, liberation involves challenging oppression (e.g., joining social action groups, practicing inclusion; Prilleltensky, 2003). As a state of being, liberation is the achievement of freedom (e.g., peace, health, social cohesion; Prilleltensky, 2003). This theory suggests that the processes and state of oppression are experienced at personal, relational, and collective levels and that psychopolitical wellness is not achieved unless it simultaneously occurs at all three levels (Prilleltensky, 2003, 2008). Prilleltensky's (2003, 2008) approach to the psychopolitical is useful for conceptualizing wellness for individuals and groups who are specifically oppressed because of aspects of their identities. The framework allows researchers and clinicians to explore Black bisexuals' sources and experiences of oppression in a holistic manner that explicitly recognizes the role of power in their suffering or ability to resist.

OPPRESSION FACED BY BLACK BISEXUALS

For Black bisexuals in the United States, barriers to psychopolitical wellness exist at every level. The psychological literature available on Black bisexuals describes how their social identities position them lower in the racial, gender, sexuality, and social class-based hierarchical systems governing the United States. The collective, relational, and personal level experiences of oppression Black bisexual people face will be reviewed herein.

Collective-Level Oppression Facing Black Bisexuals

The historical context has contributed to Black bisexuals' experience of marginalization (Bates, 2012; Greene, 1996, 2000; Pettaway, Bryant, Keane, & Craig, 2014, Rust, 2003) and stigmatization (Collins, 2004; Henderson, 2009; Pettaway et al., 2014; Rust, 2003; Scott, 2007) as a collective. As Black Americans, they contend with the legacy of European colonization, economic exploitation through slavery, the political exclusion associated with the Jim Crow era, and the mass incarceration of Black people (Alexander, 2010;

Greene, 2000; Prilleltensky 2003). These systems of domination produced multiple restrictions on how masculinity and femininity were to be performed, which did not always align with the sexual diversity and relationship modalities of pre-colonial Africa (Greene, 2000; Phillips & Stewart, 2010). Thus, for bisexuals, the collective level experience of racial and gender-based discrimination associated with Western European values and the transatlantic slave trade led to increased policing of their gender expression and sexuality (Greene, 1996; Scott, 2007).

Greene (1996, 2000) used the term "ethnosexual mythologies" to describe the gender and sexual stereotypes of Black people that reify patriarchy, heteronormativity, and White supremacy. The myths of Black hypersexuality and sexual irresponsibility that arose as ways to explain the sexual violence and exploitation that occurred during slavery were internalized by many Black and White people, creating power differentials within the Black community (Greene, 1996, 2000). A politic of respectability, rooted in White, Western middle class values, emerged wherein heteronormative attractions and behaviors and stereotypic gender roles were the only acceptable ones (Greene, 2000). Black people who romantically engaged with people of the same gender faced restrictions and opposition from the Black community (Greene, 1996; Moore, 2012; Scott, 2007).

Many Black bisexuals were discouraged from claiming a queer[2] identity, especially publicly (Bates, 2012; Greene, 2000). However, Blues singers Ma Rainey and Bessie Smith are prime examples of Black bisexuals who resisted the respectability politics that were rampant at the turn of the twentieth century (Phillips & Stewart, 2010). These bi women performed songs that were inclusive of diverse genders and sexualities and openly dated men and women at a time when bisexuality among Black people was seen as reinforcing negative stereotypes that would further marginalize the Black collective (Greene, 1996, 2000; Phillips & Stewart, 2010). Yet, despite Black bisexuals' acts of resistance throughout history, the stigma associated with identifying as a bisexual persists in the 2010s (Bates, 2012).

Unfortunately for the Black bisexual community, there is also a history of stigmatization from within the lesbian and gay communities (Dodge et al., 2012; Friedman et al., 2014). Weiss' (2003) research on bisexual and transgender individuals within the LGBT "community" makes the case that both groups have historically been excluded. Lesbian and gay individuals may be exclusionary due to perceptions of bisexuality as a transitional or a more privileged identity (Rust, 2003). In a more recent study of 645 participants, Friedman and colleagues (2014) found that gay and lesbian participants held significantly higher negative attitudes toward bisexuals than the bisexual participants. In addition, respondents showed higher negative attitudes toward bisexual men than toward bisexual women (Friedman et al., 2014).

Historically, bisexual women have had more visibility and support than bisexual men in the LGBT community (Weiss, 2003).

As a collective, Black bisexuals are not perceived as politically powerful (Rust, 2003). They lack political representation and affirmative media visibility (O'Dowd, 2013; Yoshino, 2000). Economic exploitation is another psychopolitical vulnerability that Black bisexuals face. Evidence shows that lesbian, gay, bisexual, transgender, and queer (LGBTQ) people of color "earn lower salaries and achieve less workplace advancement than White LGBTQ individuals regardless of job performance or qualification" (Elmslie & Tebaldi, 2007). Using the federal poverty line as a baseline, Badgett, Durso, and Schneebaum (2013) found that 25.9 percent of bisexual men and 29.4 percent of bisexual women surveyed were poor, a rate higher than straight, gay, or bisexual men and women. This study utilized a racially diverse sample with Black (44.7 percent), Native American (39.1 percent), Asian (16.3 percent), White (13.7 percent), and "other" (41 percent) people represented. Unfortunately, much of the available data about the financial health of LGBTQ people in the United States does not provide specific information about Black bisexuals. Thus, in the absence of data on Black bisexual poverty, we can assume that Black bisexuals, particularly women, disproportionately contend with experiences and consequences of economic oppression (Battle & Crum, 2007).

Ethnosexual myths about Black bisexuals have limited an exploration of the issues impacting this community. As such, the extant literature on Black bisexuals is often pathologizing, essentializing, and objectifying (Childs, Laudone, & Tavernier, 2010; Pettaway et al., 2014; Rust, 2003). The public health and social science literature on Black bisexuality tends to focus on sexual health and stigma associated with Black bisexual men being on the *down low* (Pettaway et al., 2014; Phillips, 2005). Rust (2003) encourages researchers to move beyond simply focusing on sexual behaviors and attend to other components of bisexuality (e.g., coming out processes, emotional feelings, relationship values, bisexual identity). Without theories of Black bisexuality, particularly Black bisexual identity development, we lack an understanding of the Black bisexual collective, from their sense of self, to their behaviors, and aspirations (Bates, 2012; Greene, 2000).

Relational-Level Oppression Facing Black Bisexuals

Institutions central to the Black community, such as the family, the church, historically Black colleges and universities; Black fraternities, sororities, and other social groups; and Black civil rights organizations have traditionally been a source of support for Black people in the face of anti-Black racism (Blank, Mahmood, Fox, & Guterbock, 2002; Campbell et al., 2007;

Dudley, 2013; Greene, 2000; Wade & Harper, 2015). However, historically Black institutions have not provided bisexuals the same support for coping with and challenging gender and sexuality-based oppression (Bates, 2012; Dudley, 2013; Garner, 2008; Moore, 2008; Pettaway et al., 2014). Black bisexuals are taught by their family and church members that same-gender attractions are taboo and are discouraged from challenging stereotypic gender norms (Bates, 2012; Greene, 1996). Traditionally, these institutions have encouraged Black bisexuals to foreclose on sexual self-exploration (Bates, 2012) for the specific purposes of maintaining the respectability of the race (Greene, 1996, 2000; Scott, 2007). Transgressing heteronormativity in the Black community can reduce social capital, resulting in Black bisexuals being cast as not Black because of their attractions (Scott, 2007). Research suggests that some Black families follow a "don't ask, don't tell" policy, allowing them to maintain relational ties but ignore or deny their family members' sexuality (Bowleg, Burkholder, Teti, & Craig, 2008; Greene, 2000). A similar process has been documented in the church (Moore, 2008; Rust, 1996). Here, a "hate the sin, but love the sinner" approach has marginalized Black bisexuals (Moore, 2008). These mantras can be harmful and Black bisexuals have struggled to find truly supportive communities.

Without support from these traditional sources to which other Black people have access, Black bisexuals may seek refuge in queer communities. Queer service organizations and gay pride events, while meant to be a safe space for queer people, are not always welcoming to bisexuals (Rust, 2003) or Blacks (Balsam, Molina, Beadnell, Simoni, & Walters, 2011). The Black community perceives these spaces as catering to White lesbian and gay individuals and racism has been reported within some of them as well (Balsam et al., 2011; Bowleg et al., 2008). Thus, for Black bisexuals there are limited sources for everyday support (Frost, Meyer & Schwarz, 2016). This lack of support may be particularly problematic for Black bisexual men who, when compared to White bisexuals and Black women, receive less support from their partners (Frost et al., 2016).

Whether they are out to an intimate partner, Black bisexuals are vulnerable to violence. Intimate partner violence (IPV), a devastating life experience which 61 percent of bisexual women and 37 percent of bisexual men experience (Department of Health and Human Services [DHHS], 2010), presents additional barriers to relational wellness (Cunningham, 2011; Wade & Harper, 2015). The research indicates that bisexuals have higher rates of IPV than lesbian, gay, or heterosexual individuals, including an increased likelihood of reporting being raped in their teens and early twenties (DHHS, 2010). Given the increased exposure to violence and other symptoms of poverty that Black people face, it makes sense that Black bisexuals as a whole and low-resource Black bisexual women in particular would be especially vulnerable to IPV (Wilson, Lamis, Winn, & Kaslow, 2014). Such consistent experiences of oppression at the relational level also have personal level costs (Prilleltensky, 2003).

Personal-Level Oppression Facing Black Bisexuals

Many studies have concluded that bisexual individuals are at greater risk for substance use than heterosexual, gay, and lesbian individuals (Ford & Jasinski, 2006; Green & Feinstein, 2012; Hughes et al., 2006; Wilsnack et al., 2008). Also, most of the available research indicates the use of substances among Black bisexual men during sexual encounters, with most studies capturing the relation of substance use as a correlate to risk for acquiring HIV risk (Benoit & Koken, 2012; Halkitis & Jerome, 2008; Jerome & Halkitis, 2014). However, as indicated by Wade and Harper (2015) in a review of 54 studies about the negative health outcomes of Black men who have sex with men (MSM), the risk related to substance abuse among Black MSM is not statistically different than that of their heterosexual counterparts. Thus, the study of substance abuse in Black bisexuals is an area that still needs much research (Wade & Harper, 2015).

Black bisexuals experience higher rates of mood disorders when compared to their White counterparts (DHHS, 2010). In a quantitative study of 603 Black sexual minority women (11 percent bisexual), Mays, Cochran, and Roeder (2004) explored their levels of distress. The researchers found that Black sexual minority women, including bisexuals, reported high levels of depression, with over 50 percent of the participants reported having experienced a chronic, distressing situation within the last six months (Mays et al., 2004). In the case of Black bisexual men, a recent study of 117 Black bisexual men, Allen, Myers, and Williams (2014) found that participants reported high levels of depressive symptoms as a result of low levels of social support and high levels of discrimination. Also, this study shows that participants with low support from parents and peers presented with more mental health concerns than those participants with higher parent and peer support (Allen et al., 2014). In the face of substance use concerns and mental health concerns, Black bisexuals need but lack quality care. Black bisexuals also report higher incidents of negative experiences with healthcare providers (Li, Matthews, Aranda, Patel, & Patel, 2015).

Although the data presented in this section are alarming, researchers point out that very few resources have been employed for the care of this population (Hussen et al., 2015; Oswalt, 2009; Talley et al., 2014). In the absence of environmental protections and supportive institutions, Black bisexual men and women have found ways to foster their own, and their siblings'[3] resilience.

DEFINING RESILIENCE

Many scholars refer to resilience as a process of (a) adapting to or bouncing back from adversity and (b) thriving, or experiencing increased wellness, despite the risk (Brodsky et al., 2011; Follins, Walker, & Lewis, 2014; Singh, 2013). Brodsky and Cattaneo's (2013) Transconceptual Model of Empowerment and Resilience (TMER) distinguishes between resilience and resistance, noting that resistance is part of resilience processes. In TMER, "resilience consists of internal, local level goals that are aimed at intrapersonal actions and outcomes—adapting, withstanding, or *resisting* the situation as it is" (emphasis added, Brodsky & Cattaneo, 2013, p. 338). Thus resilience always exists in the context of oppression and at its best, goes beyond the intrapersonal level to include the relational and/or collective level experience of resisting oppression (Brodsky & Cattaneo, 2013).

Resilience involves five components: (1) a critical awareness of risk, (2) an intention to act against risk, (3) taking thoughtful action(s), (4) continually engaging in reflection from a strengths focused perspective, and (5) enlisting varying maintenance procedures such as protection and flexibility (Brodsky & Cattaneo, 2013). This process is iterative and in certain contexts, bisexual individuals may recognize that internal change goals are not sufficient for attaining wellness personally, relationally, and/or collectively. It is important to recall that resilience only exists in oppressive, risk-enhancing contexts (Brodsky & Cattaneo, 2013). Black bisexuals are resilient, maintaining their resolve to love radically in the face of multiple oppressions (Meyer, 2010).

Research on Resiliency Factors in Black Bisexual Individuals

Studies about Black bisexuals have explored their experiences of resilience in terms of: (a) the role of religion and spirituality as sources of support and (b) coping strategies used to navigate the oppression associated with one's racial and sexual identities. In a qualitative study of 28 Black bisexual men, Jeffries and colleagues (2008) explored the role of religion and spirituality in their lives. The participants identified religion and spirituality as crucial components in their lives. In addition, regardless of disapproval from religious leaders, spirituality was instrumental for these men to cope with homophobic and biphobic messages and internalized binegativity (Jeffries, Dodge, & Sandfort, 2008). Similar findings were reported by Kubicek and colleagues (2009) in a multiracial sample of 483 MSM, with 12 percent who identified as bisexual. The participants in that study were able to reframe homophobic, biphobic, and heterosexist messages received from their religious leaders and community members and develop a strong sense of spiritual connection with a higher power. Participants reported focusing on the positive aspects of their religion such as messages of unconditional love and forgiveness by God (Kubicek et al., 2009). In a more recent study of 175 LGB men and women (59 were bisexual), Walker and Longmire-Avital (2013) found that although bisexual individuals reported higher levels of internalized binegativity than then their lesbian and gay counterparts, their resilience levels as a result of their religious faith did not differ from that of the lesbian and gay participants. Similar findings of religion and spirituality as a source of resilience, coping, and well-being among Black bisexual women were found by Gougis (2013).

The literature also highlights the importance of Black bisexuals' embrace of *role flexibility* (behaving differently in specific contexts and situations), advocating for change, and having a strong sense of racial identity as a form of resilience (Wilson & Miller, 2002). In a qualitative study with 37 Black gay and bisexual men, Wilson and Miller (2002) examined the strategies that participants used to navigate their sexual identity. The findings suggested that Black bisexual men cope with biphobic messages using strategies similar to those they use to combat racism. Specifically, participants reported six coping strategies: (a) altering one's actions, dress, and mannerisms in heterosexual environments, (b) remaining close to a higher power, (c) confronting others' overt expressions of verbal discrimination toward sexual minorities, (d) avoiding same-sex sexual behavior, (e) surrounding themselves with other Black and bisexual men, and (f) engaging in self-love and self-acceptance (Wilson & Miller, 2002).

Racial group identification has increased resilience, by providing social support for Black bisexual men in educational settings (Goode-Cross & Tager, 2011; Patton, 2011). These studies highlight acts of resilience and point to the importance of racial identity to wellness. In a qualitative study with eight Black bisexual men who attended predominantly White institutions, Goode-Cross and Tager (2011) found that racial identity was more salient than sexual orientation in creating social support. In addition, Black bisexuals discussed regularly spending time with other Black gay and bisexual individuals as a means of protection, and for encouragement and coping (Goode-Cross & Tager, 2011). Similar studies have concluded that Black bisexuals create safe spaces where they can be their authentic selves, use selective disclosures based on their assessment of environment, and avoid highly homophobic and/ or racist environments as a way to keep themselves healthy (Goode-Cross & Good, 2008, 2009; Goode-Cross & Tager, 2011; McCready, 2004; Patton, 2011; Washington & Wall, 2006).

EXAMPLES OF BLACK BISEXUAL RESISTANCE

Through Black bisexuals' resistance, "a meaningful shift in the experience of power" occurs (Cattaneo & Goodman, 2015). In the TMER model, the term "empowerment" is used to address the ways in which individuals who either experience the processes or embody the consequences of oppression resist the external forces working against their wellness (Brodsky & Cattaneo, 2013). However, the authors advance resistance in lieu of empowerment in order to (1) focus on the actions Black bisexuals take on a personal and relational level that demonstrate resilience and (2) underscore the fact that systemic changes are needed in order for power imbalances to be rectified on a collective level. The act of resistance involves using knowledge, skills, resources, and a sense of self-efficacy to work toward achieving increased psychopolitical wellness at the personal, relational, or collective level (Brodsky & Cattaneo, 2013). For Black bisexuals whose identities and social contexts are often rife with risk and adversity, resistance is a critical aspect of keeping oneself and one's siblings healthy and resilient.

Whether intentional or not, all Black bisexuals are resisters. At a minimum, they challenge "patriarchal constructions of gender and the traditional meanings of masculinity and femininity" (Scott, 2007, p. 220) by having same- and other-gender attractions. Black bisexuals resist compulsory monosexuality in psychologically and politically meaningful ways. When bisexuals claim, clarify, or ask to be addressed with a particular sexual identity label ("bisexual," "bi," "queer"), they resist by taking control of the naming process (Bates, 2012; Scott, 2006). Rust (2003) notes how some bisexuals respond to quips that they are suffering internalized homophobia by naming such assertions as biphobia. In doing so, they claim "definitional power" over both their identities and their experiences of oppression (Scott, 2007, p. 211). This process of validating oneself and one's community is one important way the community resists and becomes more resilient.

On the other hand, some Black bisexuals have resisted racism and oppression by downplaying their sexuality (Greene, 2000; Moore, 2010). Moore's (2010) study of Black LGBT people in Los Angeles highlights a distinction between those born before and after 1954. The author argues that Black LGBT people born before 1954 experienced a stigma surrounding their sexuality throughout their adult lives (Moore, 2010). Although only four out of her 25 interviewees identified as bisexual, one participant's disclosure about having "to have a certain deportment" in order to "survive" and "thrive" represented this cohort of bisexual-identified elders (Moore, 2010). Resilience for some younger Black bisexuals still relies on their willingness to resist desires for a public bisexual identity and generally downplay their sexuality (Patton, 2011). In Patton's qualitative study of six men at a historically Black college, four of the participants revealed that concerns related to biphobia and economic oppression cause them to resist publicly disclosing their bisexual identity. Participants were aware that their sexuality could result in a loss of opportunities and damage their hopes for economic stability in the future

(Patton, 2011). Across generations, Black bisexuals resist falling victim to numerous sources of oppression by making conscientious decisions regarding how they will perform in the public domain. Though victimized, they resist, survive, and try to thrive in these oppressive contexts.

Crissle West, a host on the Black- and queer-positive podcast *The Read* is an example of a Black bisexual person using definitional power in a public manner that may help keep the Black bisexual community healthy. Crissle's followers know she is bisexual because she exposes herself across social media outlets, filling a void in the media. Responding to biphobic quips that she is not "lesbian enough," Crissle writes in her blog,

> I'm a black American woman and that's enough baggage to carry around in this world without worrying about whether I'm being queer enough to be relatable. I don't feel a responsibility to serve or be accountable to anyone but myself. Naturally I want queer black girls to be proud of me, but if I have to write myself a reminder to dyke it up in order to get your approval then you can keep it. The love that I receive from black women specifically has been so overwhelming that I have been moved to tears time after time—I consider that a gift. But it is not my job to be the lesbian face that you wish to see, and I don't mind disappointing you by being myself (West, 2016).

Crissle is one example of how Black bisexual resisters use varying platforms to educate about the intersection of Blackness and queerness in the United States today (West, 2016).

The Black bisexual community also often resists anti-Black racism by remaining embedded and finding healthy ways of being within the Black community (Bates, 2012; Moore, 2010). Instead of patronizing predominantly White queer spaces, many Black bisexuals advocate for greater visibility and support within the Black community (Bates, 2012; Moore, 2010). Reflections from a pastor in Los Angeles indicate that Black bisexuals may be resisting oppression by 'coming out' more often in Black church settings (Moore, 2010). Black bisexuals may also resist being "seduced by Whiteness" and its "material rewards" (Rodriguez, 2011, p. 591) by not performing their bi identity in a manner prescribed by dominant White LGBT culture (Moore, 2010; Patton, 2011). Black bi men in Patton's (2011) study did not ascribe to the sexual identity politics common to White LGBT people, such as a focus on labels or having a fixed identity. These participants resisted by defining their sexuality more in terms of contextual factors of salience at the time (Patton, 2011). These practices, centered on authentic self-definition and racial group identification, reflect resistance as resilience.

Black bisexuals have also resisted oppressive environments by creating or joining queer communities of color (Goode-Cross & Good, 2008, 2009; Goode-Cross & Tager, 2011; McCready, 2004; Moore, 2010; Patton, 2011; Washington & Wall, 2006). The DC Bisexual Women of Color Collaborative meets at different locations in the Washington, DC, metropolitan area and many supportive spaces for Black bisexual people exist primarily online (e.g., biwoc.org, Colorlines.com). Blogs like Colorlines have provided platforms for Black bisexual men to explore their sexualities and reject the oversimplified and often racist rhetoric around Black men on the *down low*.

Black bisexuals may also engage in resistance when developing and maintaining relationships. The domination of monosexism can lead to consequences such as discrimination from biphobic partners, competition for accepting and compatible partners, and isolation in the absence of love and intimacy (Prilleltensky, 2003). To resist, Black bisexual men have created unique ways of classifying potential same gender partners, based on similarities in outness, gender performance, and other factors (Patton, 2011). One participant in Patton's (2011) study was interested in "political" types, noting that the men in this category had "as much to lose" as he did (p. 91). It is important for Black bisexuals pursuing relational wellness to avoid racist and/or biphobic people as partners. However, the limited research on Black bisexual women suggests that even when they end up in relationships with people who oppress them (e.g., pressuring them to denounce their bisexual identity), they can resist these restrictions (Bates, 2012; Greene, 2000; Rust, 2003). Participants in Bates' (2012) study resisted by leaving the relationship, engaging in identity exploration, and recognizing that their partners' biphobia should not be internalized. Researchers interested in Black bisexuality may consider exploring how bisexuals who are romantically or sexually involved with monosexuals disclose and maintain their sexual identity.

Finally, Black bisexuals' resistance is evidenced in their ability to create and experience joy and love (Bates, 2012; Moore, 2010; Wilson & Miller, 2002) in the face of the outlined barriers to wellness. A woman in Bates' (2012) study acknowledged that she took pleasure in withstanding degradation and then educating those who want to oppress her. In Moore's (2010) study, Black bisexuals intentionally integrated an ethic of love into their activism at a Martin Luther King Jr. parade, wearing White for peace and responding to discriminatory comments with loving affirmations. The men in Wilson and Miller's (2002) study coped by forming loving chosen families and through acts of self-love. Black bisexuals resist dehumanization and invisibility by showing they are deserving of love, receiving love, and by giving love in the face of biphobia (Bates, 2012; Moore, 2010; Wilson & Miller, 2002).

CONCLUSION

Through a combination of a review of the research literature, an examination of the historical context, and the inclusion of diverse Black bisexual resisters, this chapter has made the case that resistance is an important component of resilience for Black bisexuals in the United States. First, psychopolitical wellness was proffered as a framework for conceptualizing the relationship between oppression and the psychological and political components of resistance for Black bisexuals. The key factors and themes associated with resilience and resistance for Black bisexuals were highlighted, showing that despite multiple barriers to wellness, they often actively and consciously resist and maintain their wellness. Provided that Black bisexual individuals and groups are often rendered invisible in the psychological literature, this chapter incorporated concrete examples of resistance from Black bisexuals who epitomize the presented themes and embody the struggle that has kept many Black bisexual individuals healthy.

NOTES

1. Bisexual is used herein to describe a person that has same and other-gender romantic and/or sexual attractions or experiences.
2. Queer is an umbrella term used herein to indicate a person or persons who are not straight-identified.
3. "Siblings" is a gender-neutral term denoting fictive kinships and a concern for the Black collective, similar to "brothers" and "sisters" (Shabazz-El, 2015).

REFERENCES

Alexander, M. (2010). *The new Jim Crow: Mass incarceration in the age of color-blindness.* New York, NY: New Press.
Allen, V. J., Myers, H. F., & Williams, J. K. (2014). Depression among Black bisexual men with early and later life adversities. *Cultural Diversity and Ethnic Minority Psychology, 20,* 128–137. doi:10.1037/a0034128
Badgett, M. V., Durso, L. E., & Schneebaum, A. (2013). *New patterns of poverty in the lesbian, gay, and bisexual community.* Los Angeles, CA: The Williams Institute. Retrieved from: http://escholarship.org/uc/item/8dq9d947
Balsam, K. F., Molina, Y., Beadnell, B., Simoni, J., & Walters, K. (2011). Measuring multiple minority stress: The LGBT people of color microaggressions scale. *Cultural Diversity and Ethnic Minority Psychology, 17,* 163–174. doi:10.1037/a0023244
Bates, D. D. (2012). Beyond expectations: The experiences of two African American bisexual women. *Journal of Bisexuality, 12,* 404–416. doi:10.1080/15299716.2012.702622
Battle, J., & Crum, M. (2007). Black LGB health and well-being. In I. H. Meyer & M. E. Northridge (Eds.), *The health of sexual minorities: Public health perspectives on lesbian, gay, bisexual, and transgender populations* (pp. 320–352). New York, NY: Springer Science + Business Media. doi:10.1007/978-0-387-31334-4_13

Benoit, E., & Koken, J. A. (2012). Perspectives on substance use and disclosure among behaviorally bisexual Black men with female primary partners. *Journal of Ethnicity in Substance Abuse, 11*, 294–317 24p. doi:10.1080/15332640.2012.735 165

Blank, M. B., Mahmood, M., Fox, J. C., & Guterbock, T. (2002). Alternative mental health services: The role of the Black church in the south. *American Journal of Public Health, 92*, 1668–1672.

Bowleg, L., Burkholder, G., Teti, M., & Craig, M. L. (2008). The complexities of outness: Psychosocial predictors of coming out to others among Black lesbian and bisexual women. *Journal of LGBT Health Research, 4*(4), 153–166. doi:10.1080/15574090903167422

Brodsky, A. E., & Cattaneo, L. B. (2013). A transconceptual model of empowerment and resilience: Divergence, convergence and interactions in kindred community concepts. *American Journal of Community Psychology, 52*, 333–346. doi:10.1007/s10464-013-9599-x

Brodsky, A. E., Welsh, E., Carrillo, A., Talwar, G., Scheibler, J., & Butler, T. (2011). Between synergy and conflict: Balancing the processes of organizational and individual resilience in an Afghan women's community. *American Journal of Community Psychology, 47*, 217–235. doi:10.1007/s10464-010-9399-5

Campbell, M. K., Hudson, M. A., Resnicow, K., Blakeney, N., Paxton, A., & Baskin, M. (2007). Church-based health promotion interventions: Evidence and lessons learned. *Annual Review of Public Health, 28*, 213–234. doi:10.1146/annurev.publhealth.28.021406.144016

Cattaneo, L. B., & Goodman, L. A. (2015). What is empowerment anyway? A model for domestic violence practice, research, and evaluation. *Psychology of Violence, 5*, 84–94. doi:10.1037/a0035137

Childs, E., Laudone, S., & Tavernier, L. (2010). Revisiting Black sexuality in families: Problems, puzzles, and prospects. In J. Battle & S. Barnes (Eds.), *Black sexualities: Probing powers, passions, practices, and policies* (pp. 17–36). New Brunswick, NJ: Rutgers University Press.

Collins, P. H. (2004). *Black sexual politics: African Americans, gender, and the new racism.* New York, NY: Routledge.

Cunningham, N. (2011). *Lesbian, gay, bisexual, transgender and queer grantmaking by U.S. foundations.* New York, NY: Funders for LGBTQ Issues. Retrieved from http://www.lgbtfunders.org/files/2010LGBTQGrantmakingReport.pdf

Department of Health and Human Services. (2010). *Healthy People 2020.* Washington, DC: Author. Retrieved from http://www.outforhealth.org/files/all/hp2020lesbianpeople.pdf

Dodge, B., Schnarrs, P. W., Reece, M., Goncalves, G., Martinez, O., Nix, R., & … Fortenberry, J. D. (2012). Community involvement among behaviourally bisexual men in the midwestern USA: Experiences and perceptions across communities. *Culture, Health & Sexuality, 14*, 1095–1110. doi:10.1080/13691058.2012.721136

Dudley, R. J. (2013). Being Black and lesbian, gay, bisexual or transgender. *Journal of Gay & Lesbian Mental Health, 17*, 183–195. doi:10.1080/19359705.2013.768171

Elmslie, B., & Tebaldi, E. (2007). Sexual orientation and labor market discrimination. *Journal of Labor Research, 28,* 436–453.

Follins, L. D., Walker, J. J., & Lewis, M. K. (2014). Resilience in Black lesbian, gay, bisexual, and transgender individuals: A critical review of the literature. *Journal of Gay & Lesbian Mental Health, 18,* 190–212. doi:10.1080/19359705.2013.828343

Ford, J. A., & Jasinski, J. L. (2006). Sexual orientation and substance use among college students. *Addictive Behaviors, 31,* 404–413.

Friedman, M. R., Dodge, B., Schick, V., Herbenick, D., Hubach, R., Bowling, J., & … Reece, M. (2014). From bias to bisexual health disparities: Attitudes toward bisexual men and women in the United States. *LGBT Health, 1,* 309–318. doi:10.1089/lgbt.2014.0005

Frost, D. M., Meyer, I. H., & Schwartz, S. (2016). Social support networks among diverse sexual minority populations. *American Journal of Orthopsychiatry, 86,* 91–102.

Garner, G. L., Jr. (2008). *Managing heterosexism and biphobia: A revealing Black bisexual male perspective* (Doctoral dissertation). Retrieved from ProQuest Dissertations & Theses Global. (Accession No. 304558356)

Goode-Cross, D. T., & Good, G. E. (2008). African-American men who have sex with men: Creating safe spaces through relationships. *Psychology of Men and Masculinity, 9,* 221–234.

———. (2009). Managing multiple minority identities: African American men who have sex with men at predominately White universities. *Journal of Diversity in Higher Education, 2,* 103–112.

Goode-Cross, D. T., & Tager, D. (2011). Negotiating multiple identities: How African-American gay and bisexual men persist at a predominantly White institution. *Journal of Homosexuality, 58,* 1235–1254.

Gougis, D. (2013). *The effect of internal and external discrimination on the psychological well-being and self-esteem of lesbian, gay, bisexual, and queer Black women* (Doctoral dissertation). Retrieved from ProQuest Dissertations & Theses Global. (Accession No. 2015–99040–333)

Green, K. E., & Feinstein, B. A. (2012). Substance use in lesbian, gay, and bisexual populations: An update on empirical research and implications for treatment. *Psychology of Addictive Behaviors, 26,* 265–278.

Greene, B. (1996). Lesbians and gay men of color: Ethnosexual mythologies in heterosexism. In E. Rothblum & L. Bond (Eds.), *Preventing Heterosexism and Homophobia* (pp. 59–70). Thousand Oaks, CA: Sage.

———. (2000). African American lesbian and bisexual women. *Journal of Social Issues, 56,* 239–249.

Halkitis, P. N., & Jerome, R. C. (2008). A comparative analysis of methamphetamine use: Black gay and bisexual men in relation to men of other races. *Addictive Behaviors, 33,* 83–93. doi:10.1016/j.addbeh.2007.07.015

Henderson, L. (2009). Between the two: Bisexual identity among African Americans. *Journal of African American Studies, 13,* 263–282. doi:10.1007/s12111–008–9072–3

Hughes, T. L., Wilsnack, S. C., Szalacha, L. A., Johnson, T., Bostwick, W. B., Seymour, R., & ... Kinnison, K. E. (2006). Age and racial/ethnic differences in drinking and drinking-related problems in a community sample of lesbians. *Journal of Studies on Alcohol, 67,* 579–590.

Hussen, S. A., Harper, G. W., Bauermeister, J. A., & Hightow-Weidman, L. B. (2015). Psychosocial influences on engagement in care among HIV-positive young Black gay/bisexual and other men who have sex with men. *AIDS Patient Care & STDs, 29,* 77–85. doi:10.1089/apc.2014.0117

Jeffries, W. L., Dodge, B., & Sandfort, T. G. M. (2008). Religion and spirituality among bisexual Black men in the USA. *Culture, Health & Sexuality, 10,* 463–477.

Jerome, R. C., & Halkitis, P. N. (2014). An exploratory investigation of treatment strategies for Black, gay, bisexual, and heterosexual men-who-have-sex-with-men who use methamphetamine. *Journal of LGBT Issues in Counseling, 8,* 2–24. doi:10.1080/15538605.2014.853636

Kubicek, K., McDavitt, B., Carpineto, J., Weiss, G., Iverson, E., & Kipke, M. (2009). "God made me gay for a reason": Young men who have sex with men's resiliency in resolving internalized homophobia from religious sources. *Journal of Adolescent Research, 24,* 601–633.

Li, C., Matthews, A. K., Aranda, F., Patel, C., & Patel, M. (2015). Predictors and consequences of negative patient-provider interactions among a sample of African American sexual minority women. *LGBT Health, 2,* 140–146. doi:10.1089/lgbt.2014.0127

Mays, V. M., Cochran, S. D., & Roeder, M. R. (2004). Depressive distress and prevalence of common problems among homosexually active African American women in the United States. *Journal of Psychology & Human Sexuality, 15,* 27–46. doi:10.1300/J056v15n02_03

McCready, L. T. (2004). Understanding the marginalization of gay and gender non-conforming Black male students. *Theory into Practice, 43,* 136–143.

Meyer, I. H. (2010). Identity, stress, and resilience in lesbians, gay men, and bisexuals of color. *The Counseling Psychologist, 38*(3), 442–454. doi:10.1177/0011000009351601

Moore, D. (2008). Guilty of sin: African-American denominational churches and their exclusion of SGL sisters and brothers. *Black Theology, 6,* 83–97.

Moore, M. R. (2010). Articulating a politics of (multiple) identities. *Du Bois Review: Social Science Research on Race, 7,* 2, 315–334.

———. (2012). Intersectionality and the study of Black, sexual minority women. *Gender & Society, 26,* 33–39. doi:10.1177/0891243211427031

O'Dowd, P. (2013, January 1). Sinema, first openly bisexual member of Congress, represents 'changing Arizona.' NPR: All Things Considered. Retrieved from: http://www.npr.org/sections/itsallpolitics/2013/01/08/168362011/sinema-first-openly-bisexual-member-of-congress-represents-changing-arizona

Oswalt, S. B. (2009). Don't forget the" B": Considering bisexual students and their specific health needs. *Journal of American College Health, 57,* 557–560.

Patton, L. D. (2011). Perspectives on identity, disclosure, and the campus environment among African American gay and bisexual men at one historically Black college. *Journal of College Student Development, 52*, 77–100.

Pettaway, L., Bryant, L., Keane, F., & Craig, S. (2014). Becoming down low: A review of the literature on Black men who have sex with men and women. *Journal of Bisexuality, 14*, 209–221. doi:10.1080/15299716.2014.902346

Phillips, L. (2005). Deconstructing "down low" discourse: The politics of sexuality, gender, race, AIDS, and anxiety. *Journal of African American Studies, 9*(2), 3–15.

Phillips, L., & Stewart, M. (2010). Nontraditional, nonconforming, and transgressive gender expression and relationship modalities in Black communities. In J. Battle & S. Barnes (Eds.), *Black sexualities: Probing powers, passions, practices, and policies* (pp. 17–36). New Brunswick, NJ: Rutgers University Press.

Prilleltensky, I. (2003). Understanding, resisting, and overcoming oppression: Toward psychopolitical validity. *American Journal of Community Psychology, 31*, 195–201. doi:10.1023/A:1023043108210

———. (2008). The role of power in wellness, oppression, and liberation: The promise of psychopolitical validity. *Journal of Community Psychology, 36*, 116–136.

Rodriguez, D. (2011). Silent rage and the politics of resistance: Countering seductions of Whiteness and the road to politicization and empowerment. *Qualitative Inquiry, 17*, 589–598. doi:10.1177/1077800411413994

Rust, P. C. (1996). Managing multiple identities: Diversity among bisexual women and men. In B. A. Firestein (Ed.), *Bisexuality: The psychology and politics of an invisible minority* (pp. 53–83). Thousand Oaks, CA: Sage.

———. (2003). Finding a sexual identity and community: Therapeutic implications and cultural assumptions in scientific models of coming out. In L. D. Garnets & D. C. Kimmel (Eds.), *Psychological perspectives on lesbian, gay, and bisexual experiences* (2nd ed.) (pp. 227–269). New York, NY: Columbia University Press.

Scott, R. L. (2007). Addressing social invalidation to promote well-being for multiracial bisexuals of African descent. In B. A. Firestein (Ed.), *Becoming visible: Counseling bisexuals across the lifespan* (pp. 207–228). New York, NY: Columbia University Press.

Shabazz-El, W. (2015, August 10). "We gonna be alright": An HIV activist at the 1st national movement for Black lives convening [Blog post]. Retrieved from https://pwnusa.wordpress.com/2015/08/10/we-gonna-be-alright-an-hiv-activist-at-m4bl/

Singh, A. A. (2013). Transgender youth of color and resilience: Negotiating oppression and finding support. *Sex Roles, 68*, 690–702.

Talley, A. E., Hughes, T. L., Aranda, F., Birkett, M., & Marshal, M. P. (2014). Exploring alcohol-use behaviors among heterosexual and sexual minority adolescents: Intersections with sex, age, and race/ethnicity. *American Journal of Public Health, 104*, 295–303.

Wade, R. M., & Harper, G. W. (2015). Young Black gay/bisexual and other men who have sex with men: A review and content analysis of health-focused research between 1988 and 2013. *American Journal of Men's Health, 1*, 1–18. doi:10.1177/1557988315606962

Walker, J. J., & Longmire-Avital, B. (2013). The impact of religious faith and internalized homonegativity on resiliency for Black lesbian, gay, and bisexual emerging adults. *Developmental Psychology, 49,* 1723–1731. doi:10.1037/a0031059

Washington, J., & Wall, V. (2006). African American gay men: Another challenge for the academy. In M. Cuyjet (Ed.), *African American men in college* (pp. 174–188). San Francisco, CA: Jossey-Bass.

Weiss, J. T. (2003). GL vs. BT: The archaeology of biphobia and transphobia within the U.S. gay and lesbian community. *Journal of Bisexuality, 3*(3–4), 25–55. doi:10.1300/J159v03n03_02

West, C. M. (2016). My-Self [Blog post]. Retrieved from http://crissle.com/myself/

Wilsnack, S. C., Hughes, T. L., Johnson, T. P., Bostwick, W. B., Szalacha, L. A., Benson, P., & … Kinnison, K. E. (2008). Drinking and drinking-related problems among heterosexual and sexual minority women. *Journal of Studies on Alcohol and Drugs, 69,* 129–139.

Wilson, B. D. M. & Miller, R. L. (2002). Strategies for managing heterosexism used among African American gay and bisexual men. *Journal of Black Psychology, 28,* 371–391.

Wilson, C. K., Lamis, D. A., Winn, S., & Kaslow, N. J. (2014). Intimate partner violence, spiritual well-being, and parenting stress in African-American women. *Journal of Spirituality in Mental Health, 16,* 261–285. doi:10.1080/19349637.20 14.957604

Yoshino, K. (2000). The epistemic contract of bisexual erasure. *Stanford Law Review,* 353–461.

Chapter 5

Narratives of Health among Black Trans Men

An Exploratory Intersectional Analysis

Tonia C. Poteat and Lourdes Dolores Follins

Transgender (trans) men are individuals assigned a female sex at birth who identify along a masculine spectrum.[1,2] Many trans men in the United States contend with stigma, discrimination, violence, and isolation based on others' reactions to their gender identities and presentations (Grant et al., 2011). Where there is research, the data demonstrate high rates of violence, mental health problems, social service needs, and barriers to health care among trans men (Conron, Scott, Stowell, & Landers, 2012; Keuroghlian, Reisner, White, & Weiss, 2015; Peitzmeier, Khullar, Reisner, & Potter, 2014; Reisner, Katz-Wise, Gordon, Corliss, & Austin, 2016; Singh, 2013; Stephens, Bernstein, & Philip, 2011; Thomas, 2016).

Over the last fifteen years there has been an increase in the amount of research on trans men's healthcare needs and experiences (MacCarthy, Reisner, Nunn, Perez-Brumer, & Operario, 2015). Frequently explored topics in trans men's health include HIV/STI risk (Reisner, Perkovich, & Mimiaga, 2010; Sevelius, 2009); mental health (Bockting, Miner, Swinburne Romine, Hamilton, & Coleman, 2013); and access to and utilization of health care (Rachlin, Green, & Lombardi, 2008; Roller, Sedlak, & Draucker, 2015; Rounds, McGrath, & Walsh, 2013; Shires & Jaffee, 2015).

Most participants in these studies have been well-educated and employed with health insurance. Despite these advantages, many reported being refused or having difficulty obtaining medical care. Studies have found that trans men may either avoid or delay seeking medical care because of prior negative experiences with the healthcare system (Grant et al., 2011). These experiences range from mis-gendering, ignorance about trans healthcare, and insurance obstacles to outright stigma, maltreatment, and refusal of care (Lambda Legal, 2010; Rounds et al., 2013).

The majority of studies on transmasculine health include very few Black trans men. The dearth of research with this population precludes identification of the breadth of health needs and experiences of trans masculine communities. The simultaneous interaction of marginalized identities along lines of race, gender, sexuality, and socioeconomic status shape the health and healthcare experiences for Black trans men in ways that cannot be understood through studies of White trans men. Black trans men "have remained absent from mainstream discussions of health disparities" (Hussey, 2006, p. 130). Learning more about Black trans men's health and healthcare experiences can help providers, policy makers, and program administrators determine how best to address their specific needs. This chapter uses an intersectional lens to give voice to eight Black trans men's descriptions of their healthcare needs experiences and makes recommendations to improve service delivery and advance research with Black trans masculine communities.

METHODS

Data collection took place in Baltimore, Maryland—a mid-Atlantic city with well-known racial, economic, and health disparities. Baltimore also has visible activism related to racial and gender injustice, having recently received notoriety for the community uprising in response to the death of Freddie Gray—a Black cisgender man who died in police custody. Baltimore has a politically and socially active transgender community with several transgender-led support groups and advocacy organizations. Baltimore has had a gender non-discrimination ordinance since 2002, and Maryland passed similar legal protections in 2014.

We analyzed a subset of data from a larger study of gender and health among transgender adults in Baltimore. Purposive sampling was used to identify participants, and individual in-depth interviews took place from January to July 2011. Field notes were handwritten immediately after each interview and typed once transcription was complete. Participants were recruited by placing flyers in the city's LGBT health center, during announcements at trans support group meetings, and by word-of-mouth. All participants provided verbal informed consent; and all interviews were audio taped and transcribed verbatim. The Institutional Review Board at Johns Hopkins Bloomberg School of Public Health provided ethical approval for this study. To maximize confidentiality, no individual identifiers were collected. Verbal consent was obtained, and no written consent forms were used.

For this analysis, inclusion criteria were being age eighteen years or older, residing in the Baltimore metropolitan area, having been assigned female at birth, currently identifying as trans or as a gender different from their birth-assigned sex, and identifying as Black or African American. Each potential participant was screened over the telephone. Participants meeting the inclusion criteria were scheduled for an interview at the project office located in a central area of the city, accessible by public transportation. One individual in-depth interview was conducted with each participant. Each interview lasted between 45 and 180 minutes with an average duration of 90 minutes. Each person received $25 for taking part in the study.

At the conclusion of the interview, participants answered a few demographic questions and completed a 10-item scale designed to measure enacted stigma (discrimination) based on gender identity (Bockting et al., 2013). Participants were asked to respond "yes" or "no" to statements about experiences of mistreatment related to their gender identity. However, two of the 10 items were not applicable to any of the participants in this study. These items included problems getting HIV prevention services because of gender identity or presentation and problems getting alcohol or drug treatment because of gender identity or presentation. Because none of the participants had attempted to seek these services, these items were excluded from analysis. The statements in the resulting 8-item scale are listed in Table 5.2.

Interviews elicited detailed narratives of individual experiences and perceptions. Specifically, participants were asked about their family and social life, gender identity, sexual orientation and practices, healthcare experiences, as well as experiences of stigma and discrimination. Data for qualitative analysis included transcripts of audio recordings from the in-depth interviews as well as typed reflexive notes from all data collection activities. The first author conducted all of the interviews, and the second author led data analysis. Both are cisgender Black women who work in academic institutions. The first author lived and worked in the Baltimore community for several years prior to and during data collection. In addition to her academic work, she provides medical care for members of the LGBTQ community and participates in local community advocacy. The second author lives and works in New York where she has provided social services as well as participated in research and advocacy with LGBTQ communities of color.

Transcripts were hand-coded using a summative content analysis approach (Hsieh & Shannon, 2005). Codes were discussed between the two coders until consensus was reached, then the final codebook was created. Codes related to healthcare experiences were extracted and examined for patterns as well as co-occurring and recurring themes. These themes were then examined in light of individual narratives for context. Memos were used to organize themes, link themes to narratives, and track the analytic process. Preliminary findings were discussed with Black trans men in the community during a dissemination workshop, and their feedback was incorporated into the final manuscript.

Table 5.1   Participant Characteristics and Scores on 8-Point Scale of Enacted Stigma

ID	Age	Identity*	Education	Housing**	Healthcare+	Medical Transition	Enacted Stigma
P17	30	Straight Black male	Some college	Yes	Yes	Yes	3
P18	23	Mixed AA Queer male	Some college	Yes	Yes	Yes	4
P20	57	AA straight male	Associate degree	Yes	Yes	Yes	3
P23	48	Black male heterosexual	HS diploma	Yes	Yes	No	2
P36	22	Straight Black male	Some college	Yes	Yes	Yes	2
P56	26	West Indian Trans Queer	Masters	Yes	No	No	2
P57	46	Black AA male who prefers women 100 percent	HS diploma	No	Yes	No	6
P58	41	Black/Italian/Native American Male Lesbian and Heterosexual male	Some college	Yes	No	No	3

*All identity terms listed were named by the participants, for example, "Straight" and "West Indian." **Housing = regular place to live; +Healthcare = regular source of healthcare; AA = African American; HS = high school.

Table 5.1 summarizes participant characteristics. The average age of study participants was thirty-seven years (range twenty-two to fifty-seven). All were high school graduates, and all but two had at least some college. All but one were stably housed; and all but two had a regular source of healthcare. While all participants identified as Black or African American, two participants also identified as "mixed" race and one identified as West Indian. Most participants identified as heterosexual and/or preferred only female partners. Two participants identified as Queer, and one participant identified as both a lesbian and a heterosexual male. Six of eight participants had engaged in some form of medical transition such as testosterone injections or chest reconstruction surgery.

FINDINGS

Social Context: Intersectional Stigma/Discrimination

All participants reported experiencing at least two of the eight forms of gender identity discrimination assessed, with three being the median and six being the highest number of experiences (Table 5.2). All of the participants reported experiencing verbal abuse or harassment because of their gender identities while no one reported experiencing arrest because of their gender identity. Half of the participants had been physically abused or beaten because of their gender identity, and seven out of eight had problems getting a job because of their gender identity or presentation.

Table 5.2 Frequency of Reported Enacted Stigma Experiences

Types of Discrimination	% (n=8)
1. Problems getting a job because of gender identity or presentation	87.5
2. Lost a job because of gender identity or presentation	33
3. Denied housing or thrown out because of gender identity or presentation	28.5
4. Problems getting health or medical services because of gender identity or presentation	12.5
5. Physically abused or beaten because of gender identity or presentation	50
6. Verbally abused or harassed because of gender identity or presentation	100
7. Sexually abused or assaulted because of gender identity or presentation	12.5
8. Arrested because of gender identity or presentation	0

While none of the eight participants were asked specifically about race, six people raised the topic spontaneously. Two participants asserted that trans people were more likely to be accepted by White people than Black people and provided examples from the workplace and within multiracial families when this had happened. Others raised race in the context of their experiences of racism. One participant eloquently described the intersectional nature of his experience as a Black trans man.

I don't think it's just gender-wise. I think it's everything, the whole package. So being that people are ignorant to a lot of things, they're not open-minded to other things. So, if everyone had come with an open mind, everybody is everybody—really doesn't matter if you're orange, green, brown. Everything would be fine. (p. 17)

Participants varied in how their gender was perceived by others, and this impacted their experiences of stigma and discrimination. Several participants reported a reduction in stigma that came with physical transition (i.e., going from being perceived as a masculine gay woman to being perceived as a cisgender male). At the same time, this new gender presentation came with the need to deal with the stigmatizing stereotypes associated with being a Black man.

But I'm still considered the black guy-- the Black male. You know how they say, "Black males, it's hard for them to work, yada, yada." But I think a Black male is better than being gay and dominant. It's not being gay and feminine; it's being gay and dominant. (p. 17)

However, being seen as male was not protective when perceived in the context of femininity. For example, one participant described being attacked on the street by a group of men because they thought he was a gay man.

I have to realize that I'm not seen as a butch lesbian anymore . . . because I'm seen as a gay male now, it's like, "Oh, I'mma beat this little faggot's ass." And it was really bad. It was six guys. (p. 18)

Health in the Context of Discrimination

Surviving at the nexus of multiple stigmatized identities took its toll on the health of participants. Despite their relative young age, most were dealing with chronic medical conditions ranging from recurrent tendonitis, migraine headaches, diabetes, and depression. While not every participant explicitly linked his social context with his health, this particular participant described how dealing with transphobia impacted his well-being:

> [So much to deal with] every day. And I'm getting to the point it's like I'm getting real frustrated. I think my ulcer is beginning to start hurting because I'm having stomach problems and I say, okay, I think that's my ulcer begin to start hurting again. Where do trans people go where they can be accepted? Don't have to worry about the bathrooms or worry about somebody looking at them weird. Where can you go? Where can you work at? Everybody got to work. You've got to eat. You've got to live. Where do I go? (p. 23)

Mental Health

Every participant described prior, current, or ongoing mental health challenges including major depression and bipolar disorder. In some cases, these challenges were precipitated by major life events such as the death of a loved one, the loss of a relationship, or efforts to deal with a history of sexual abuse.

> I do have bipolar, but I'm not really sick with it. It's very much managed. I still work with—I take medication and stuff like that, but it hasn't been a problem in my relationships with people. . . . I haven't had any episodes. I used to be terrible with it, trying to get adjusted to medicine, and just being angry. I was sexually abused, and all that stuff I had going on. . . . it turned out to be okay. I mean, I take my medicine. (p. 20)

Most participants were able to find a mental healthcare provider or system that provided what they needed to cope. One participant describes stressors leading up to a mental health crisis and his surprise at finding a mental health provider who was sensitive to his needs:

> I had a lot of my own personal issues going on—a really bad breakup, and just moving was completely stressful, sick relatives—and everything just came to a

head at that point. It triggered a major depressive episode, and I was exhibiting a lot of suicidal ideation, and. . . . I had to go to the emergency room and got an assessment and everything. But surprisingly, [the hospital] was really sensitive to mental health issues and gender issues, more importantly, and sexual orientation issues, . . . there was no referral to pronouns, which I was like, "Wow." And there was no assumption regarding who my partner was. Which was nice. It was a welcome change. (p. 56)

Healthcare Experiences

Unlike their mental health experiences, almost every participant described a negative encounter with a non-mental health medical provider or system. One participant called his insurance company to ask about coverage for transition-related services. The person at the insurance company had never heard the word "transgender" and did not understand what he was asking. Likewise, several participants described disclosing their transgender identity to health-care providers who were uninformed and unprepared to meet their needs in a competent and respectful fashion. Often, it was difficult for participants to tell whether they received substandard care due to race, gender, the interaction between the two, or some other factor. This participant described an experience with a provider who tried to deny racial discrimination while their actions suggested otherwise:

> They tried to protect themselves and said, "This doesn't have anything to do with color." And I said, "You're a damn liar. That White boy just walked in here and he was all doped up, and you gave him something. . . where I was in so much excruciating fucking pain, you're going to tell me, 'Oh, we can't give you anything in this waiting room. You're going to have to wait until the doctor sees you.'" (p. 57)

When mistreatment came from a Black provider, it was even more painful. This participant describes his experience of having specifically selected a Black woman provider because he expected her to be more understanding. However, his experience was quite different:

> She paid no attention to my gender stuff, still kept calling me "She," oh, I think she just actually stopped using gender when referring to me with the assistant person. She was really quick, she didn't even like look at me, like I didn't feel like she looked in my eyes, you know, at all. I felt like she kind of blew off like—I don't know, I just felt really dismissed. Yeah, so that sucked, because I felt like she just didn't see me or hear me or anything I said at all. And that she was black really, you know, made it cut—just cut that much deeper, you know? (p. 58)

Healthcare Seeking

Prior experiences of mistreatment or fear of mistreatment led some participants to avoid healthcare. However, many of the reasons provided for delaying or avoiding health care were not related to transgender identities. Challenges with health insurance coverage, financial limitations, and fear of medical institutions were commonly cited. Several participants describing delaying treatment for emergent and chronic conditions until pain became unbearable or the condition precluded their ability to function.

A few participants asserted a strong desire to seek preventive care, even in the face of potential mistreatment or fear of medical intervention. For example, one participant stated, "I dealt with it, because regardless to what I may feel, I know the kind of body that I have. So I have to take care of it, regardless" (p. 18). Sometimes seeking care meant having to search for a provider who would treat him with respect and dignity. Other times it meant avoiding disclosure. A participant who had a particularly negative interaction with a provider stated he would still continue to get care at the same health center, just not with that particular person. Another participant felt he had to hide his transgender identity in order to get the care he needed:

> She's like the top at [the hospital] when it's coming to colon cancer. And it took me forever to get an appointment with her. So I'm not going to say, "I'm trans, respect me, that's who I am." Sometimes you have to keep your mouth shut to get decent help and it's sad. (p. 23)

Participants were consistent in describing what they wanted from a healthcare provider. Several reported that they would be happy with someone who had no transgender care experience, but who was supportive of their identity and willing to learn. However, the best provider would not only be accepting, but also knowledgeable, experienced, personable, and not make assumptions based on their appearance. Ideally, the participant wanted a situation where they would not have to always explain themselves. However, the reality of low competency in transgender health made finding their ideal provider seem daunting. This participant described:

> Not a lot of people understand the trans community. So, am I going to find a nice doctor that looks me in the eye and talks to me and that I feel is really looking at me right then and there as a person and looking at my needs, and then he's not going to understand my trans situation? So, that's kind of scary, you know, so I need them to be knowledgeable of my community and what I'm going through, physically, and psychologically, but at the same time, you know, having that personal touch. (p. 36)

Coping, Resilience, and Social Support

Participants demonstrated remarkable resilience. As described above, everyone had completed high school. All but one were stably housed; and all but one had a regular source of healthcare. Having survived major depression, suicide attempts, medical maltreatment, social stigma, and violence as well as systemic racism, sexism, and heterosexism, their existence was often a testament to their resilience. This resilience was frequently understated with many participants summing things up in a fashion similar to P18 who stated: "I made it through so I'm okay."

In the face of intersecting matrices of oppression, participants used coping strategies that ranged from drug use to dancing to prayer.

I can't continue to be bitter, because it's killing me . . . So what I do now, just turn everybody over to God, and just ask him to help me to forgive, and prayer, and help me to forgive and, but boy, also strengthen me to do the right thing, (p. 20)

Social support was critical for coping with life's challenges as well as for access to resources and information that fostered resilience. A few participants found this support in family members and/or partners. However, almost everyone described another trans masculine individual or group that helped him to navigate transition, cope with stressors, or access healthcare services.

I had joined a trans fraternity, they accept me for who I am. And I didn't know—they're like, man, we really love you. You're cool. (p. 23)

For a while, I didn't think that it [transition] was a possibility for me. I was kind of like maybe ashamed of those feelings. But then I met my friend and he been through the whole process and I got to see his outcome and what he looks like and the life that he leads and the happiness that he has. And he basically showed me the steps and told me what to do. And since I had the information, I took it and I followed it and did it because I wanted the same thing for myself. (p. 36)

One participant took specific pride in his role connecting isolated trans men of color to social support.

I go to BTMA [a trans masculine support group]. So, I try to take a few of the guys. Because it's a lot of guys of color that don't know about the meeting. So if the information's not being broadcast, they don't know. So I'm trying to be that marketing, advertising guy. I'm the go-to guy about all the programs in the area. And it's another responsibility, but I wear the hat proudly. (p. 18)

DISCUSSION

The health of Black trans men cannot be understood outside the social and historical context of race and gender in the United States. An intersectional analysis requires us to center the experiences of these men when considering how the complex interplay of oppression and privilege operate to impact their health (Bowleg, 2012; Crenshaw 1993). While the Black trans men who are perceived as men by others may no longer experience sexism aimed at women, they now face stigmas associated with stereotypes of Black men as lazy, violent, and threatening (Gayle, 2012; Kang, 2010; Welch, 2007). Black trans masculine individuals who challenge gender binaries in their identity or presentation (e.g. requiring gynecological services, appearing "effeminate," etc.) face simultaneous racism, sexism, transphobia, and homophobia. Given what we know about the impact of oppression on health, it is no surprise that the Black trans men in this study, despite their relative young age, experienced a multitude of chronic and/or disabling physical and mental health conditions.

Every participant in this study faced mental health challenges significant enough to require medical intervention. It is heartening to note these men were able to access supportive and accepting mental health services. However, this is unlikely to be true for Black trans men living in places without legal protections or visible active Black and trans communities. Clearly, there is a strong need for preventive services, crisis intervention, and mental health care that can address the complexity of stressors Black trans men experience. The resilience exhibited by this study's participants may lie in their access to a network of other Black trans men who understood their experience, showed them that it was possible to express their authentic gender, and connected them to resources and a sense of community.

When describing what they needed from healthcare, participants articulated compassionate, knowledgeable, and person-oriented providers that, in practice, would be ideal for all. Instead, they often experienced unwelcoming, unprepared, and judgmental healthcare providers who were unable to hear or understand their needs, even when they clearly articulated them. Recent improvements in access to care provided by the Affordable Care Act and solidified in recent Medicaid rulings confirming access to gender-affirming care, may do little to improve health for Black trans men without a radical restructuring of how that care is provided.

Study Limitations

This study was limited by the small sample size that precluded the ability to reach data saturation. Most study participants were recruited by word-of-mouth; therefore, participants were, by default, connected to at least one other trans person who referred them to the study. While the goal of this analysis was to approach the data with an intersectional lens, neither the enacted stigma scale nor the interview guide asked specific questions about intersecting identities. For example, none of the participants reported being arrested because of their gender identity on the enacted stigma scale. However, two of the participants spontaneously described histories of arrest during their narratives, suggesting that intersecting factors beyond gender played a role in their arrest. Previous research has indicated that asking direct questions about intersectionality may not be the best way to access intersectional experiences (Bowleg, 2012); therefore, being able to draw indirectly from narratives of gender can provide important information about how living at the nexus of being Black, transgender, and masculine impacts health. Despite some limitations, the centering of Black trans masculine voices in narratives of health provides an essential starting point for exploration of their healthcare needs. These data touch only the tip of the iceberg of Black trans men's health. More research is needed to provide both greater depth and breadth to this information, as well as to inform potential interventions to address specific disparities faced by Black trans men.

RECOMMENDATIONS

Black trans men in this study reported experiencing a higher number of types of enacted stigma compared to a national study that used the same scale. Bockting et al.'s (2013) Internet study of transgender people found the median number of enacted stigma experiences for trans men was one (n = 464, 2.6 percent Black). Among the Black trans men in this study, the median number was three. Future research should assess not only the number of types of stigma experiences, but also aspects of intersectional and layered stigma, as well as frequency and saliency of those experiences. Beyond documenting stigma, it will also be important to examine carefully the associations and causal pathways between intersectional oppressions and health outcomes. In particular, expanding current LGBT health frameworks, such as the Minority Stress Model, to more clearly account for intersectionality in research with gender and sexual minority populations is critical to its applicability to transgender people of color.

Research among transgender people has increased exponentially in the last several years, with the majority of studies focused on mental health (Reisner, Poteat, et al., 2016). However, few of these studies have included significant numbers of Black trans men. This gap in the literature leaves mental health providers with few resources to address the particular needs of this population. The narratives presented in this study provide some insight into the health challenges Black trans men face and the coping strategies that support their resilience. Specifically, healthcare providers should seek out knowledge about the Black trans masculine community, rather than relying on their patients to educate them. Providers should be aware of local as well as national and online resources available to provide critical social support for their patients and clients. In that spirit, a list of relevant national and online resources is provided below.

NOTES

1. Acknowledgments: The authors gratefully acknowledge the courage and honesty of the Black trans men who contributed their narratives to this study. We would also like to thank Nick Hadikwa Mwaluko for his insightful feedback on drafts of this manuscript.

2. Resources: The Brown Boi Project http://www.brownboiproject.org/ https://www.facebook.com/brownboiproject/; Free Ourselves: A Guide to Health and Self Love for Brown Bois by the Brown Boi Project http://www.gladdaybookshop.com/products/freeing-ourselves-a-guide-to-health-and-self-love-for-brown-bois; Black Transmen Incorporated http://www.blacktransmen.org/; https://www.facebook.com/blackties.

REFERENCES

Bockting, W. O., Miner, M. H., Swinburne Romine, R. E., Hamilton, A., & Coleman, E. (2013). Stigma, mental health, and resilience in an online sample of the US transgender population. *American Journal of Public Health, 103*(5), 943–951. doi:10.2105/AJPH.2013.301241

Conron, K. J., Scott, G., Stowell, G. S., & Landers, S. J. (2012). Transgender health in Massachusetts: Results from a household probability sample of adults. *American Journal of Public Health, 102*(1), 118–122. doi:10.2105/ajph.2011.300315

Gayle, G. L. (2012). *Black man's burden: An interpretative phenomenological analysis of how pervasive negative stereotypes in the media affect the psychology of African American men.* (Doctoral dissertation). Available from ProQuest Dissertations and Theses database. (UMI No. 3537464).

Grant, J. M., Mottet, L. A., Tanis, J., Harrison, J., Herman, J. L., & Keisling, M. (2011). *Injustice at every turn: A report of the national transgender discrimination survey.* Retrieved from: http://www.thetaskforce.org/downloads/reports/reports/ntds_full.pdf

Hsieh, H.-F., & Shannon, S. E. (2005). Three approaches to qualitative content analysis. *Qualitative Health Research, 15*(9), 1277–1288.

Hussey, W. (2006). Slivers of the journey: The use of photovoice and storytelling to examine female to male transsexuals' experience of health care access. *Journal of Homosexuality, 51*(1), 129–158. doi:10.1300/J082v51n01_07

Kang, S. (2010). *Beyond the double jeopardy hypothesis: Examining the interaction between age- and race-based stereotypes across the lifespan*. (Doctoral dissertation). Available from ProQuest Dissertations & Theses Global: Social Sciences. (UMI No. 1344123282).

Keuroghlian, A. S., Reisner, S. L., White, J. M., & Weiss, R. D. (2015). Substance use and treatment of substance use disorders in a community sample of transgender adults. *Drug and Alcohol Dependency, 152*, 139–146. doi:10.1016/j.drugalcdep.2015.04.008

Lambda Legal. (2010). *When health care isn't caring: Lambda legal's survey on discrimination against LGBT people and people living with HIV*. Retrieved from www.lambdalegal.org/health-care-report

MacCarthy, S., Reisner, S. L., Nunn, A., Perez-Brumer, A., & Operario, D. (2015). The time is now: Attention increases to transgender health in the United States but scientific knowledge gaps remain. *LGBT Health, 2*(4), 287–291. doi:10.1089/lgbt.2014.0073

Peitzmeier, S. M., Khullar, K., Reisner, S. L., & Potter, J. (2014). Pap test use is lower among female-to-male patients than non-transgender women. *American Journal of Preventive Medicine, 47*(6), 808–812. doi:10.1016/j.amepre.2014.07.031

Rachlin, K., Green, J., & Lombardi, E. (2008). Utilization of health care among female-to-male transgender individuals in the United States. *Journal of Homosexuality, 54*(3), 243–258. doi:10.1080/00918360801982124

Reisner, S. L., Katz-Wise, S. L., Gordon, A. R., Corliss, H. L., & Austin, S. B. (2016). Social epidemiology of depression and anxiety by gender identity. *Journal of Adolescent Health*. doi:10.1016/j.jadohealth.2016.04.006

Reisner, S. L., Perkovich, B., & Mimiaga, M. J. (2010). A mixed methods study of the sexual health needs of New England transmen who have sex with nontransgender men. *AIDS Patient Care and STDs, 2*(8), 501–513.

Reisner, S. L., Poteat, T., Keatley, J., Cabral, M., Mothopeng, T., Dunham, E., . . . Baral, S. D. (2016). Global health burden and needs of transgender populations: A review. *Lancet*. doi:10.1016/s0140–6736(16)00684-x

Roller, C. G., Sedlak, C., & Draucker, C. B. (2015). Navigating the system: How transgender individuals engage in health care services. *Journal of Nursing Scholarship, 47*(5), 417–424. doi:10.1111/jnu.12160

Rounds, K. E., McGrath, B. B., & Walsh, E. (2013). Perspectives on provider behaviors: A qualitative study of sexual and gender minorities regarding quality of care. *Contemporary Nurse, 44*(1), 99–110. doi:10.5172/conu.2013.44.1.99

Sevelius, J. (2009). "There's no pamphlet for the kind of sex I have": HIV-related risk factors and protective behaviors among transgender men who have sex with nontransgender men. *Journal of the Association of Nurses in AIDS Care, 20*(5), 398–410. doi:10.1016/j.jana.2009.06.001

Shires, D. A., & Jaffee, K. (2015). Factors associated with health care discrimination experiences among a national sample of female-to-male transgender individuals. *Health & Social Work, 40*(2), 134–141. doi:10.1093/hsw/hlv025

Singh, A. A. (2013). Transgender youth of color and resilience: Negotiating oppression and finding support. *Sex Roles, 68*(11), 690–702. doi:10.1007/s11199–012–0149-z

Stephens, S. C., Bernstein, K. T., & Philip, S. S. (2011). Male to female and female to male transgender persons have different sexual risk behaviors yet similar rates of STDs and HIV. *AIDS Behavior, 15*(3), 683–686. doi:10.1007/s10461–010–9773–1

Thomas, S. P. (2016). Hate crime, medical care, and mental health care for transgender individuals. *Issues in Mental Health Nursing, 37*(4), 209–210. doi:10.3109/01 612840.2016.1150738

Welch, K. (2007). Black criminal stereotypes and racial profiling. *Journal of Contemporary Criminal Justice, 23*(3), 276–288. doi:10.1177/1043986207306870

Chapter 6

Balancing Act

Identity Management and Mental Health among Black LBT Women

Siobhan Brooks

Scholars have explored the correlation between mental health and sexuality among white identified LGB individuals (Bostwick, Boyd, Hughes, West, & Mccabe, 2014), and Black gay men (Mount, Amponsah, Graham, & Lambert, 2014) in the United States. However, little research has been conducted on the impact of identity management on mental health among Black LBT women (Greene, 2002). This chapter provides a historical overview of how same sex sexual behavior, gender nonconformity, and Blackness have been viewed in the United States and how the pathologization of LGBT people and Blacks has influenced the health and well-being of contemporary LBT Black women in the United States. This is followed by a description and examination of how six Black LBT women in Philadelphia managed multiple oppressions (e.g., sexism, transphobia, heterosexism, and homophobia), the related mental health ramifications of those oppressions, and how Black LBT women maintain their emotional well-being. The chapter concludes with some strategies that social workers and counselors working in Black communities can use when creating services for these Black LBT women.

SAME SEX RELATIONS, DEVIANCE, AND MENTAL ILLNESS

legalized

Historically, gay and lesbian sexual behavior was viewed as sinful, criminalized by the legal system, and later categorized as a mental illness (Meyer, 2013). For Black LGBT people, this was all complicated by racial ideologies because enslaved Blacks were viewed as mentally ill or deficient for attempting to escape enslavement (Washington, 2006). Proponents of slavery viewed Africans as possessing a deviant sexuality consisting of nakedness, polygamy, abnormal genitalia, and same-sex relations; as a result, they had to be civilized by Christianity (Abdur-Rehman, 2006, p. 224). According to Aliyyah I. Abdur-Rehman (2006) in her article, "The Strangest Freaks of Despotism: Queer Sexuality in Antebellum African American Slave Narratives:"

> While it would oversimplify the case to suggest that homosexuality encompasses all forms of sexual deviance, the specific resonance of homosexuality within blackness can be traced, in part, to the belief in slavery that, as descendants of Ham, black people were doomed to generation enslavement precisely for the historic crimes of incest and homosexuality. (p. 224)

belief of preexisting homosexuality

Blackness was associated with various forms of deviant sexuality that threatened ideas of a pure heterosexual white identity.

US religious, legal, and medical systems were used to legitimize the discrimination against LGBT people. Historic and current religious support for homophobia includes interpretations of the Bible framing homosexuality as a sin, institutionalizing anti-gay policies within some churches, and encouraging hatred of gays and lesbians (Clark, Brown, & Hochstein, 1989). This religious prejudice subsequently found its way into laws. In 1656, New Haven colony prohibited women from having sex with other women, and after 1890 criminalization of sodomy for women became more prevalent in the American colonies (Eskridge, 2008). During the postwar years, same sex relationships were transformed from sin and vice to a medical illnesses—from punishment to treatment (Mumford, 2016).

During this time, LGBT people in the United States were subject to incarceration in mental institutions where they were forced to undergo electric shock, conversion therapy, and psychoanalysis (Meyer, 2013). These treatments reinforced the idea that same sex relationships were deviant, and instead encouraged heterosexual relations, thus increasing the risk of low self-esteem and suicide among LGBT patients (Meyer, 2013). It was not until 1974 that same sex desire officially ceased to be categorized as a mental illness in the Diagnostic and Statistical Manual (DSM) of the American Psychiatric Association (Silverstein, 2009). While most of the medical attention to homosexuality during the 1950s focused on men, because of the assumption that lesbians were asexual, this anti-gay climate also affected women—including Black LB women (Lorde, 1982). Audre Lorde, in her biomythography *Zami,* provides accounts of Black LB women who were punished by society (e.g., police harassment in gay clubs, pressure to marry men, and isolation leading to alcoholism and suicide) for not conforming to traditional gender roles (Lorde, 1982).

Transgender people also experienced prejudice throughout much of US history. Dr. Harry Benjamin coined the term "transsexuality" in the 1950s to refer to someone using surgery to change their gender (Stryker, 2006). He distinguished homosexuals, transvestites, and transsexuals, believing that *merely disorientation = "confusion"* (handwritten annotation)

transsexuals possessed the most disorientation relating to their gender, but viewed all as disorders having to do with gender role disorientation (Johnson, 2007). For Black transgender women during this time, the intersections of various marginal identities made them targets of state control. Carlett A. Brown was the first Black intersexed woman to have gender reassignment surgery during the 1950s in Denmark (Jet Magazine, 1954). Prior to surgery, Brown served in the US Navy and was a shake dancer at nightclubs where she was arrested on charges of "deviant dress codes" (Bruno, n.d.). The criminalization of Black transgender women was common during the 1950s and 1960s, leading to social movements to fight against police brutality of transgender people such as the 1966 Compton's Cafeteria riot in San Francisco and the 1969 Stonewall riots in New York. The aforementioned structural discrimination has implications for contemporary Black LBT women's experiences including sexual and gender identity conflict as well as interpersonal marginalization due to race, sexuality, and gender.

IDENTITY MANAGEMENT AMONG BLACK LESBIAN AND BISEXUAL WOMEN

Black lesbian and bisexual women are subjected to at least three forms of oppression: homophobia, racism, and sexism (Greene, 1996). The intersections of these identities make the experiences of heterosexism unique and more challenging for Black LB women than their white counterparts. Meyer, Schwartz, and Frost (2008) found that Black and Latina LB women face more stressors based on race and class than white LBs. LB women of color in that study also had fewer social support resources. In addition, Black LB women may face Christian-based homophobia from their church (Mays, Cochran, & Rhue, 1993), employment discrimination, and prejudice at social establishments in white lesbian communities (Bridges, Selvidge, & Matthews, 2003).

Historically, Black churches have been pillars of strength and the cornerstones for community values for US Blacks (Griffin, 2000). However, for Black LB women, religion can also be a source of oppression and lead to negative mental health outcomes (Walker & Longmire-Avital, 2013). Many Black LB women from religious families struggle to reconcile their sexuality with anti-gay and transphobic messages they receive from their church and interpretations of the Bible that are understood to be homophobic and heterosexist (Miller & Stack, 2014). For Black LB women, this conflict can produce stress regarding being a member of a racialized religious community and being out as a member of the LB community. *have to chose* (handwritten annotation)

Black LB women have fewer spaces for affirmation of their identities than white gays and lesbians. The creation of a Black LB community is a necessity for the emotional survival and community building for Black LB women (Moore, 2006). In these spaces, Black LB women can integrate all aspects of their identities without feeling they have to hide parts of their identity (Loia-cano, 1989). Scholars have noted several strategies that Black LB women use in managing their sexual and racial identities (Brooks, 2016; Miller, 2011). For example, Black lesbian identity management within some Black families emphasizes the "don't ask, don't tell" model (DADT)—women are accepted as long as they don't mention their sexuality or bring girlfriends to their relatives' houses (Miller, 2011). Black lesbians' use of the DADT model can also be beneficial in maintaining economic benefits, where sexual orientation disclosure in the workplace may result in job loss or covert on-the-job marginalization (Bowleg, Brooks & Ritz, 2008). Black lesbian and bisexual women have also employed the following strategies of identity management: passing as straight or perceived gender when in "straight" spaces, educating straight Blacks about LB issues, disengaging from LB politics, and organizing in Black "straight" spaces around issues that affect Black people, such as police brutality (Bowleg et al., 2008; Brooks, 2016).

↳ only address half of identity

IDENTITY MANAGEMENT AMONG BLACK TRANSGENDER WOMEN

Black transgender women also use various identity management strategies. In my own research, I found that many Black transgender women identified as straight women and integrated into Black neighborhood settings by presenting as cisgender[1] women. Others use the term "transgender" as a political statement moving in and out of white LBT spaces, yet preferring Black straight and transgender spaces (Brooks, 2016). Although the reviewed research represents a small step toward inquiry into the lives of Black LBT women, more research needs to be done in the area of Black LBT women's identity management. Effective identity management strategies can help Black LBT women remain resilient in the face of several forms of systematic oppression based on sexuality and gender presentation.

METHODS

This study was approved by the Institutional Review Board at California State Fullerton and used ethnographic methods and semi-structured interviews based on a sample of 10 Black LBT women in the Philadelphia area. Active, primary recruitment was conducted at Black LGBT Pride events in Philadelphia. Secondary recruitment was done through snowball sampling

(Rocco, 2003), meaning women interviewed in my study also recruited other women from Black LGBT organizations in Philadelphia. Participants who reported that they occupied multiple spaces in their family and work lives, and therefore offered a broad perspective of the ways homophobia, transphobia, sexism, and heterosexism affected their mental health were included in the study. I identified myself as a Black lesbian who was also from the inner-city to gain the trust the women who were suspicious of being interviewed for the project, especially by a researcher, even after I told them that I got their information from someone they also knew. Some preconceived notions I had going into this study were that the women would not want to disclose any mental health challenges they have had in the past, so the strategy I used was to ask open-ended questions about their backgrounds, families, and slowly ease into questions about mental health. This approach helped me build a connection with the women so that they would open up about their mental health struggles. My research questions were:

• How would you describe the relationship with your family?
• How long have you been out as lesbian/bi/transgender?
• What role does religion have in your life?
• How has your relationship changed with your family?
• Do you experience mental health challenges? If so what kind?
• Where do you go to seek services?
• Do you have family/community support?
• What keeps you going in the face of challenging times?
• How do you take care of your emotional/physical health?

I changed participants' names in this chapter to protect their identity. To analyze my data, I used a coding system categorizing mental health challenges into two groups: Anxiety and Depression with schizoid-affective disorder being placed as a subheading under depression. I also grouped women by sexual orientation, education, religion, age, and class.

RESULTS

One woman identified as Puerto Rican and Nicaraguan of African descent, one as a Jamaican, and eight as African American. All women had a high school education or equivalent, with three women holding master's degrees and three women with a college degree or some college. Six women identified as lesbian, one as bisexual, one as a masculine lesbian woman (who was often viewed as a transman), and two heterosexual transgender-identified women. Most of the women came from strong religious backgrounds, with two who

Table 6.1   Sample Demographics

	n	%
Ethnicity		
African American	8	80
Jamaican	1	10
Puerto Rican	1	10
Highest Education Obtained		
High school	4	40
Some college or College degree	3	30
Master's degree or higher	3	30
Sexual Identity		
Lesbian	7	70
Bisexual	1	10
Heterosexual	2	20
Gender Identity		
Cisgender	7	70
Transgender/GNC	3	30
Religious Affiliation		
Baptist	5	50
Catholic	2	20
Pentecostal	1	10
No particular religion	2	20

n =10. *Note.* GNC = gender nonconforming.

were raised Catholic, one Pentecostal, and five Baptist. All women were working at the time of the interview and three were in romantic partnerships (see Table 6.1). The names used in this chapter are pseudonyms and are used in order to protect the anonymity and confidentiality of the participants.

All women reported having mental health challenges which were directly related to stress and rejection from families and communities because of their sexual and/or gender identity. Five women were diagnosed with depression, three had anxiety disorder, and one had schizoid-affective disorder. Coping strategies included: drugs and alcohol, food, and attempting suicide. Most of the women found support in other Black LBT female friends and by seeking psychotherapy.

Black Church Involvement and Feelings of Rejection

Sandra is a twenty-four-year-old Puerto Rican and Nicaraguan woman of African descent, and she is currently getting a master's in school counseling at a Christian university on the East Coast. Her mother is a school principal, while her father works for a sanitation company. Both her parents are very religious and met in church in New York City. When I asked her how she experiences being a lesbian in a religious family, she responded with the following statement:

I loved going to church because it connected me with my mom and also I was involved in a youth group in the church, it gave me a sense of belonging, until I started coming out to myself, then I started to question everything: the church, my sexuality. I was hearing mixed messages from the pastor, like 'Homosexuality is a sin, but we love everyone.' You know—love the sinner, but hate the sin.

double standard

The homophobia in Sandra's church took a toll on her mental health and she started drinking heavily at the clubs and smoking cigarettes to ease her pain of rejection by her religious community. Sandra recounted to me that drinking has been a problem for her in the past because she felt God didn't love her:

> I even cried sometimes while clubbing because I felt God didn't love me and I was living in sin. Even when people have handed me flyers about gay friendly churches, I didn't want to go because of the conflict of my sexuality and what the church says about it.

I asked her if she has sought out counseling and she reported that she has, but prior to that decision, she and her mother held prayer circles in hopes of changing her sexuality. She now prays on her own in addition to attending psychotherapy. Sandra's story illustrates the contradictions many Black LBT women encounter in their religious communities. She had challenges merging her religious and sexual identities. She believed that she was living in sin by being in a relationship with a woman, which explains her refusal to attend LGBT-friendly churches.

However, not all LBT women are affected by homophobic church sermons. Some are able to reframe the church experience to be affirming to them. Irene is a thirty-two-year-old lesbian parent who attends Black churches with homophobic sermons:

message change

> Sometimes I go to a Black church and the preacher will say homosexuality is a sin, but it does not bother me because I know God loves me the way I am.

This selective attentiveness to the sermon allows women like Irene to participate in Black churches as a lesbian and focus on what would be an otherwise uplifting sermon minus the homophobia. *bits + pieces taken*

Rejection and Rights in the Family Context

Cheri, a twenty-eight-year-old Black lesbian living with her mother and sister in a Philadelphia suburb, described her home environment as stressful. She reported that she tries to avoid gay topics, but finds it difficult to do because same-sex marriage is still a popular topic of discussion. She described eating with her family at the dinner table and feeling anxious when gay topics are in the news:

I hate when the news is on and something about gay people comes up, like with President Obama's endorsement of gay marriage. I try to talk over the television or distract them from it because my mother will have something negative to say about being gay.

She reported that she has experienced distress in connection with her sexuality and tense relationship with her mother. She suffered weight gain, anxiety, and depression, which eventually lead to a suicide attempt in 2009:

My mother and I were having problems because of my sexual orientation and I was in a bad place. I had just broken up with my girlfriend and felt like I didn't want to be here any longer. I was taken to a mental institution. For a while after that my mother tried to be more supportive, but within a few months she was back to her ways.

Angela, a twenty-four-year-old Black lesbian from Jamaica, shared that in spite of graduating from a prestigious college and applying to medical school, her mother has not gotten over the fact that she is a lesbian:

My mother tried to put me in counseling to change me; over the years she is nicer to me, but does not accept this part of me. I can never bring a partner over to meet her; she just won't accept them. This has caused me a lot of depression, which I am working on.

Yuri is a forty-three-year-old masculine-identified woman from North Philadelphia. She was homeless during the ages of eleven to sixteen after running away from an abusive home and lived in her friend's basement. During this time, she had bouts of depression because she could not express her sexuality as she feared the loss of her friend's support:

I was really depressed because as a teen I knew I had feelings for girls, but I couldn't express it, because I was homeless and needed all the support I could get. While on the streets I got pregnant and had to go back to my abusive home environment. I started using drugs to cope with what I was feeling, which were the fears of being a new parent, and having to go back to the home I ran away from. I would sell sex for drugs, and while doing that I got pregnant again, this time by a trick, and feel into a deeper suicidal depression. Over the years, recovery and therapy have helped me a lot; I don't have to hide who I am to the world.

Yuri's depression was exacerbated by homelessness, homophobia, and being a young homeless parent battling drug addiction. Yuri's narrative illustrates that multiple oppressions intertwine and affect the mental health of Black LBT women.

Tamara, eighteen years old, was raised in a Black middle class family and currently lives in the suburbs. She reported experiencing depression, which runs in her family and was exacerbated by her being a lesbian:

> I was hospitalized last year with schizo-affect disorder, which I think is the effect of the altering of identity between Black and lesbian. In my home Blacks must not act low-class, we are marginalized in white environments. My father discussed racism a lot in the military; that he would be of a higher rank if it weren't for racism. The message I grew up with was: Don't be proud to be gay because it is linked to Black people as a group—Black respectability. Also, when you Black you are supposed to be strong, handle anything. I had a breakdown, which adds to the shame of not living up to Black respectability.

[handwritten: black strength]

Tamara's statement underscores the intersectionality between sexuality, class, and Black respectability politics. Her identity as a Black woman is discussed in the context of systemic racism that her father contended with in the military, which prevented him from moving up in rank. Tamara's father understands a lesbian identity to be a barrier to Blacks assimilating into white middle class culture (Hill, 2005, p. 99). In this hostile home environment, Tamara's racial identity was affirmed at the expense of her lesbianism, thus resulting in her mental health crisis and inability to merge the two identities.

[handwritten: → blacks can't show LGBTQ b/c poor view on blacks]

Mental Healthcare Challenges: Black Transgender Women

Adrienne, an HIV-positive twenty-five-year-old trans-identified Black woman felt that transwomen are targeted as an at risk group for HIV, but their overall health needs are not accounted for at queer-inclusive health centers:

> Most transwomen just get their hormones at queer health centers, but even there they don't have any trans staff there, so it is more queer friendly than other health clinics, but with the trans population they just try and get you in and out; hook you up with your hormones, test you for HIV, but those are not the only health issues we have. Side effects of hormones, drug abuse, lack of housing, and inclusive health care are still a battle.

Another challenge for transwomen is being labeled as having Gender Dysphoria, a diagnosis currently in the DSM-5. Rhonda, a forty-four-year-old transgender woman, stated that many transgender women who are pre-operative wouldn't go to psychotherapy because transgenderism is listed as Gender Dysphoria in the DSM manual:

> The label Gender Identity Disorder [the former term for gender dysphoria] makes you sound crazy, and we have already heard that. So we think that if

[handwritten: reinforces heteronormativity by having that as a diagnosis]

we go to therapy it is because there is something wrong with us because of this label.

The diagnosis may make some transwomen feel marginalized and not use psychotherapy, but Rhonda noted that in order to get hormones and name changes for identification cards, a trans person must accept this label to receive services.

Resiliency and Social Services for Black LBT Women

Some members of the Black LGBT community are trying to be of service for Black LBT women facing mental health challenges. Brittney, a twenty-eight-year-old bisexual woman who was a master's of social work student, stated that:

> I have noticed in our community a lot of mental health issues, especially sub-stance abuse. That is one reason why I am getting my master's in social work, at University of Pennsylvania to help serve the community regarding mental health. Also, I am hearing about more suicides than in recent years among Black lesbians. There was one woman who was really successful as an engineer who killed herself. No one knows why, she had a house, car, partner—all the trap-pings of success and killed herself at 27!

Brittney's observation, along with the above testimonies of the challenges and state of Black LBT women's mental health is disturbing.

Some Black LBT women have been successful with finding a queer-friendly therapist that understands life at the intersections of race and sexual identity. Toni, a thirty-two-year-old Black working-class identified lesbian, works at an LGBT center. She has an associate's degree and reported that she is working on her bachelor's degree. She has faced family rejection based on her sexuality, which has increased her anxiety and depression. She finds that a combination of therapy and medications helps:

> I use a combination of prescribed anti-depressants and anti-anxiety medications. I also visit with a psychiatrist every 3 months. I was formally in bi-weekly therapy—so this is helping me.

Angela disclosed that she thinks queer mental health services help create safe places for lesbians, especially those who have had negative experiences of counseling in the past:

> I go to an LGBT counseling center in downtown Philly and feel like I belong there and that my lesbianism is not questioned. I have had negative experiences

need belonging

with therapy in the past, family sending me to counseling to try and change me, so it is refreshing to feel like I can actually be myself.

In spite of challenges, many women in this study were resilient when it came to challenging heterosexism, transphobia, racism, and classism. Toni, who also identifies as working class, reported having a strong support system of friends that make her feel loved in her community:

> I am consistently trying to find community while dealing with financial issues and family strains. I have been trying to get my BA for over ten years, but it is hard when you have to work to support yourself. I find strength in my partner who loves me. Also, my friends have become my family.

Rhonda cited the House Ball scene as a place where Black transgender women build community:

> Some transgender women build community in the ball scene performing for money. It is fun and empowering to put yourself out there performing and making money—you feel good about yourself. *financial worth*

Some Black LBT women use their personal spirituality to help them overcome homophobia from religious sources. Sandra stated:

> I recently began going to church again where I see God's love from a very different perspective than the one I grew up learning about. In the past I saw God as very domineering, forthright, and strict. Now I am able to identify God as a loving entity that accepts me. This is how I find peace within myself. Also, my friends help a lot with supporting me.

Angela reported that she now challenges the homophobic messages she encounters in religious settings:

> When I hear people talking about how homosexuality is a sin I remind them that God is about loving people, not hating them. I am a child of God because I am a good caring person, and the Bible teaches that we should be caring towards each other. *TRUE?*

DISCUSSION

Many Black LBT women face mental health challenges when managing their sexual and gender identities. In spite of media attention to LGBT-related issues, such as gay marriage or the recent bathroom laws in North Carolina (Lee, 2016), many Black LBT women continue to face rejection and marginalization. Black LBT women receive conflicting messages within the church about love and acceptance, mixed with the labeling of a lesbian or bisexual identity as sinful. This tension between their religious, gender, and sexual identities can cause psychological distress for some Black LBT religious women. Family rejection in the face of increasing media coverage of LGBT issues is another situation that produces stress for many Black LBT women negotiating their sexuality and family membership.

While the labeling of gay and lesbian sexuality as pathology has decreased in the medical field, Black transgender women are still viewed as having a mental disorder (gender dysphoria). Many Black transgender women often avoid therapy fearing they will be further pathologized, or that providers will reproduce stereotypes that transgender people are dysfunctional (Vance et al., 2010). Moreover, when Black transgender women seek mental health services they are treated for physical health concerns associated with transgender women (i.e., HIV testing, hormone intake), and not mental health treatment (Gorton & Grubb, 2014). The focus of some transgender health services providers on only physical ailments rather than mental health reinforces assumptions of transgender women being hypersexual. While it is true that HIV/AIDS is a health issue for many Black working-class transgender women who are often forced into survival sex work because of job and housing discrimination, this is not the only issue transgender women face. Poor and working-class Black transgender women also need mental health services and social support. They would also benefit from access to resources such as safe housing, jobs, and affirming educational opportunities (Gorton & Grubb, 2014).

More research needs to be done in the area of mental health and Black LBT women, but the experiences of the women interviewed for this study provide some insight into the challenges and possible avenues for mental health care. Many Black LBT women come from religious backgrounds, so encouragement of attending LGBT-friendly churches, along with working among church pastors within Black communities to address and end homophobia, transphobia, and heterosexism can improve the mental well-being of Black LBT women. A reformation of traditional Black churches that focuses on the eradication of homophobia can have a positive effect on the communities in which these women live. Furthermore, homoinclusive and homoaffirming education for healthcare and allied health students will help future providers focus on strength-building and inclusiveness instead of pathologizing sexual and non-gender conforming identities (Singh, 2010). Black transgender women need to have inclusive mental health care at clinics, thus requiring more training for social service providers about issues that affect Black transgender women.

In addition to social services, the families of Black LBT women can foster positive mental health by showing unconditional love and acceptance. Black heterosexual family members of Black LBT women should be encouraged to engage in journeys of self-discovery *with* their LBT loved ones, starting with accepting partners, using religion to uplift and not oppress, and attending LBT-related events to educate themselves on issues affecting this population. Members of the Black LBT communities will also benefit from helping each other. Black transgender women can share resources with one another, be supportive, and accepting regardless what stage of transition a woman is in. For example, some transgender women ostracize other transwomen that do not appear to pass as cisgender. Transgender Black women can share information about various resources in the community with each other. Similarly, Black lesbians and bisexual women can offer each other, and transwomen, support, friendship, and share resources related to jobs, housing, and social events.

CONCLUSION

This chapter highlighted challenges to and resiliency in Black LBT women's positive mental health, focusing on religious, family, and medical settings. Many LBT women in the United States suffer from homophobia, heterosexism, and transphobia in religious, familial, and medical environments. However, many Black LBT women are also taking care of their mental health needs by forming caring communities, engaging in psychotherapy, and advocating for social services. With more education, awareness, and social support, the mental health for many Black LBT women in the United States will improve.

NOTE

1. Cisgender refers to someone born biologically male or female and also identifies with that gender.

REFERENCES

Abdur-Rahman, A. I. (2006). " The strangest freaks of despotism:" Queer sexuality in antebellum African American slave narratives. *African American Review, 40*(2), 223–237.

Bostwick, W. B., Boyd, C. J., Hughes, T. L., West, B. T., & McCabe, S. E. (2014). Discrimination and mental health among lesbian, gay, and bisexual adults in the United States. *American Journal of Orthopsychiatry, 84*(1), 35–45.

Bowleg, L., Brooks, K., & Ritz, S. F. (2008). "Bringing home more than a paycheck" An exploratory analysis of Black lesbians' experiences of stress and coping in the workplace. *Journal of Lesbian Studies, 12*(1), 69–84.

Bridges, S. K., Selvidge, M. M., & Matthews, C. R. (2003). Lesbian women of color: Therapeutic issues and challenges. *Journal of Multicultural Counseling and Development, 31*(2), 113–131.

Brooks, S. (2016). Staying in the hood: Black lesbian and transgender women and identity management in North Philadelphia. *Journal of Homosexuality,* 1–21. doi: 10.1080/00918369.2016.1158008

Bruno, K. (n.d.). Carlett Brown: The extreme marginalization of transwomen of color. [Website] Retrieved from http://outhistory.org/exhibits/show/tgi-bios/carlett-brown

Clarke, J. M., Brown, J. C., & Hochstein, L. M. (1989). Institutional religion and gay/ lesbian oppression. *Marriage & Family Review, 14*(3–4), 265–284.

Eskridge, W. N. (2008). *Dishonorable passions: Sodomy laws in America, 1861–2003.* Westminster, London: Penguin.

Gorton, N., & Grubb, H. M. (2014). General, sexual, and reproductive health. In L. Erickson-Schroth (Ed.), *Trans bodies, trans selves: A resource for the transgender community* (pp. 215–239). New York, NY: Oxford University Press.

Greene, B. (1996). Lesbian women of color: Triple jeopardy. *Journal of Lesbian Studies, 1*(1), 109–147.

———. (2000). African American lesbian and bisexual women. *Journal of Social Issues, 56*(2), 239–249.

Griffin, H. (2000). Their own received them not: African American lesbians and gays in Black churches. *Theology & Sexuality, 2000*(12), 88–100.

Jet Magazine. (1954, April). *Are homosexuals becoming respectable?* Retrieved from https://www.flickr.com/photos/vieilles_annonces/1295157599

Johnson, K. (2007). Transsexualism: Diagnostic dilemmas, transgender politics and the future of transgender care. In V. Clarke & E. Peel (Eds.), *Out of psychology: Lesbian, gay, bisexual, trans and queer perspectives* (pp. 445–461). Hoboken, NJ: John Wiley & Sons.

Lee, C. (2016). The fight for children's 'safety' in North Carolina. *The Brown University Child and Adolescent Behavior Letter, 32*(6), 8–8.

Loiacano, D. K. (1989). Gay identity issues among Black Americans: Racism, homophobia, and the need for validation. *Journal of Counseling & Development, 68*(1), 21–25.

Lorde, A. (1982). *Zami: A new spelling of my name.* New York, NY: Random House.

Mays, V. M., Cochran, S. D., & Rhue, S. (1993). The impact of perceived discrimination on the intimate relationships of Black lesbians. *Journal of Homosexuality, 25*(4), 1–14.

Meyer, I. H. (2013). Prejudice, social stress, and mental health in lesbian, gay, and bisexual populations: Conceptual issues and research evidence. *Psychological Bulletin, 129*(5), 674.

Meyer, I. H., Schwartz, S., & Frost, D. M. (2008). Social patterning of stress and coping: Does disadvantaged social statuses confer more stress and fewer coping resources? *Social Science & Medicine, 67*(3), 368–379.

Miller, S. J. (2011). African-American lesbian identity management and identity development in the context of family and community. *Journal of Homosexuality, 58*(4), 547–563.

Miller, S. J., & Stack, K. (2014). African-American lesbian and queer women respond to Christian-based homophobia. *Journal of GLBT Family Studies, 10*(3), 243–268.

Moore, M. R. (2006). Lipstick or timberlands? Meanings of gender presentation in Black lesbian communities. *Signs, 32*(1), 113–139.

Mount, D. L., Amponsah, A. A., Graham, L. F., & Lambert, M. C. (2014). Factors associated with label preferences and mental health quality of life among college-aged African American sexual minority men. *Journal of African American Males in Education, 5*(1), 75–95.

Mumford, K. (2016). *Not straight, not white: Black gay men from the march on Washington to the AIDS crisis.* Chapel Hill, NC: University of North Carolina Press.

Rocco, T. S. (2003). Shaping the future: Writing up the method on qualitative studies. *Human Resource Development Quarterly, 14*(3), 343–349.

Silverstein, C. (2009). The implications of removing homosexuality from the DSM as a mental disorder. *Archives of Sexual Behavior, 38*(2), 161–163.

Singh, A., & McKleroy, V. S. (2011). "Just getting out of bed is a revolutionary act": The resilience of transgender people of color who have survived traumatic life events. *Traumatology, 17,* 34–44.

Stryker, S. (2006). (De)subjugated knowledges: An introduction to transgender studies. In S. Stryker & S. Whittle (Eds.), *The transgender studies reader* (pp. 1–17). New York, NY: Routledge.

Vance Jr, S. R., Cohen-Kettenis, P. T., Drescher, J., Meyer-Bahlburg, H. F., Pfäfflin, F., & Zucker, K. J. (2010). Opinions about the DSM gender identity disorder diagnosis: Results from an international survey administered to organizations concerned with the welfare of transgender people. *International Journal of Transgenderism, 12*(1), 1–14.

Walker, J. N. J., & Longmire-Avital, B. (2013). The impact of religious faith and internalized homonegativity on resiliency for Black lesbian, gay, and bisexual emerging adults. *Developmental Psychology, 49*(9), 1723–1731.

Washington, H. A. (2006). *Medical apartheid: The dark history of medical experimentation on Black Americans from colonial times to the present.* New York, NY: Doubleday Books.

Chapter 7

Rainbows or Ribbons?

Queer Black Women Searching for a Place in the Cancer Sisterhood

LaShaune P. Johnson and Jane A. McElroy

In a darkened, smoky room in 1999, there's a sound of soft rattling, ruffling of skirts, and panted prayers. A disembodied, guttural voice says:

Papa Legba ouvre baye pou mwen, Ago eh!
Papa Legba ouvre baye pou mwen,
Ouvre baye pou mwen, Papa
Pou mwen passe, Le'm tounnen map remesi Lwa yo![1]

The room is suddenly illuminated and begins to pulsate with thunderous and hypnotic drumming. Dancers enter the room, in a sea of red, yellow, white, and blue, representing a range of expression from old to young, from masculine to coquettish and feminine. The sudden burst of color, light, and sound leaves all in the room breathless, disoriented. The audience is on its feet. As the dizzying flurry of brightly colored dancers march across the stage, the lines between the audience and the performers, the living and dead, become blurred. In this moment, there is unlimited power and possibility; we are rapt with boundless joy and all become temporarily healed, from wounds known and unknown. It was a song dedicated to Papa Legba, the opener of doors, the shape-shifting trickster, the keeper of the gate between the living and the dead. Men and women of all ages, colors, and body sizes leave their cares at the feet of Legba, and everyday differences disappear. It is from moments like these—found in the ordinary and extraordinary—that queer cancer patients and survivors of color may find that they can draw their strength and resilience.

Legba is the spirit who holds a protective hand over those who find themselves at the crossroads, and at the intersection of the Black communities and queer[2] communities is where we begin this chapter. We are not the first theorists to reflect on the dizzying experience being queer, Black, and facing cancer. Most famously, Audre Lorde chronicled her walk at the border between life and death as a cancer patient, and her life as a member of the rarely intersecting Black communities and queer communities. While Lorde spent her life refusing to settle for highlighting one identity, she understood the complex juggling act that queer Black people have to perform to be able to live fully in all of their identities (1984). As one queer Black woman illustrated when talking about multiple social identities:

> One of the things I've been talking about is, when I go to church, my church is open and affirming so I can bring all of me there, but there's certain places you can't always bring all of you. You go here, you have to be the Black person. You go here, here you're the gay person. You go here and you're the religious person. And to be able to bring your whole self to the table . . . I think we were allowed to do that here. It didn't matter which part; you didn't feel like you had to check it at the door. So I do think we felt very comfortable in bringing our whole selves here where there's a lot of places you don't. (McElroy, Washington, Wintemberg, Williams, & Redman, 2016, p. S68)

Many queer women of color are asked to shapeshift to fit into one-dimensional settings around them, even as they simultaneously experience discrimination against those identities (Remedios & Snyder, 2015). Just as Du Bois (1903) suggested in his early theorizing about "double consciousness," these conflicting allegiances "warring" inside the queer woman of color are a heavy burden to bear and are heavier during times of illness. The illness that is the focus of this chapter is cancer. These women's opposing allegiances are to a diverse set of communities: Black, queer, and various cancer organizations that appear along the cancer care continuum. In this chapter we will open the gate to a new way of thinking about queer Black women on the cancer continuum of care by highlighting relevant literature about intersectionality among both Black women and queer women. We present examples from our work that underscores the cross-cutting issues facing the Black and queer communities when addressing Black women's cancer disparities. Finally, we propose ways that each of these communities (Black, queer, and cancer) can improve the experiences of queer Black women facing cancer.

CANCER STATISTICS FOR BLACK WOMEN

Black women have a lower probability of developing invasive cancer, but have worse survival and higher death rates than White women when combining data from all cancer sites (American Cancer Society [ACS], 2016). According the ACS's 2016–2018 *Cancer Facts & Figures for African Americans,* the mortality rates for endometrial cancer for Black women are significantly higher than White women—1 in 108 compared to 1 in 184 (ACS, 2016). The median survival time for Black women facing endometrial cancer is also significantly shorter than that for White women (61 months vs. 121 months; Madison, Schottenfeld, Schwartz & Gruber, 2004). The rates of diagnosis are likely similar for many other cancers (i.e., breast, lung and bronchus, kidney, non-Hodgkin's lymphoma, thyroid, leukemia) among Black women. One important determinant of racial/ethnic differences in cancer survival is stage at diagnosis (Madison et al., 2004; Setiawan, Pike, Kolonel, Nomura, Goodman, & Henderson, 2007). However, Maxwell and colleagues (2008) reported racial differences in cancer survival even for women who were diagnosed at the same stage. Connell, Rotmensch, Waggoner & Mundt (1999) evaluated a large cohort of surgically staged and uniformly treated endometrial cancer patients and found that Black women had worse outcomes which traditional prognostic factors could not predict.

Researchers agree that the factors contributing to the disparities in overall survival rates in Black women are multifactorial and poorly understood (Allard & Maxwell, 2009; Connell et al., 1999; Maxwell, Tian, Risinger, Hamilton, & Barakat, 2008; Setiawan et al., 2007; Yap & Matthews, 2006). The observed racial disparity in endometrial and other cancer survival may be not only due to unevenness in stage, grade, histology, socioeconomic status, adjuvant therapy, known risk factors, and comorbidities (Cote et al., 2015), but also due to Black women's cultural and social environmental factors (ACS, 2016; Connell et al., 1999; Madison et al., 2004; Oliver at al., 2011; Randall, 2003). For example, difficulties in cross-racial patient-physician communication, differences in diet, high-risk social habits, and unique environmental stressors faced by Black women (Freeman, 2004).

SEXUAL AND GENDER MINORITY WOMEN'S CANCER STATISTICS

There is evidence that queer women face increased risk for many cancers due to higher prevalence of cancer risk factors and less access to care compared to non-queer populations (Institute of Medicine [IOM], 2011). Queer populations have the highest rates of tobacco use and excessive alcohol consumption (IOM, 2011). Lesbians and bisexual women are consistently reported to be more likely to be overweight or obese (Boehmer, 2007; Eliason et al., 2015; Struble, Lindley, Montgomery, Hardin, & Burcin, 2011). Members of the queer community have lower levels of preventive health behaviors, such as screening and access to care (Diamant, 2000). Boehmer and colleagues (2005) reported that sexual minority women face exposure to negative societal attitudes, prejudice, discrimination and stigma, and indicate that stigma, as a cultural barrier, can interfere with access to care. Two other risk factors for many chronic diseases—physical activity and dietary choices—also vary by sexual orientation (Minnis et al., 2016). Finally, queer individuals have higher stress levels compared to those outside of the queer community (McElroy et al., 2016), which may also influence cancer survival.

QUEER WOMEN'S CANCER EXPERIENCES AND TREATMENT JOURNEYS[3]

Much of the cancer research has centered on non-queer survivors or caregivers. From the limited qualitative research in which queer participants discuss disclosing their sexual orientation and gender identity, many of the queer Black women surveyed report fears about coming out to healthcare providers (Kamen, Mustian, Dozier, Bowen, & Li, 2015; Woody, 2014). A sixty-six-year-old Black woman shared her concern about selectively coming out to healthcare professionals,

> I don't just go into it. If it comes up, [I'll share]. I'm African American; you can see that, and a woman. But somehow things happen that comes up and I just say I'm a lesbian . . . I don't care what they say first do no harm and you're a human being first with biases. . . and who knows . . . once they find out they gonna kill me anyway. Right, so it's a double question mark [gay and Black]. (Woody, 2014, p. 153)

In a small endometrial case-control study with a White sample, a pattern of feeling responsible for initiating the conversation about one's sexual orientation identity was observed (Cote, 2015). Of the 18 White queer participants, women with endometrial cancer were 1.5 times more like to be out to their doctor compared to women without endometrial cancer. However, of those that were out, 75 percent initiated that conversation. In another small study of White queer breast cancer survivors who opted to not have reconstructive breast surgery, all were out to their surgeon (Brown & McElroy, 2016). For several of these women, the disclosure of their queer identity helped their providers to understand the reasoning behind this surgical choice. One participant said,

> I think [provider awareness of sexual orientation and gender identity] influenced me in a positive way. Knowing that I was in a same-sex relationship with a partner whose child I was raising played into the choices I made about treatment, and they respected that. Also, my decisions regarding surgery (I had a bilateral mastectomy) seemed more in keeping with my gender identity and my surgeon got that. I was fortunate to have a surgeon who is a queer woman of color. (Brown & McElroy, 2016)

Whereas others faced difficulties when navigating the healthcare system. As one participant noted:

I think [my healthcare providers] were respectful, but didn't know how to react to the decisions I made [choosing to not have reconstructive breast survey] because of my sexual identity. They discourage me in my decision and brought it up in follow-ups as a drastic move that wasn't needed! This was my Oncologist! "(Brown & McElroy, 2016)

Boehmer and colleagues (2014) have reported some particularly useful findings for thinking about how queer women cope during the cancer continuum of care. They found that in comparison to heterosexual women, queer women reported less anxious preoccupation, hopelessness, and cognitive avoidance coping. The authors theorized that these response patterns were possibly "a reflection of skills learned in the context of exposure to minority stress, which they transferred to the cancer experience" (Boehmer et al., 2014, p. 234). While their findings seem to be more reflective of the White participants (approximately 90 percent of the sample), this is an idea worth exploring with queer Black women who experience a larger matrix of oppression (Collins, 1990).

PINK RIBBON CULTURE

There are organized national and local communities designed to offer support, advocacy, and education to people along the cancer continuum of care. National organizations such as Susan G. Komen for the Cure (for breast cancer) or the American Cancer Society (for all cancers) offer support and educational materials for all stages of the continuum, as well as financial resources for research and community projects. In addition to being known for their educational work, these groups' fundraising endeavors provide money for research. Filling in the gaps for the mainstream organizations are specialized factions that educate and support particular subgroups of survivors. For instance, the Sisters Network, Inc. is a national organization that addresses breast cancer disparities for Black women. The LGBT Cancer Network does parallel work for the general queer community. Regardless of their focus population, most groups offer the creation of in-person and virtual support groups for patients/survivors/caretakers, educational materials for patients, survivors, caretakers, and providers, resources for finding providers, and legal information. When someone is newly diagnosed with cancer, one resource often recommended by providers are support groups which have been shown to be an effective forum for providing psychosocial support

(Davison, Pennebaker, & Dickerson, 2000). However, less than 10 percent of patients attend support groups (Stalker, Johnson, & Cimma, 1990).

A lack of participation in support groups may be because the organizations are unwelcoming for those who are people of color, poor, and sexual and gender minorities (King, 2008; Sulik, 2011). This exclusion from mainstream cancer communities comes at a time when breast and gynecological cancer survival disparities between Black and White women are increasing (Hunt, Whitman, & Hurlbert, 2014)—in spite of medical advances and increased access to care for the previously un(der)insured (Berry et al., 2005; Danforth, 2013). In addition, many queer Black women do not find a home in national Black cancer organizations. A telephone call by one of the authors to the Linda Creed Breast Cancer Foundation, which has a robust Black support group ("Safe Circle"), revealed that its LGBTQ support group ("Rainbow Circle") leadership was unable to provide narratives or references for women of color who were part of the Rainbow Circle (personal communication, June 28, 2016).

A more troubling telephone conversation which possibly reflects the reality for queer Black women seeking assistance occurred when one of the authors contacted the Black Women's Health Imperative. The retired Black lesbian founder, Byllye Avery, once mentioned in an interview that she "never felt that the Black women rejected me so much as they didn't know what to do with me. By the time I got to the Black Women's Health Project, there were several women on the planning committee who were lesbian, and one of the things we worked on was homophobia" (Correspondent, 2015). Yet, in a recent telephone call inquiring about queer Black women, the staff member remarked, "We serve Black women, not queer women." When co-author Johnson said, "Well, I'm quite sure there are queer Black women," the staff member responded by telling Johnson to call the queer cancer organizations and said, "We don't ask women that stuff" (personal communication, June 30, 2016).

A scan of two national African American cancer organizations' (Sister Network, Inc. and Witness Project) materials reveals nothing specific to queer community health needs. In a search of the Sisters Network, Inc. national website, one can read about their general program and targeted programming for young women and teens, but there is no such program for queer women. Additionally, although websites list some of the commonly understood lifestyle and biological risks for developing breast cancer, nothing is listed about the special risks for queer populations, in spite of that information being available on the website of its primary source.[4] Scores of cancer-related websites, marathons, and other marketing campaigns flood televisions, social media, and shopping carts. One need not look far for an inspirational "cancer journey" story. Yet, finding a cancer story or blog online that reflects the social identities of queer Black women is daunting, if not impossible.

Culturally appropriate and equitable access to cancer prevention, as well as detection and treatment are important (Hunt et al., 2014), but they are only part of the story. While recent research (Giwa & Greensmith, 2012; Isoke, 2014; Petzen, 2012; Stone & Ward, 2011) has highlighted queer Black women and their outsider roles in the queer and Black communities, less is understood about how these women view, enter, and participate in the cancer care continuum. In the maelstrom of often-changing cancer screening recommendations, multilayered tumor diagnoses, and complex treatment regimes, how and where do queer Black women find solace, information, and support during their time on the cancer continuum of care?[5]

Besides the lack of inclusion, these programs have a darker side. The events that they host are sometimes critiqued for promoting a "tyranny of cheerfulness" (King, 2008). This overarching perspective does not allow for anger (at disparities or diagnosis), questions about the causes of cancer (including debated environmental factors), and conversations about death (King, 2008). According to King, this cheerful emphasis also reduces the likelihood of addressing complicated social justice issues related to experiences and access to cancer screening, diagnosis, treatment, and survival for different classes, races, ethnicities, gender identities, and sexual orientations. The second prong of the major cancer organizations is secondary prevention through screening which allows for early detection of cancer. However, the founders of Breast Cancer Action argue that the emphasis on awareness campaigns and screenings diverts attention from the broader, social, economic, policy and environmental causes of breast cancer (King, 2008).

FAITH AND BLACK WOMEN'S CANCER JOURNEYS

Womanist theology offers Black women the strength to cope with life's hardships and allows Black women to center their experiences in Western faith practices. Numerous studies have shown that the illness explanations, coping, and healing are linked to faith in Black communities (Mytko & Knight, 1999; Laubmeier, Zakowski, & Bair, 2004; Stroman, 2000). For example, a 2.5-year Black breast cancer survivor provided evidence of the importance of faith in coping with cancer diagnosis: "If it hadn't been for God, I couldn't cope with nothing" (Holt et al., 2009, p. 6). Among queer women of faith who have an accepting community, numerous aspects of coping with cancer can be supported through their belief system (Holt et al., 2009).

In a study of Black cancer patients and their caregivers, Sterba and colleagues (2014) found three overarching themes in the patients' and their caretakers' discussions about the role of faith in their experiences with cancer. After treatment, religiousness and spirituality played a major role in both survivors' and caregivers' lives by: "1) providing global guidance, 2) guiding illness management efforts and 3) facilitating recovery" (Sterba et al., 2014, p. 1). Faith did not immobilize or deter the believers, but provided them with the confidence that they would be healed by a higher power, often through the Christ-guided hands of their provider (Sterba et al., 2014). Womanist theology also gives Black women a way to push back against one-dimensional descriptions of them and their beliefs (i.e., all Black women are fatalistic about cancer). It gives them an opportunity in religious and broader settings to turn the "sassy Black woman" stereotype on its head (Davis, 2015). They do so with the stealth and skill acquired after generations of their voices being silenced by Black men, White men, and White women. Hotz (2014) cites the work of Mitchem (2005):

> Attitude is a protective stance, a kind of preventive medicine against the world's cruelty. Both sassiness and attitude are modes of Black women's operations in the world as independent agents . . . Sassiness, in other words, is not simply a disposition or a culturally specific form of expression, but also a mode of resistance that encourages agency. Sass can express itself in ways we might traditionally recognize as a form of 'attitude,' but it also manifests as a fierce, persistent will to endure in spite of circumstances that would cause others to give up. (Mitchem, 2005, cited in Hotz, 2014, p. 2217)

This sassiness and attitude can be understood from the perspective of Black women, but oppression based on sexual orientation and gender identity also provides an impetus for assuming this protective stance. This review of the literature has illustrated a severe lack of information about and support for queer Black women along the cancer continuum. Informed by these facts, the authors of this chapter created and implemented a faith-based breast cancer healthy lifestyle program for women and girls in Central Missouri that ran from 2012 to 2013.[6] The theories of intersectionality (Pastrana, 2006), Black feminism (Collins, 1986), and womanist theology (Davis, 2015; Harvey, Johnson, & Heath, 2013) provided the theoretical frameworks from which we developed the program.

WALKING IN THE SPIRIT, SHOUTING IN A WOMANIST VOICE

This program was created in response to breast cancer disparities faced by Black women and used public health critical race (PHCR) methodology. The PHCR methodology, which is an adaptation of Critical Race Theory, allows researchers to improve the conceptualization and measurement of racism's effects on health (Ford & Airhihenbuwa, 2010, p. 1397). As an exercise of disciplinary self-critique, it calls for the contributions of those in racial and ethnic minority communities; as a result, the conceptualization of effects on health is made more robust by the theorizing of those living the experiences. The sharing of lived experiences provides depth to the theory and potentially introduces new variables into the understanding of health disparities. The program was implemented in two cities in Central Missouri and was co-designed with community members to give Black women and girls an opportunity to be empowered about their health. The symbol for the program included a dove that represented the Holy Spirit. In the Christian Bible, the dove appears during Jesus' baptism, and also plays a prominent role in the Noah flood story. The program's symbol also included a footprint, invoking both walking and the "Footprints in the Sand" poem (Zangare, 1984) that was familiar to many of the church members.

The use of the footprint was also intended to remind community members of the Bible verse: "If we live in the Spirit, let us also walk in the Spirit" (Galatians 5:25, KJV). This verse appeared on all of the materials. Understanding the Black community's sometimes troubled history with mainstream cancer organizations generally (and specifically Komen[7]), it was essential to co-create a project that would be sustainable and that felt "true" to the community. We understood that the project had to be attendant to health literacy, ethnic diversity within the Black community, and if possible, create ties between Black community, the two authors and facilitators' university, and funding agencies.

While many in leadership positions in these close-knit Black communities understood the importance of breast cancer and had participated in "Pink Sunday" events, cancer education and prevention fell far down on the priorities list of many women. The lead author was regularly told that women did not have time for breast cancer in their lives. As suggested by secondary marginalization theory (Pastrana, 2006), at the start of the project, breast cancer felt like an issue of importance to the educated elites of the community (i.e., pastors' wives, sorority members, pink collar professionals[8] with health insurance), and a problem to be ignored by the rest of the Black community. In order not to leave any of the women behind, the authors made explicit that the project's goals were addressing disparities in the Black community by encouraging awareness and discussion; acknowledging broader social, economic, and health issues in the community (e.g., poverty, food insecurity, diabetes, heart disease, violence); and integrating faith into health outreach.

Over the span of a year, we created several events that took place at churches, health departments, and other community organizations. These events were planned with community liaisons assigned from each church. As promised to the community, all of the events had a spiritual health moment along with its physical health focus. The spiritual health moment, just like the physical health theme, had an accompanying worksheet with suggestions for spiritual exercises such as prayer, Bible study, meditation, and kind acts. The following is an excerpt from one of the spiritual health moments, which featured passages from the Biblical chapters of John and Matthew[9] and was titled: "Not your ordinary fish tale." It begins with a summary of the story in John about Christ creating food for masses when there was very little and ends with a summary of the Sermon on the Mount. These summaries were approved by the church liaisons, and were connected to the event of the month (e.g., cooking demonstration, barbeque). The themes in the spiritual moment reflected themes found in other studies about the role of faith for African American breast cancer patients. A qualitative study by Holt and colleagues (2009) found that reliance on God for healing and the importance of prayer and scripture study were among some of the important elements for coping with cancer. These themes appear to have resonated with the community members—often, they would ask to take extra copies of the spiritual health worksheets to take home with them, for sharing with other family members and friends.

Using the PHCR methodology, our program agenda aligned to its foci in this way: Focus 1) Contemporary Patterns of Racial Relations: We had frank discussions about the history of Black community with Susan G. Komen, the history of Black community food deserts, structural racism, and others' lack of understanding of diversity within the Black community. For Focus 2) Knowledge Production, we engaged community members in critical discussions of the racism and classism of the "pink ribbon" culture. We encouraged them to find more like-minded communities that would support them as Black women. Focus 3) Conceptualization and Measurement: In thinking about how to measure success, co-author Johnson and the community liaisons discussed how to talk about breast cancer along with broader chronic health conditions in the community in order to achieve increased breast cancer screening. Johnson was encouraged by community liaisons to think about health disparities as the new Civil Rights issue, with the Black Church in the center of organizing. Focus 4) Action: During the twelve months of the project, Johnson encouraged community partners to learn grant writing skills and to look for partners to help them continue the work after the *Walking in the Spirit* grant was over.

Throughout the project, the women of the community were honest and very sassy—calling out the dietician's first cooking efforts as being "too white" because it included ingredients that were uncommon and unfamiliar in Black soul food staples; pushing against a guest speaker for her patronizing tone when speaking to a community well-versed in heart disease; and chastising Johnson for not recognizing the cultural difference between Christian denominations when setting up Zumba classes.[10] Integrated into the process from the beginning, the Black women used this program as what Patricia Hill Collins (1990, p. 114) calls a "site of resistance." The participants adapted the single-issue organization's purpose–focus on breast cancer—to meet their needs and concerns. Throughout the project, the women of *Walking in the Spirit* remained defiantly Christian, sassy, and Black. They actively participated in the project and shared the information with others, but they did it their way, making their allegiances and priorities clear. Although this program did not specifically engage queer Black women, the authors believe the basic tenets of the program would be appropriate. Specifically, co-designing the program with community members so that their needs were addressed; having frank discussion about the intersection of multiple social identities—Black, queer, cancer survivor; and lastly being responsive to community feedback would be important components for success.

THE WAY FORWARD

We began this chapter in the giddy embrace of one of the Vodun *lwa* Papa Legba, imploring him to provide us safe passage to a place in the cancer continuum of care where queer Black women can embrace their racial and queer identities. Much like the dancers in the Introduction, we breathlessly struggled to maintain our footing through a vertiginous formation of relevant literatures and of cancer- and queer-serving organizations that did not lead us to that safe place for queer Black women. While the answer was not found, the call still rings in our ears, and we leave the reader with a map for the way forward. We provided evidence about cancer in Black women and cancer risk factors in queer women, and pointed out that there is little research focusing on queer Black women impacted by cancer. In addition, no current models allow for a multilayered approach to understanding and addressing the needs of queer Black women seeking cancer care. What does a queer-friendly Black cancer education and support structure look like? How do we create that golden moment, where the gates are open to all who seek entry and healing is collective and empowering? A model might have the following elements:

- Strategically provide medically accurate and accessible information written in conjunction with members of the queer Black community.
- Lovingly embrace women of all ages, genders, sexualities, body sizes, and abilities and allow space to honor their histories and struggles.
- Critically reflect the PHCR methodology and be attuned to the broader social, economic, and political struggles facing queer Black women and their families.

- Constantly challenge mainstream cancer culture and demand respect for queer Black women's "sass" and gender nonconforming ways of being.
- Willingly position itself in religious and secular places, recognizing that not all women are Christian or religious, but accept the importance of gathering places for sisterhood.
- Regularly disrupt and communicate with the larger queer community so that it acknowledges the contributions of queer Black people in its broader history, and understands that issues of race must remain a part of the larger dialogue of the community.
- Boldly demand "a seat at the table" with healthcare providers to insist on a healthcare system that treats queer Black bodies with respect and humanity.

Embracing queer Black female cancer patients requires a shift within and outside several communities—the queer community, the Black community, the cancer survivor community, and the medical community. Reducing cancer disparities among queer Black women requires the inclusion of voices from queer Black cancer patients and increased acceptance of all cancer patients' multiple social identities. The lessons learned from the *Walking in the Spirit* program have great potential to help healthcare professionals create more inclusive spaces for queer Black women along the cancer continuum.

NOTES

1. *"Papa Legba, open the gate for me, Ago eh*
Papa Legba, open the gate for me
Open the gate for me, Papa
For me to pass, when I return I will thank the Lwa!"
This is a common prayer for the Vodun Iwa (spirit), Papa Legba. He is the first Iwa invoked in the Vodu ceremonial order.

2. For consistency, the authors of this chapter have chosen to use the term "queer" to represent the members of the LGBTQ/sexual and gender minority (those who identify as lesbian, gay, bisexual, transgender, queer, questioning, or other labels) communities. We recognize that this not the preferred term for all members of the community or for all researchers.

3. In a 2013 study on LGBTQ patient-centered outcomes, the authors called for systematic changes in the support of cancer LGBTQ cancer patients and survivors, citing their poorer outcomes. In their conclusion, they state: "A well-intentioned one-size-fits-all approach too often gives a message of unwelcome to LGBT patients, leading those who can avoid the system to do so, and suggesting to others that they need to remain silent about their lives, their support systems and their needs" (p. 29). This study has limitations, however: the sample was comprised of only 9 percent people of color. http://www.cancer-network.org/downloads/lgbt-patient-centered-outcomes.pdf

4. The American Cancer Society, which serves as one of the primary sources for the website, has documents specific to the queer community and cancer: http://www.cancer.org/healthy/findcancerearly/womenshealth/cancer-facts-for-lesbians-and-bisexual-women

5. San Diego Affiliate of the Susan G. Komen for the Cure's Continuum of Care Model: http://komensandiego.org/wp-content/uploads/2014/06/2012Continuum_of_Care_Model.pdf

6. Funded by Susan G. Komen Mid-Missouri Affiliate (PI: Jane A. McElroy; post-doctoral fellow, LaShaune Johnson; Dr. Johnson took leadership on the project and met regularly with Dr. McElroy about the project.)

7. At the time, the national Susan G. Komen brand had taken a hard hit within the Black community due it its controversial decision—and ultimate reversal—to break its relationship with Planned Parenthood, often one of the only sources of preventive care in underserved communities. http://www.cnn.com/2012/02/03/politics/planned-parenthood-komen-foundation/

8. Pink collar jobs are ones traditionally held by women. For instance: customer service work, childcare/teaching, healthcare, administrative, and beauty industry positions.

9. John 6:35 (KJV) "And Jesus said unto them, I am the bread of life: he that cometh to me shall never hunger; and he that believeth on me shall never thirst." Matthew 5:6 (KJV) "Blessed are they which do hunger and thirst after righteousness: for they shall be filled."

10. One of the churches was more conservative and its pastor was nervous about the "sexual" tone of Zumba. Fortunately, the Zumba instructor was able to adapt the movements to something more acceptable to the community.

REFERENCES

Allard, J. E., & Maxwell G. L. (2009). Race disparities between Black and white women in the incidence, treatment, and prognosis of endometrial cancer. *Cancer Control, 16*(1), 53–56.

American Cancer Society. (2016). *Cancer facts and figures for African Americans 2016–2018.* Atlanta, GA: Author

Berry, D. A., Cronin, K. A., Plevritis, S. K., Fryback, D. G., Clarke, L., Zelen, M., ... Feuer, E. J. (2005). Effect of screening and adjuvant therapy on mortality from breast cancer. *New England Journal of Medicine, 353*(17), 1784–1792. doi:10.1056/nejmoa050518

Boehmer, U., Bowen, D. J., & Bauer, G. R. (2007). Overweight and obesity in sexual-minority women: Evidence from population-based data. *American Journal of Public Health, 97*(6), 1134–1140. doi:10.2105/ajph.2006.088419

Boehmer, U., Glickman, M., Winter, M., & Clark, M. A. (2014). Coping and benefit finding among long-term breast cancer survivors of different sexual orientations. *Women & Therapy, 37*(3–4), 222–241. doi:10.1080/02703149.2014.897548

Boehmer, U., Freund, K. M., & Linde, R. (2005). Support providers of sexual minority women with breast cancer. *Journal of Psychosomatic Research, 59*(5), 307–314. doi:10.1016/j.jpsychores.2005.06.059

Brown, M., & McElroy, J. A. (under review) Sexual and gender minority breast cancer patients choosing bilateral mastectomy without reconstruction: "I feel like I now have a body that fits me. *Women & Health.*

CNN Wire Staff. (2012, February 4). Komen foundation reverses funding decision of planned parenthood. Retrieved from http://www.cnn.com/2012/02/03/politics/planned-parenthood-komen-foundation/

Collins, P. H. (1986). Learning from the outsider within: The sociological significance of Black feminist thought. *Social Problems 33*(6): S14–S32. doi: 10.2307/800672

———. (1990). *Black feminist thought: Knowledge, consciousness, and the politics of empowerment.* Boston, MA: Unwin Hyman.

Connell, P., Rotmensch, J., Waggoner, S. E., & Mundt, A. J. (1999). Race and clinical outcome in endometrial carcinoma. *Obstetrics & Gynecology, 94*(5), 713–720. doi:10.1016/s0029-7844(99)00381-6

Cote, M. L., Alhajj, T., Ruterbusch, J. J., Bernstein, L., Brinton, L. A., Blot, W. J., ... Olson, S. H. (2015). Risk factors for endometrial cancer in Black and white women: A pooled analysis from the epidemiology of endometrial cancer consortium (E2C2). *Cancer Causes & Control, 26*(2), 287–296. doi:10.1007/s10552-014-0510-3

Danforth Jr, D. N. (2013). Disparities in breast cancer outcomes between Caucasian and African American women: A model for describing the relationship of biological and nonbiological factors. *Breast Cancer Research, 15*(3), 208. doi:10.1186/bcr3429

Davis, S. M. (2015). The "Strong Black woman collective": A developing theoretical framework for understanding collective communication practices of Black women. *Women's Studies in Communication, 38*(1), 20–35. doi:10.1080/07491409.2014.953714

Davison, K. P., Pennebaker, J. W., & Dickerson, S. S. (2000). Who talks? The social psychology of illness support groups. *American Psychologist, 55*(2), 205–217. doi:10.1037/0003-066x.55.2.205

Diamant, A. L. (2000). Health behaviors, health status, and access to and use of health care: A population-based study of lesbian, bisexual, and heterosexual women. *Archives of Family Medicine, 9*(10), 1043–1051. doi:10.1001/archfami.9.10.1043

Du Bois, W. E. B. (1903). *The souls of Black folk.* Chicago, IL: A. C. McClurg.

Eliason, M. J., Ingraham, N., Fogel, S. C., McElroy, J. A., Lorvick, J., Mauery, D. R., & Haynes, S. (2015). A systematic review of the literature on weight in sexual minority women. *Women's Health Issues, 25*(2), 162–175. doi: 10.1016/j.whi.2014.12.001

Fitzgerald, K. (2015, March 21). Thirty years of health advocacy, and still going strong. Wicked Local Provincetown. Retrieved from http://provincetown.wickedlocal.com/article/20150321/NEWS/150329699

Ford, C. L., & Airhihenbuwa, C. O. (2010). The public health critical race methodology: Praxis for antiracism research. *Social Science & Medicine, 71*(8), 1390–1398. doi: 10.1016/j.socscimed.2010.07.030

Freeman, H. P. (2004). Poverty, culture, and social injustice: Determinants of cancer disparities. *CA: A Cancer Journal for Clinicians, 54*(2), 72–77. doi:10.3322/canjclin.54.2.72

Giwa, S., & Greensmith, C. (2012). Race relations and racism in the LGBTQ community of Toronto: Perceptions of gay and queer social service providers of color. *Journal of Homosexuality, 59*(2), 149–185. doi:10.1080/00918369.2012.6 48877

Harvey, I., Johnson, L., & Heath, C. (2013). Womanism, spirituality, and self-health management behaviors of African American older women. *Women, Gender, and Families of Color, 1*(1), 59–84. doi:1. Retrieved from http://www.jstor.org/stable/10.5406/womgenfamcol.1.1.0059 doi:1

Holt, C. L., Caplan, L., Schulz, E., Blake, V., Southward, P., Buckner, A., & Lawrence, H. (2009). Role of religion in cancer coping among African Americans: A qualitative examination. *Journal of Psychosocial Oncology, 27*(2), 248–273. doi:10.1080/07347330902776028

Hotz, K. G. (2014). "Big Momma had sugar, Imma have it too": Medical fatalism and the language of faith among African–American women in Memphis. *Journal of Religion and Health, 54*(6), 2212–2224. doi:10.1007/s10943–014–9969–1

Hunt, B. R., Whitman, S., & Hurlbert, M. S. (2014). Increasing Black: White disparities in breast cancer mortality in the 50 largest cities in the United States. *Cancer Epidemiology, 38*(2), 118–123. doi: 10.1016/j.canep.2013.09.009

Institute of Medicine. (2011). *The health of lesbian, gay, bisexual, and transgender people: Building a foundation for better understanding.* Washington, DC: National Academies Press.

Isoke, Z. (2014). Can't I be seen? Can't I be heard? Black women queering politics in Newark. *Gender, Place & Culture: A Journal of Feminist Geography, 21*(3), 353–369. doi:10.1080/0966369X.2013.781015

Kamen, C., Mustian, K. M., Dozier, A., Bowen, D. J., & Li, Y. (2015). Disparities in psychological distress impacting lesbian, gay, bisexual and transgender cancer survivors. *Psycho-Oncology, 24*(11), 1384–1391. doi:10.1002/pon.3746

King, Samantha. (2006). Pink *ribbons, inc.: Breast cancer and the politics of philanthropy.* Minneapolis, MN: University of Minnesota Press.

Mytko, J. J., & Knight, S. J. (1999). Body, mind and spirit: Towards the integration of religiosity and spirituality in cancer quality of life research. *Psycho-Oncology, 8*(5), 439–450. doi:10.1002/(sici)1099–1611(199909/10)8:5<439:aid-pon421>3.0.co;2-1

Laubmeier, K. K., Zakowski, S. G., & Bair, J. P. (2004). The role of spirituality in the psychological adjustment to cancer: A test of the transactional model of stress and coping. *International Journal of Behavioral Medicine, 11*(1), 48–55. doi:10.1207/s15327558ijbm1101_6

Lorde, A. (1984). *Sister outsider: Essays and speeches.* Trumansburg, NY: Crossing Press.

Madison, T., Schottenfeld, D., James, S. A., Schwartz, A. G., & Gruber, S. B. (2004). Endometrial cancer: Socioeconomic status and racial/ethnic differences in stage at diagnosis, treatment, and survival. *American Journal of Public Health, 94*(12), 2104–2111. doi:10.2105/ajph.94.12.2104

Margolies, L., & Scout N. F. N. (2013). LGBT patient-centered outcomes: Cancer survivors teach us how to improve care for all. National LGBT Cancer Network and The Network for LGBT Health Equity. Retrieved July 23, 2016, from http://www.cancer-network.org/downloads/lgbt-patient-centered-outcomes.pdf

Maxwell, G. L., Tian, C., Risinger, J. I., Hamilton, C. A., & Barakat, R. R. (2008). Racial disparities in recurrence among patients with early-stage endometrial cancer. *Cancer, 113*(6), 1431–1437. doi:10.1002/cncr.23717

McElroy J. A. (2014, August). *Endometrial cancer risk for sexual and gender minority women in the HEER study.* Poster session presented at the International Society for Environmental Epidemiology, Seattle, WA.

McElroy, J. A., Washington, K. T., Wintemberg, J. J., Williams, A. S., & Redman, S. (2016). "I have to age in this body": Lesbian and bisexual older women's perspectives on a health behavior intervention. *Women's Health Issues, 26*, S63–70. doi:10.1016/j.whi.2016.03.011

Minnis, A. M., Catellier, D., Kent, C., Ethier, K. A., Soler, R. E., Heirendt, W., … Rogers, T. (2016). Differences in chronic disease behavioral indicators by sexual orientation and sex. *Journal of Public Health Management and Practice, 22*, S25–S32. doi:10.1097/phh.0000000000000350

Oliver, K. E., Enewold, L. R., Zhu, K., Conrads, T. P., Rose, G. S., Maxwell, G. L., & Farley, J. H. (2011). Racial disparities in histopathologic characteristics of uterine cancer are present in older, not younger Blacks in an equal-access environment. *Gynecologic Oncology, 123*(1), 76–81. doi: 10.1016/j.ygyno.2011.06.027

Pastrana, A. (2006). The intersectional imagination: What do lesbian and gay leaders of color have to do with it? *Race, Gender & Class, 13*(3/4), 218–238. Retrieved from http://www.jstor.org/stable/41675182

Petzen, J. (2012). Queer trouble: Centering race in queer and feminist politics. *Journal of Intercultural Studies, 33*(3), 289–302. doi:10.1080/07256868.2012.673472

Randall, T. C. (2003). Differences in treatment and outcome between African-American and White women with endometrial cancer. *Journal of Clinical Oncology, 21*(22), 4200–4206. doi:10.1200/jco.2003.01.218

Remedios, J. D., & Snyder, S. H. (2015). How women of color detect and respond to multiple forms of prejudice. *Sex Roles, 73*(9–10), 371–383. doi:10.1007/s11199-015-0453-5

San Diego Affiliate of Susan G. Komen for the Cure. (2014) *Continuum of Care Model.* Retrieved from: http://komensandiego.org/wp-content/uploads/2014/06/2012Continuum_of_Care_Model.pdf

Setiawan, V. W., Pike, M. C., Kolonel, L. N., Nomura, A. M., Goodman, M. T., & Henderson, B. E. (2006). Racial/ethnic differences in endometrial cancer risk: The multiethnic cohort study. *American Journal of Epidemiology, 165*(3), 262–270. doi:10.1093/aje/kwk010

Stalker, M. Z., Johnson, P. S., & Cimma, C. (1990). Supportive activities requested by survivors of cancer. *Journal of Psychosocial Oncology, 7*(4), 21–31. doi:10.1300/j077v07n04_02

Sterba, K. R., Burris, J. L., Heiney, S. P., Ruppel, M. B., Ford, M. E., & Zapka, J. (2014). "We both just trusted and leaned on the Lord": A qualitative study of religiousness and spirituality among African American breast cancer survivors and their caregivers. *Quality of Life Research: An International Journal of Quality of Life Aspects of Treatment, Care and Rehabilitation, 23*(7), 1909–1920. doi: 10.1007/s11136–014–0654–3

Stone, A. L., & Ward, J. (2011). From 'Black people are not a homosexual act' to 'gay is the new Black': Mapping White uses of blackness in modern gay rights campaigns in the United States. *Social Identities, 17*(5), 605–624. doi:10.1080/13 504630.2011.595204

Stroman, C. A. (2000). Explaining illness to African Americans: Employing cultural concerns with strategies. In B. B. Whaley (Ed.), *Explaining illness: Research, theory, and strategies* (pp. 297–314). Mahwah, NJ: Lawrence Erlbaum.

Struble, C. B., Lindley, L. L., Montgomery, K., Hardin, J., & Burcin, M. (2010). Overweight and obesity in lesbian and bisexual college women. *Journal of American College Health, 59*(1), 51–56. doi:10.1080/07448481.2010.483703

Sulik, G. A. (2011). *Pink ribbon blues: How breast cancer culture undermines women's health.* New York, NY: Oxford University Press.

Woody, I. (2013). Aging out: A qualitative exploration of ageism and heterosexism among aging African American lesbians and gay nen. *Journal of Homosexuality, 61*(1), 145–165. doi:10.1080/00918369.2013.835603

Yap, O. W., & Matthews, R. P. (2006). Racial and ethnic disparities in cancers of the uterine corpus. *Journal of the National Medical Association, 98*(12):1930–1933.

Zangare, B. (1984). The official footprints in the sand page. Retrieved July 5, 2016, from http://www.footprints-inthe-sand.com/index.php?page=Poem/Poem.php

Chapter 8

Status Quo

Intersectionality Theory, Afrocentric Paradigms, and Meeting the Healthcare Needs of Gay and Bisexual African American Men

Dante' D. Bryant

Gay and bisexual African American men occupy a unique space within the American healthcare system. On the one hand, as racial and sexual minorities, they are more likely than European American men, regardless of sexual orientation, to experience issues related to suicide, substance abuse, co-occurring disorders, and HIV/AIDS infection and mortality (Centers for Disease Control and Prevention [CDC], 2014; Feldman, 2010; Fleming & Karon, 2002; Institute of Medicine [IOM], 2011; Millet, Peterson, Wolitski, & Stall, 2006; O'Donnell, Meyer, & Schwartz, 2011). On the other hand, gay and bisexual African American men are less likely than European American heterosexuals to access healthcare resources, receive adequate care, report positive experiences with healthcare practitioners, or exhibit positive healthcare outcomes (Komaromy et al., 1996; Phillips & Malone, 2016; Smedley, Stith, & Nelson, 200). Although there is a growing body of medical research that explores the access to care, quality of care experiences, and healthcare outcomes of gay and bisexual African American men, it has largely focused on a series of variables (e.g., economic barriers, social practices, cultural differences, sexual orientation) that are external to the healthcare system (Commission on Social Determinants of Health, 2008; Williams & Purdie-Vaughns, 2016). Researchers such as Cole (2009) have argued that the tendency to focus on individual variables may be attributed to each field's—particularly psychiatry and psychology—desire to simplify models for the sake of parsimony (Betancourt & López, 1993; Silverstein, 2006).

Although this particular approach offers significant insights into the various problems confronting these communities, it lacks the complexity necessary to resolve them. In addition, limiting the conversation to variables which are external to the healthcare system reinforces current biased and inequitable healthcare practices and reinforces the status quo. In an effort to develop a more comprehensive understanding of the healthcare challenges confronting gay and bisexual African American men, researchers must also examine the actual healthcare *system.* More specifically, there is a need to investigate the relationship between our healthcare system's ideological assumptions of health, the historical treatment of African Americans as patients, and their cumulative impact on the healthcare outcomes for gay and bisexual African American men. In an effort to address this gap in the literature, the following chapter examines how these varying aspects of the healthcare system intersect and inform the treatment, healthcare experiences, and health outcomes of gay and bisexual African American men. To accomplish this task, Intersectionality Theory (IT) and Afrocentric paradigms are applied in an effort to identify and promote a more comprehensive, culturally appropriate response to the healthcare needs of gay and bisexual African American men.

This chapter is divided into four sections. Section 1: Setting the stage, explores the healthcare system's ideological assumptions and historical treatment of African Americans and sexual minorities. Section 2: Theoretical Overview, provides a brief description of IT and Afrocentric paradigms. Section 3: Analysis, examines the relationship between social identifiers, the historical treatment of African Americans and sexual minorities, treatment practices, and healthcare experiences and outcomes for gay and bisexual African American men. Section 4: Changing Paradigms, uses IT and Afrocentric paradigms to critique and identify alternative educational strategies for training healthcare providers to respond to the needs of gay and bisexual African American men. Section 4 also provides recommendations for future research targeting gay and bisexual African American men.

SETTING THE STAGE

Ideological Assumptions and Healthcare Practices

Like all social systems and institutions, the healthcare system is based on a series of ideological assumptions regarding what it means to be human and healthy (Foucault, 1965). Because these ideas are communicated and reinforced throughout every level of the profession, they often go unexamined and unacknowledged (Burger & Luckman, 1966). The general pervasiveness and acceptance of specific definitions of humanness and health inevitably shape how healthcare providers perceive, categorize, and respond to each person who walks through their doors (Burger & Luckman, 1966; Goff,

Williams, Eberhardt, & Jackson, 2008). Unfortunately, these definitions have historically and almost exclusively been based on the aesthetic presentation as well as the psychological and behavioral practices of European, heterosexual men (Akbar, 2003; West, 1994). As a result, African Americans and sexual minorities have not only been historically excluded from normative definitions of humanness and health, but they have been systematically marginalized by a series of dehumanizing stereotypes (e.g., intellectually inferior, lazy, aggressive, sexual deviants, etc.) which can shape practitioners' responses, ". . . even when people do not personally endorse them . . ." (Akbar, 2003; Goff et al., 2008, p. 294).

It is clear that the healthcare system has actively sought to move beyond its history of misrecognition and exploitation of African Americans and sexual minorities. However, what is less apparent, is the degree to which the healthcare system's previous acts of marginalization and stereotyping continue to subtly and implicitly shape healthcare outcomes and experiences for many gay and bisexual African American men. In order to better understand the healthcare systems' contribution to the challenges that confront gay and bisexual African American men, it is important to examine how it's ideological assumptions have historically shaped perceptions and treatment of African Americans and sexual minorities.

Historical Treatment of African Americans and Sexual Minorities

The relationship between African Americans and the American healthcare system has always been contentious (DuBois, 1899; Washington, 2006). In "Medical Apartheid," Washington (2006) states, ". . . dangerous, involuntary, and nontherapeutic experimentation upon African Americans has been practiced widely and documented extensively at least since the eighteenth century" (p.7). The historical tradition of medical misrecognition, marginalization, and exploitation of African Americans has been documented by researchers and historians such as Herbert Morais (1968), Robert Blakely and Judith Harrington (1997), Susan Reverby (2000), and a host of others. Although each of these scholars focused on discrete instances of medical exploitation, collectively they speak to a healthcare tradition shaped by definitions of humanness and heath that relegated African Americans to a subhuman status.

The diminished value of African Americans was informed by a variety of socially contrived and medically supported assumptions about what it meant to be human (Reverby, 2000; Washington, 2006). To the extent that African Americans were unable to approximate European aesthetics, they were subject to an array of misdescriptions and medical exploitation. In the 1700s and 1800s, assumptions regarding the inherent laziness of African Americans contributed to them being diagnosed with *malingering*, the exaggeration of mental or physical symptoms for personal gain. In 1852, assumptions about African Americans' intellectual and moral inferiority, and inherent need for supervision led Dr. Samuel A. Cartwright to suggest that slaves who attempted to escape bondage suffered from *drapetomania*, a mental illness that caused African American slaves to flee captivity (Kevin, 2002). According to Hamilton and colleagues (2015), in the 1960s and 1970s, similar assumptions contributed to schizophrenia becoming the prominent mental health diagnosis ascribed to African American men—a trend that continues today (Metzl, 2009). Hamilton et al. (2015) also suggest that the pervasiveness of schizophrenia among this population has been informed by medical professionals' attempts to explain the distrust African American men have for European Americans.

The healthcare system's past participation in the dehumanizing of African Americans was not only consistent with the cultural ethos of seventeenth–twentieth centuries, but it was also profitable (Harrington, 1997; Reverby, 2000; Washington, 2006). The diminished value of African American bodies provided healthcare professionals with expendable human subjects that could be used to advance the medical profession and the general economy (Reverby, 2000; Washington, 2006). In the 1800s, noted physician J. Marion Sims, often touted as the father of gynecology, frequently purchased African American female slaves for the sole purpose of performing experimental vaginal surgeries, often without anesthesia (McGregor, 1989). As a result, Sims was able to advance the medical profession by perfecting surgical interventions such as vesicovaginal fistula removal (McGregor, 1989). However, despite the various ways Sims exploited the diminished status of African American female slaves, contemporary physicians such as L. L. Wall (2006) have argued that his methods were consistent with the accepted medical and ethical practices of his time. In addition, medical practitioners who either conducted or supported the Tuskegee Study of Untreated Syphilis in the Negro Male (1932–1972), the Plutonium Experiments of the 1940s, 1960s and 1970s, and the Holmesburg Prison Experiments from 1950 to 1970 made similar arguments (Hornblium, 1998; Welsome, 1987; Reverby, 2000).

The historical persistence of medically marginalized African American bodies suggest that the American healthcare system has consistently failed to separate its views and treatment of African Americans from the ones held by mainstream society. As a result, healthcare's treatment of African Americans has consistently mirrored the culturally pejorative views of African Americans that dominated each era. The significance of healthcare's cultural reflexivity is magnified the moment the social pervasiveness of negative stereotypes, which continue to haunt African Americans, intersect with the persistence of inadequate care and poor healthcare outcomes for African Americans (Anderson et al., 2000; CDC, 2015; Hamilton et al., 2015; Smedley, Stith, & Nelson, 2002; Williams & Purdie-Vaughns, 2016).

Although aesthetically less identifiable, non-African American sexual minorities have also been victims of the healthcare system's reflexive relationship with socially pejorative views of European American sexual minority men. Prior to 1973, the American Psychiatric Association (APA) classified homosexuality as a mental disorder (APA, 1972). The misidentification of sexual minorities led to a series of medically endorsed treatment practices such institutionalization, conversion therapy, psychotherapy, hypnosis, electric shock therapy, and chemical castration (David, 1999; Freud, 1991; Haldeman, 2002; Milar, 2011). Although many of these techniques were not exclusively used for the purpose of "curing" same-gender sexual impulses, individuals who were identified as such were unjustly subjected to them (Haldeman, 2002). Although medical institutions have largely dismissed the idea that sexual minorities are psychologically unfit, dehumanizing stereotypes and heterosexual biases persist.

In his 2013 work, "Homosexuality and the Mental Health Professions," Drescher identified practice habits, within psychotherapy, that prioritize heterosexism and disenfranchise individuals who identify as gay or bisexual. The danger of persisting negative stereotypes surrounding racial and sexual minorities is compounded by the healthcare system's historical inability to differentiate its professional practice ethics from normative assumptions about health and humanity.

THEORETICAL OVERVIEW

Intersectionality Theory

In 1989, African American feminist and legal scholar Dr. Kimberlé Crenshaw coined the term *intersectionality* (Carastathis, 2014; Crenshaw, 1989; Jane, 2001). Drawing from a tradition of African American female critical social analysis (i.e., Sojourner Truth, The Combahee River Collective), Crenshaw (1989) sought to address the prolonged exclusion of African American women from European American feminist and anti-racist discourses (Marable & Mullings, 2000). Over the past decade, IT has gained popularity among disciplines such as gender and culture studies, religious studies, sociology, and social work (Hutchison et al., 2011). The recent appeal of IT may be attributed to its ability to identify and analyze how various social labels (e.g., gender, race, sexual orientation, ability, socioeconomic status, etc.) intersect with power and shape individual and group experiences of oppression and inequality (Collins, 1989; Hutchison et al., 2011; Floyd-Thomas, 2006). In addition, IT provides researchers with a framework that not only prioritizes the experiences of marginalized communities, but calls into question pejorative and oppressive views/definitions of society (Floyd-Thomas, 2006; Hutchison, 2011).

Afrocentric Paradigms

Although there is considerable debate regarding the origins of Afrocentricity and Afrocentric paradigms, their emergence in mainstream and academic discourses is generally attributed to Dr. Molefi Asante (Asante, 1980; Mazama, 2001). According to Asante (1980, 1990), Afrocentrism assumes that African Americans have been intellectually, culturally, and spiritually dislocated. More precisely, African Americans have uncritically accepted European values, perceptions, and definitions of reality (Asante, 1980, 1990, 1991). As a result, African Americans see themselves and the world they inhabit, through Eurocentric eyes (Asante, 1991). Therefore, the primary objective of Afrocentricity is to systematically displace Eurocentric views from the consciousness of African Americans while providing them with a new, Afrocentric lens through which to view themselves and the world around them (Asante, 1990, 1991). According to Asante (1991, 1996), the ultimate act of liberation is defining oneself on one's own terms. However, this can only be accomplished if an individual operates from a worldview and set of values that are consistent with their ancestry, culture, and historical experiences. Throughout the remainder of this chapter, IT and Afrocentric paradigms will be used in an effort to identify, diagnose, and respond to the persistence of negative healthcare experiences and outcomes associated with gay and bisexual African American men.

ANALYSIS

The negative healthcare outcomes and experiences of gay and bisexual African American men are not only informed by a history of dehumanization and misdescription, but they are also shaped by intersecting and often unacknowledged social categories. Although it is clear that gay and bisexual African American men exist as racial and sexual minorities, what is frequently overlooked is their simultaneous identification as patients. Although the category of "patient" is easily taken for granted, its relationship to power is not fixed (Foucault, 1965). Studies conducted by Demoulin and colleagues (2004, 2005) and Gaunt, Leyens, and Demoulin (2002) found that, regardless of their racial group, individuals were more likely to attribute secondary human qualities (e.g., empathy, jealousy, hope, etc.) to people who looked more like them. The significance of these findings is profound when one considers that 74 percent of practicing physicians in the United States identify as White (Boukus, Cassil, & O'Malley,

2009). The significance is further amplified when one takes into consideration that humanness is associated with trust (Parker, 2015). Given these findings, it is safe to assume that practicing physicians in the United States are more likely to trust European American patients' versus African American patients' descriptions of their symptoms (Anderson et al., 2000). These findings also suggest that race plays a role in the amount of *expert power*[1] physicians ascribe to patients. Conversely, it is possible that when the amount of expert power assigned to patients is diminished, healthcare practitioners are more likely to engage in misrecognition, misdiagnosis, and improper treatment.

While African Americans are at an increased risk of medical misrecognition, as a group, gay and bisexual men are more likely than their heterosexual counterparts to receive diminished care (Durso & Meyer, 2013). While conducting interviews with primary care physicians in North Carolina, Bryant (2016) found that gay and bisexual men were less likely to be offered anal Pap smears than women. The failure of healthcare providers to provide comprehensive care to gay and bisexual men increases their likelihood of developing anal cancer (Arain, Walts, Thomas, & Bose, 2005; IOM, 2011). IT reminds us that the significance of a social label is its respective relationship to power (Collins, 1991; Crenshaw, 1989; Davis, 2008). Therefore, in an effort to provide a more comprehensive understanding of how healthcare systems contribute to poor healthcare outcomes for gay and bisexual African American men, we must identify the unique set of labels that have been ascribed to this particular population. In doing so, we are able to properly situate them and their experiences in relation to distinct levels of social power. More precisely, we are able to better understand how documented medical exploitation, reduced patient testimony, heightened potential of misrecognition, and a lack of comprehensive care intersect to inform the healthcare experiences and outcomes for gay and bisexual African American men.

While IT calls attention to the relationship between history, social categories, power, and experiences, Afrocentric paradigms remind us that the categorical values ascribed to the social labels of "gay," "bisexual," "African American," and "men" are not fixed (Asante, 1990; Collins, 1989; Floyd-Thomas, 2006; Mazama, 2001). To the contrary, these labels and their subsequent values are products of European culture, values, perceptions, and social paradigms (Asante, 1980, 1987, 1990). To this extent, Afrocentricity argues that labels and their categorical values have been chosen. Therefore, these labels and their relationship to power can be unchosen and redefined (Asante, 1991). Asante (1991) argues that in order to choose differently, African Americans must accept that European culture and its values are not universal. In addition, they must also be taught to value alternative cultural paradigms (Asante, 1990, 1991; Mazama, 2002). Failing to acknowledge either of these realities relegates African Americans and other categorically disenfranchised groups to a marginalized social status within American society (Asante, 1991). Mazama (2001) captures this point clearly when he eloquently states,

> Our failure to recognize the roots of such ideas in the European cultural ethos has led us, willingly or unwillingly, to agree to footnote status in the White man's book . . . We do not exist on our own terms, but on borrowed European ones. (p. 387)

Improving the healthcare experiences of gay and bisexual African American men requires that the US healthcare systems acknowledge the plasticity of categorical values informed by Eurocentrism. According to Asante (1991), the moment we begin to examine the relationship between Eurocentrism and existing social labels, we gradually become aware of each category's inherent malleability. Noting that social labels and their categorical values can be changed is not unique to Afrocentrism (see Burger & Luckman, 1966; Foucault, 1972, 1977; Gadamer, 1975; Sartre, 1957). However, what is unique to Afrocentrism is the idea of systematically displacing Eurocentric views with cultural paradigms that are unique to each community. Although it is important to note that Afrocentrism focuses on African Americans and the need to prioritize African paradigms, it does not discourage other ethnic or racial groups from engaging in a similar process (Asante, 1990, 1991). To the contrary, Afrocentrism suggests that, like Eurocentrism, Afrocentrism is just one of many cultural views. According to Asante (1991), each culture provides its participants with a unique social perspective. In addition, every culturally specific paradigm is capable of liberating its participants from labels and categorical values that are non-indigenous and oppressive (Asante, 1990, 1991; Mazama, 2002).

CHANGING PARADIGMS

It is undeniable that the healthcare system has made considerable improvements regarding its treatment of racial and sexual minorities (Cohen, Gabriel, & Terrell, 2002; Mechanic, 2002). Despite these improvements, disparities in the healthcare outcomes and experience for gay and bisexual African American men persist (Cohen et al., 2002; Durso & Meyer, 2012). The limited success of current interventions may be attributed to their tendency to target issues outside of the healthcare system. However, even when researchers examine and apply interventions directed at healthcare institutions (e.g., requiring cultural competency and diversity sensitivity training courses), minimal change is observed (Cohen et al., 2002).

According to IT and Afrocentrism, these interventions have fallen short of their desired outcomes because they fail to fully consider and address the relationship between gay and bisexual African American men's healthcare outcomes, their historical relationship to the healthcare system, social labels, power, and Eurocentric values, perspectives and cultural paradigms. As a result, the causes of negative healthcare care experiences and outcomes for gay and bisexual African American men are not only misunderstood, but remain unaddressed. One of the great insights provided by Kuhn's (1962) construction of paradigms is that all intellectual inquiry, including research, is based on a series of assumptions about the world. By doing so he systematically negated the existence of scientific neutrality. Although Kuhn (1962) is not the only person to call attention to this point, it is one that is often overlooked when attempting to define and address issues surrounding healthcare outcomes; particularly as they relate to racial and sexual minorities (Foucault, 1972, 1977; Gadamer, 1975).

According to Afrocentrism, what is often overlooked and seldom discussed, is the degree to which the current cultural ethos prioritizes Eurocentric views of non-European cultures (Asante, 1980, 1987, 1990). To put it differently, the elevated status of Eurocentrism does not allow us to view gay and bisexual African American men through the eyes of gay and bisexual African American men. To the contrary, the pervasiveness of Eurocentrism demands that we view non-European cultural realities as alternatives or deviations from the "norm." Defining the cultural experiences of non-dominant groups in this way passively reinforces their de-legitimation and marginalization while simultaneously promoting and reinforcing the status quo (Asante, 1990, 1991; Collins, 1989; Floyd-Thomas, 2006; Hutchison et al., 2011; Robbins et al., 2006). Therefore, true cultural competency requires that we call into question all practices that are informed by Eurocentrism (Asante, 1980, 1987, 1991). In addition, it demands that Eurocentric paradigms be systematically displaced from their elevated status of normal and rendered one perspective among many (Asante, 1990, 1991). Prioritizing Eurocentric paradigms, omitting healthcare's socially reflexive nature, and neglecting the historical classification and treatment of racial and sexual minorities severely limits the healthcare system's ability to properly and fully address the problems that inform the poor healthcare outcomes of gay and bisexual African American men. In an effort to address the challenges facing this population, researchers cannot take anything for granted. To the contrary, researchers must begin to question and explore everything.

Educational Strategies

IT and Afrocentric paradigms are critical lenses capable of aiding the healthcare system's efforts to more adequately identify and respond to gay and bisexual African American men's poor healthcare outcomes. Therefore, the following recommendations uses these two approaches to provide a more holistic approach to these issues. The following recommendations should not be considered comprehensive and will focus exclusively on pedagogical strategies designed to improve how medical providers and other helping professionals approach cultural competency and diversity education. Traditionally, cultural competency and diversity trainings have focused on exposing and investigating non-dominant cultures while briefly examining the impact of colonialism (Griggs, 2014). However, this approach runs the risk of perpetuating the marginalization of non-dominant groups while reifying the status quo. In an effort to displace Eurocentric views from their elevated status of "normal," the author recommends that educators reimagine these courses through the lens and process of Pedagogical Displacement. Pedagogical Displacement is an instructional approach that was created by the author which moves beyond the traditional views of cultural competency and diversity trainings by focusing on the process of displacing normative ideas and social categories. This process consists of seven steps: Step 1. Identifying the dominant social norms (i.e., systems of classification); Step 2. Assessing the legitimacy of dominant cultural values among students; Step 3. Examining the historical development and implications of social labels such as gay, bisexual, African American, heterosexual, European, and male and how they contribute to varying social experiences. This includes the discipline's historical identification and treatment of all persons impacted by these labels. Step 4. Re-assessing the legitimacy of traditionally normative ideas and categories among students; Step 5. Exploring alternative non-culturally specific ways of viewing society; Step 6. Exploring non-dominant cultural systems of classification and their subsequent effects on their respective society; and Step 7. Exploring how cultural and non-culturally specific paradigms (steps 1, 5, and 6) can be fused to enhance healthcare practitioners' engagement in more equal and equitable treatment of gay and bisexual African American men.

Pedagogical Displacement should be divided into a minimum of two distinct courses for healthcare practitioners in the United States. The first course should focus exclusively on colonialism and its impact on non-European cultures (Steps 1, 2, and 3). The second course should consist of a brief review of course 1 (concluding with Step 5), then focus exclusively on non-European cultures (Steps 6 and 7). It is important that the course retain this order and that the second course present non-European cultures independent of colonialism. Presenting non-European cultures independent of colonial influence allows students to view the viability of these cultures prior to the impact of Eurocentrism. In addition, ordering the course in this way helps reduces the tendency to view non-Eurocentric cultures (especially African American culture) as subordinate to more mainstream Eurocentric perspectives.

The premises for these recommendations are based on the current demographics of healthcare providers, particularly physicians (74 percent of which identify as White) and the distinction between *cultural exposure* and *cultural reflection* (Boukus et al., 2009). While cultural exposure grants students the opportunity to learn about diverse cultures, it does not necessitate cultural reflection. Cultural reflection requires that a person examine the aspects of their cultural environment that are taken for granted. Furthermore, this process entails examining socially constructed ideas of "normal," the historical nature of these ideas, and how they impact distinct aspects of society differently. Providing students with the opportunity and skills to critically reflect on Eurocentrism, prior to engaging non-Eurocentric cultures, contributes to the process of *displacement* (a process similar to demythologizing). Properly displacing the elevated status of Eurocentric views is essential. If educators fail to aid students in facilitating Eurocentric displacement, students will be relegated to viewing African American culture and other non-European cultures through an unexamined and elevated Eurocentric social paradigm. However, if educators are successful in this process, they will equip healthcare professionals with a critical lens that will promote a more balanced view of cultural differences and their normative legitimacy. In addition, this form of educational engagement can empower future healthcare practitioners by providing them with a more inclusive and analytical lens which ". . . means, precisely, the end to the status quo" (Baldwin, 1972, p. 87).

Healthcare professionals who participate in this form of education should emerge viewing healthcare practices with a more critical lens. The critical examination of healthcare practices is a skill set which includes examining and calling into question the legitimacy of current and historical practices, the role power plays in defining what is normal, and the identification, development, and exploration of alternative practices, strategies, and approaches. A healthcare provider who is able to demonstrate the aforementioned skills will ultimately be more capable of identifying, assessing, engaging and responding to the needs of gay and bisexual African American men.

Research Recommendations

Research on Pedagogical Displacement should be conducted with nursing students, graduate psychology and psychiatry students, as well as medical students and current medical providers. While Pedagogical Displacement is an instructional approach which has been developed and successfully utilized by this author, there is a dearth of research examining its ability to effectively contribute to the sustained displacement of elevated Eurocentric categories, labels and values among students. In addition, research targeting students' responses regarding the effectiveness of Pedagogical Displacement is also warranted. Investigations into either component of Pedagogical Displacement can aid in the development of a more comprehensive and refined approach to diversity and culturally competency training for medical providers who work with gay and bisexual African American men.

NOTE

1. Expert power: When someone has knowledge or skills that someone else requires. A necessary component for collaboration (Raven, 2008).

REFERENCES

Akbar, N. (2003). *Akbar: Papers in African psychology*. Tallahassee, FL: Mind Productions.

American Psychiatric Association. (1972). *Diversity mental health month: Cultural competency key to better outcomes*. Retrieved from: https://www.psychiatry.org/

Anderson, K. O., Mendoza, T. R., Valero, V., Richman, S. P., Russell, C., Hurley, J.... Cleeland, C. S. (2000). Minority cancer patients and their providers: Pain management attitudes and practice. *Cancer, 88* (8), 1929–1938.

Arain, S., Walts, A., Thomas, P., & Bose, S. (2005). The anal pap smear: Cytomorphology of squamous intraepithelial lesions. *CytoJournal, 2*(1), 4.

Asante, M. (1980). *Afrocentricity (revised)*. Trenton, NJ: Africa World Press.

———. (1987). *The Afrocentric idea*. Philadelphia, PA: Temple University Press.

———. (1990). *Kemet, Afrocentricity and knowledge*. Trenton, NJ: Africa World Press.

———. (1991). The Afrocentric idea in education. *Journal of Negro Education, 60*(2), 170–179.

Baldwin, J. (1972). *No name in the street*. New York, NY: Vintage Books.

Balsam, K., Molina, Y., Beadnell, B., Simoni, J., & Walters, K. (2011). Measuring multiple minority stress: The LGBT people of color microaggressions Scale. *Cultural Diversity and Ethnic Minority Psychology, 17*(2), 163–174.

Betancourt, H., & López, S. R. (1993). The study of culture, ethnicity, and race in American psychology. *American Psychologist, 48*(6), 629–637.

Blakely, R., & Harrington, J. (1997). *Bones in the basement: Postmortem racism in nineteenth century medical training*. Washington, DC: Smithsonian Institution Press.

Boukus, R., Cassil, A., & O' Malley, A. (2009). *A snapshot of U.S. physicians: Key findings from the 2008 health tracking physician survey, Data Bulletin No. 35*. Retrieved from: http://www.hschange.com/CONTENT/1078/#table1

Bryant, D. (2016). *Sexual minorities and health care: Physician interviews*. Unpublished raw data.

Burger, P., & Luckman, T. (1966). *The social construction of reality: A treatise in the sociology of knowledge*. New York, NY: Anchor Books.

Carastathis, A. (2014). The concept of intersectionality in feminist theory. *Compass, 9* (5), 304–314.

Centers for Disease Control and Prevention. (2014). *HIV by group.* Retrieved from: http://www.cdc.gov/hiv/group/index.html

Centers for Disease Control and Prevention. (2015). *Data and Statistics.* Retrieved from: http://www.cdc.gov/datastatistics/index.html

Cohen, J., Gabriel, B., & Terrell, T. (2002). The case for diversity in the health care workforce. *Health Affairs, 21*(5), 90–102.

Collins, P. H. (1998). The tie that binds: Race, gender, and US violence. *Ethnic and Racial Studies, 21* (5), 917–938.

Commission on Social Determinants of Health. (2008). *Closing the gap in a generation: health equity through action on the social determinants of health. Final Report of the Commission on Social Determinants of Health.* Geneva: World Health Organization. Retrieved from http://apps.who.int/iris/bitstream/10665/69832/1/WHO_IER_CSDH_08.1_eng.pdf

Crenshaw, K. (1989). Demarginalizing the intersection of race and sex: A Black feminist critique of antidiscrimination doctrine, feminist theory and antiracist politics. *The University of Chicago Legal Forum 140*, 139–167.

Davis, K. (2008). Intersectionality as buzzword: A sociology of science perspective on what makes a feminist theory successful. *Feminist Theory, 9*(1): 67–85.

Demoulin, S., Leyens, J., Paladino, M., Rodriguez-Torres, R., Rodriguez-Perez, A., & Dovidio, J. (2004). Dimensions of "uniquely" and "non-uniquely" human emotions. *Cognition & Emotion, 81*(1), 71–96.

Demoulin, S., Leyens, J., Rodriguez-Torres, R., Rodriguez-Perez, A., Paladino, P., & Fiske, S. (2005). Motivation to support a desired conclusion versus motivation to avoid an undesirable conclusion: The case of infra-humanization. *International Journal of Psychology, 40*(6), 416–428.

DuBois, W. (1899). *The Philadelphia negro: A social study.* Philadelphia, PA: Pennsylvania Press.

Durso, L., & Meyer, H. (2013). Patterns and predictors of disclosure of sexual orientation to healthcare providers among lesbians, gay men, and bisexuals. *Sexuality Research and Social Policy, 10*(1), 35–42.

Feldman, B. (2010). A critical literature review to identify possible causes of higher rates of HIV infection among young Black and Latino men who have sex with men. *Journal of the National Medical Association, 102*(12), 1206–1226.

Floyd-Thomas, S. (2006). *Deeper shades of purple: Womanism in religion and society.* New York, NY: New York University Press.

Follins, L., Walker, J., & Lewis, M. (2013). Resilience in Black lesbian, gay, bisexual, and transgender individuals: A critical review of the literature. *Journal of Gay & Lesbian Mental Health, 18*(2), 190–212.

Foucault, M. (1965). *Madness and civilization: A history of insanity in the age of reason.* New York, NY: Vintage Books.

———. (1972). *The archology of knowledge and the discourse on language.* New York, NY: Harper.

———. (1977). *Discipline and punishment: The birth of the prison.* New York, NY: Vintage Books.

Freud, S. (1991). *On Sexuality: Volume 7*. London, UK: Penguin Books.

Gadamer, H. (1975). *Truth and method*. New York, NY: Continuum.

Gaunt, R., Leyens, J., & Demoulin, S. (2002). Intergroup relations and the attribution of emotions: Control over memory for secondary emotions associated with the ingroup and outgroup. *Journal of Experimental Social Psychology, 38*(5), 508–514.

Goff, P., Williams, J., Eberhardt, J., & Jackson, C. (2008) Not yet human: Implicit knowledge, historical dehumanization, and contemporary consequences. *Journal of Personality and Social Psychology, 94*(2), 292–306.

Grulich, A. (2012). The epidemiology of anal cancer. *Sexual Health, 9*(9), 504–508.

Haldeman, D. (2002). Gay rights, patient rights: The implications of sexual orientation conversion therapy. *Professional Psychology: Research and Practice, 33*(3), 260–264.

Hornblum, A. (1998). *Acres of skin: Human experiments at Holmesburg prison* (1st ed.). New York, NY: Routledge.

Institute of Medicine. (2011). *Select populations and health disparities*. Retrieved from: http://www.nationalacademies.org/hmd/Global/Search.aspx?q=sexual+minorities&outp=xml_no_dtd&client=iom_frontend&site=iom&proxyreload=1

Komaromy, M., Grumbach, K., Drake, M., Vranizan, K., Lurie, N., Keane, D., & Bindman, A. (1996). The role of Black and Hispanic physicians in providing health care for underserved populations. *New England Journal of Medicine, 334*(20), 1305–1310.

Kuhn, T. (1962). *The structure of scientific revolutions*. Chicago, IL: Chicago University Press.

Marable, M., & Mullings, L. (2000). *Let nobody turn us around: Voices of resistance, reform and renewal*. New York, NY: Rowman & Littlefield.

Maza, A. (2001). The afrocentric paradigm: Contours and definitions. *Journal of Black Studies, 31*(4), 387–405.

McGregor, D. (1989). *Sexual surgery and the origins of gynecology: J. Marion Sims, his hospital, and his patients*. New York, NY: Garland.

Metzl, J. (2009). *The protest psychosis: How schizophrenia became a Black disease*. Boston, MA: Beacon Press.

Milar, K. (2011). The myth buster. *Monitor on Psychology, 42*(2), 24.

Millett, G., Peterson, J., Wolitski, R., Stall, R. (2006). Greater risk for HIV infection of Black men who have sex with men: A critical literature review. *American Journal of Public Health, 96*(6), 1007–1019.

Morais, H. (1968). *The history of the negro in medicine*. New York, NY: International Library of Negro Life and History.

O'Donnell, S., Meyer, I., & Schwartz, S. (2011). Increased risk of suicide attempts among Black and Latino lesbians, gay men, and bisexuals. *American Journal of Public Health, 101*(6), 1056–1059.

Phillips, J., & Malone, B. (2014). Increasing racial/ethnic diversity in nursing to reduce health disparities and achieve health equity. *Public Health Reports, 129* (Suppl 2), 45–50. Retrieved from: http://www.ncbi.nlm.nih.gov/pmc/articles/PMC3863700/?tool=pmcentrez

Raven, B. H. (2008). The bases of power and the power/interaction model of interpersonal influence. *Analyses of Social Issues and Public Policy, 8*(1), 1–22.

Reverby, S. (2000). *Tuskegee's truths: Rethinking the Tuskegee syphilis study (Studies in social medicine).* Chapel Hill, NC: University of North Carolina Press.

Sartre, J. (1957). *Existentialism and human emotions.* New York, NY: Kensington.

Smedley, B., Stith, A., & Nelson, A. (2003). *Unequal treatment: Confronting racial and ethnic disparities in health care.* Washington, DC: National Academies Press.

Wall, L. (2013). The medical ethics of Dr. J Marion Sims: A fresh look at the historical record. *Journal of Medical Ethics, 32*(6), 346–350.

Washington, H. (2006). *Medical apartheid.* New York, NY: Doubleday Broadway.

Welsome, A. (1999). *The plutonium files: America's secret medical experiments in the cold war.* New York, NY: Broadway.

West, C. (1994). *Race matters.* New York, NY: Vintage Books.

Williams, D., & Purdie-Vaughns, W. (2016). Needed interventions to reduce racial/ethnic disparities in health. *Journal of Health Politics Policy and Law, 41*(3), 627–651.

Yoshino, K. (2002). Covering. *Yale Law Journal, 111*(4), 769–939.

Chapter 9

Identity, Sexual Identity Disclosure, and HIV Risk in Black Sexual Minority Men

A Conceptual Overview

Rahwa Haile, Mark B. Padilla, and Edith A. Parker

The impact of social stigma on health and disease has been central within the social determinants literature, in which researchers have identified social stigma as both a potential fundamental cause of health disparities and a requirement for the perpetuation of social inequalities (Parker & Aggleton, 2003; Stuber, Meyer, & Link, 2008). Moreover, the existing domestic and global public health literature suggests that there is a strong relationship between stigma and HIV-related risk and vulnerability among sexual minority men (SMM; Diaz, Ayala, Bein, Henne, & Marin, 2001; Padilla et al., 2008; Wilson & Yoshikawa, 2004). The impact of sexual stigma and its management on HIV/AIDS among black SMM has been explored. Sexual stigma is the deeply embedded ideology which devalues and deems non-normative sexual desires, behaviors, and identities invalid (Herek, Chopp, & Strohl, 2007). Similarly, stigma management techniques are described as concrete strategies that stigmatized groups adopt in order to cope with stigmatization (Goffman, 1963). Within the HIV-related literature that focuses on black SMM, some of the core sexual stigma management techniques proposed include those related to gay identity and disclosure.

In a seminal review, Millett and colleagues reviewed dominant hypotheses posed to explain black-white disparities in HIV/AIDS among SMM (Millett, Peterson, Wolitski & Stall, 2006). One stigma management hypothesis explored was that black SMM are less likely than other SMM to identify as gay or to disclose their sexual identity, which may lead to increased HIV risk behavior (Millett et al., 2006). The pattern of findings regarding this hypothesis are deeply contradictory. Some researchers have found no relationship between claiming a gay self-identity, sexual identity disclosure, and sexual risk behavior in black SMM, and while others suggest that higher levels of gay identity and community engagement are associated with higher levels of sexual risk behavior (Crawford, Allison, Zamboni, & Soto, 2002; Hart & Peterson, 2004; Mutchler et al., 2008; Wheeler, Lauby, Liu, Van Sluytman, & Murrill, 2008).

In order to better understand why the findings have been so mixed, this chapter examines how some studies addressing this hypothesis conceptualize key constructs. The premise of this review is that the ways in which key constructs are conceptualized form the boundaries within which the problem of stigma and HIV in black SMM can be addressed and understood. In this chapter, we summarize some trends in *how* authors conceptualize race, sexuality, and racial and sexual stigma and inequality. This is followed by a critical discussion of these trends in light of structural approaches to understanding health and illness, as well as in light of intersectionality theory.

METHOD

This study involved a conceptual overview of the HIV-related literature examining black-white differences in sexual identity and sexual identity disclosure among SMM, and the relationships between these constructs and HIV-related risk in black SMM. To identify these studies, we searched the literature in MEDLINE and PsycINFO from 1990 to 2016, using the terms "black or African American," "white or racial disparities," "homosexual or bisexual or men who have sex with men or MSM or gay or same gender loving or non-gay identified or down-low or sexual identity or sexual orientation," and "HIV." We also supplemented our search by reviewing the citations of other published studies. Consistent with Millett's critical literature review (2006), the focus was on studies that assessed (1) black-white differences in sexual identity among SMM, (2) black-white differences in sexual identity disclosure among SMM, (3) the relationship between sexual identity and HIV-related risk in black SMM, and (4) the relationship between sexual identity disclosure and HIV-related risk in black SMM. In examining these studies, the focus was on the major trends in the ways in which race, sexuality, and racial and sexual stigma and inequality are described.

RESULTS

In the forty-two articles reviewed, several general patterns emerged.[1] Both race and sexuality were described in individualistic terms. Similarly, racial and sexual stigma and inequality were described in a de-politicized and additive fashion. Below we describe specific trends within the literature examined.

Race

In all of the studies reviewed, black race is conceptualized as reflecting either an independent variable or risk group. However, race as a social process is not discussed. Although the overall trend is for race to be described as belonging to individuals, in some instances (n = 4), race is described as reflecting cultural variation (Chng & Geliga-Vargas, 2000; Heckman, 1999; Magnus et al., 2010; Warren et al., 2008). For example, Warren and colleagues (2008) argue that interventions need to be developed in ways that respond to the cultural milieu of black men. In rare instances (n = 2), race is explicitly discussed as a proxy for fewer economic resources, thus directly discussed in terms of its relationship to socioeconomic and ecological inequalities (Ostrow et al., 1991; Sullivan et al., 2014).

Sexuality

Sexuality is also theorized in individualistic terms and specifically, in relationship to the gender of those with whom an individual engages in sexual acts. Men who have sex with men (MSM) and with men and women (MSMW) are described as constituting a high risk group (n = 32). Researchers have also explored gay identity and gay identity disclosure, two sexual stigma management techniques that are theorized to protect against HIV risk. Gay identity is conceptualized as protective for sexual health for several different reasons. First, because identifying as gay may reflect successful transcendence of internalized homophobia (Dodge, Jeffries, & Sandfort, 2008; Wolitski, Jones, Wasserman, & Smith, 2006). Second, claiming a gay identity is described as facilitating access to a visible gay community, where HIV prevention programming is targeted (Bernstein et al., 2008; Martinez & Hosek, 2005; Mutchler et al., 2008; Pathela et al., 2006; Rietmeijer, Wolitski, Fishbein, Corby, & Cohn, 1998; Williams et al., 2008). A third reason that gay identity is theorized to be protective is that those who identify as gay and participate in gay culture may have access to healthy sexual norms present within the gay community (Chng & Geliga-Vargas, 2000; Goldbaum et al., 1998; Heckman, 1999; Wohl et al., 2002). A final route through which claiming a gay identity is deemed protective is that it may increase the likelihood that individuals perceive themselves as at risk of HIV infection (Bernstein et al., 2008; Williams et al., 2008).

Similarly, disclosure of same-sex desire, orientation, or behavior is hypothesized as protective because it may promote political organizing (Kennamer, Honnold, Bradford, & Hendricks, 2000). Kennamer and colleagues (2000, p. 520) contextualize their study by stating a key assumption—that "to the degree that Blacks are not 'out' and are not organized, then they are unable to participate to the same degree as white gay and bisexual men in the fight against HIV/AIDS." Disclosure of same sex desire is also discussed as signaling personal liberation from internalized homophobia (CDC, 2003), as well as freeing MSM from secrecy (Simoni, Mason, & Marks, 1997). Similar to the ways in which race and sexuality are discussed, sexuality-related psychosocial factors are discussed as individual characteristics which individuals can freely choose to adopt.

Racial Stigma and Inequality

Racial stigma and inequality are defined as discrimination (Crawford et al., 2002; Halkitis & Jerome, 2008) or sexual objectification (Warren et al., 2008). When discussed, racism is typically described in terms of its presence within gay communities and gay-identified venues (Crawford et al., 2002; Heckman, 1999; Rosario, Schrimshaw, & Hunter, 2004; Warren et al., 2008). In other words, racism is most often discussed insofar as it is perpetrated by the mainstream white gay community. Ostrow and colleagues (1991) state that black SMM face isolation as a result of perceived racism in white gay organizations. In this way, racism is taken to be an attribute of the larger, mostly white gay community. Moreover, racial inequality was explicitly discussed in only a small number of articles (n= 7).

Sexual Stigma and Inequality

Sexual stigma and inequality are described as lack of tolerance for and negative attitudes about same-sex behavior (Bernstein et al., 2008; McKirnan et al., 1995), rejection of same-sex behavior as not masculine (Ross, Essien, Williams, & Fernandez-Esquer, 2003; Siegel, Schrimshaw, Lekas, & Parsons, 2008), and discrimination (CDC, 2003; Crawford et al., 2002; Kennamer et al., 2000; Mutchler et al., 2008; Warren et al., 2008; Williams et al., 2008). Some researchers suggest that homophobia is an integral part of black culture (Kennamer et al., 2000) and that high levels of homophobia in the black community are a consequence of conservative religious beliefs (Crawford et al., 2002) or the need to maintain respectability in the face of racism (Kennamer et al., 2000). Although less common, some suggest that homophobia is an institutionally rooted phenomenon (Simoni et al., 1997). In general, sexual stigma and inequality tend to be discussed as though they are particularly endemic to the black community.

Racial and Sexual Stigma and Inequality

Some researchers note that racial and sexual stigma are constructs that merge in the lives of black SMM (Chng & Geliga Vargas, 2000; Crawford et al.,

2002; Kennamer et al., 2000; Martinez & Hosek, 2005; Mason, Simoni, Marks, Johnson, & Richardson, 1997; Mutchler et al., 2008; Siegel et al., 2008; Stokes & Peterson, 1998; Williams et al., 2008). One way in which these constructs are said to merge is in creating a social context in which black SMM grapple with simultaneous exposure to two distinct forms of discrimination—interpersonal racial discrimination and interpersonal homophobic discrimination (Crawford et al., 2002; Martinez & Hosek, 2005; Mason et al., 1997; Mutchler et al., 2008; Siegel et al., 2004; Williams et al., 2008). Some describe these multiple levels of stigma in terms of their potential to create high levels of stress (Crawford et al., 2002; Kennamer et al., 2000; Mutchler et al., 2008). However, researchers also posit that either racial or sexual forms of stigma and inequality are ultimately more likely to increase levels HIV risk and vulnerability. Chng & Geliga-Vargas (2000) suggest that there may be fundamental conflicts between ethnic minority cultures and gay culture, and that these cultural conflicts may become particularly salient through the process of assimilation into the mainstream gay community. Furthermore, it has been suggested that ethnic minority SMM who are highly affiliated with their ethnic identity may isolate themselves from the larger gay community (Chng & Geliga-Vargas, 2000), thus limiting their access to safer sex norms and potentially affirming gay social networks. From this perspective, one can infer that for SMM of color, identification with one's ethnic culture may be fundamentally more damaging to sexual health.

DISCUSSION

There are some major trends regarding how key constructs within this literature are conceptualized. Black race is presented in individualistic terms and as a simple independent variable. However, the political dimensions of race or racism are rarely addressed (exceptions include Ostrow et al., 1991 and Sullivan et al., 2014). Rather, race is understood to be fairly self-explanatory, the property of individuals. Although researchers do not suggest that race is a biological or genetic construct, race figures as a personal, private attribute within this literature. Sexuality also tends to be described in individualistic and behavioral terms, in relationship to the gender of those with whom individuals engage in sexual acts. The sexual stigma management techniques of gay identification and gay identity disclosure are generally presented as protective insofar as they facilitate access to a visible gay community. This access is in turn described as health-promoting in that it can provide access to safer sex norms and accurate self-perception of sexual risk.

Racial stigma and inequality are discussed less often within this literature than sexuality and sexual stigma and inequality. When addressed, racial stigma is presented as interpersonal discrimination, most often perpetrated by the mainstream gay community. Similarly, sexual stigma is most often presented as interpersonal discrimination, most often perpetrated by the black community. Thus, descriptions of the structural dimensions of sexual and racial stigma are generally absent. When examined in tandem, racial and sexual stigma are presented as discrete and additive, as opposed to intersectional (Bowleg, 2008) forms of inequality, which sometimes expose black SMM to a higher overall quantity of discrimination.

De-politicization of Racial and Sexual Stigmatization

Two major underlying conceptual assumptions of this literature may help account for its contradictory findings, which suggest that gay identity and disclosure may be linked to higher levels of sexual risk behavior among black SMM. The first conceptual limitation is its additive and sometimes oppositional approach to racial and sexual stigma and inequality, and the second conceptual limitation is the de-politicized way in which racial and sexual stigma and inequality are understood. This literature also discusses racial stigma and inequality as a feature of the white gay community, and sexual stigma and inequality as a feature of the black community. This primarily cultural mode of characterizing racial and sexual inequality as existing primarily in the acts of members of already marginalized communities may be symptomatic of larger trends in the study of sexual and racial stigma and inequality in the United States. As Vaid argued (2008), the visibility of gay and black political leaders makes it appear that sexual and racial inequalities are a thing of the past. In fact, at a time in which same sex marriage is legal, circumstances have truly improved for certain subsets of these communities (Vaid, 2008). However, the subjugation of many people of color, sexual minorities, and sexual minorities of color continues unabated (Vaid, 2013). Racial and sexual stigma and inequality do not however solely exist within LGBT and black social spaces. On the contrary, racial and sexual stigma and inequality structure the *entire* world of social interactions, not solely or primarily those which occur within the identifiable black and gay communities. In support of this claim, some qualitative work suggests that black SMM experience discrimination as ubiquitous rather than confined to the black and gay communities, and include settings like schools, clinics, and social welfare organizations (Haile, Padilla, & Parker, 2011).

In addition, as black men living in the United States, black SMM are no less subject than other subgroups of blacks to the economic, social, and health consequences of racism. Black SMM experience socioeconomic outcomes similar to blacks in general, and far poorer socioeconomic outcomes as compared to their white counterparts (Battle, Cohen, Warren, Fergerson,

& Audam, 2002; Dang & Frazer, 2005). Building on these patterns, a critical next step in developing a more nuanced understanding of the social epidemiology of HIV/AIDS in Black sexual minority men demands asking questions about how structural and political dimensions of racism impact HIV risk and vulnerability.

Similarly, although there have certainly been increased legal and social benefits accorded to same-sex relationships, many researchers have argued that in the process of gay "normalization," certain racialized homosexualities (e.g., BSMM) continue to be seen as unredeemable, illegitimate, pre-modern, or "unliberated" vis-à-vis "homonormative" gay identity formations (Duggan, 2002; Ferguson, 2005; Manalansan, 1997). Regardless, homophobic attitudes do not fully reflect the totality of heteronormative inequality. Instead, heteronormativity permeates structural, cultural, and interpersonal relationships, and in many instances remains supported through laws, institutions, and social ideologies, which in turn legitimize the stigmatization of black SMM and other groups (Cohen, 1997). Despite the fact that gains have been made in the rights of sexual minorities as a group, to experience same-sex desire as a black SMM in a heteronormative society remains stigmatized, and acting on or publicly claiming one's same-sex desire remains a fundamentally politicized act.

This state-sanctioned denial of full citizenship, social validation of familial relationships, and protection in the event of interpersonal and institutional forms of discrimination profoundly influences the quality of life for black SMM. It facilitates and justifies acts of prejudice. Thus, overall levels of stress are increased and coping resources are decreased. The deleterious health consequences of institutional forms of discrimination for sexual minorities have been established in national cross-sectional and prospective studies (Hatzenbuehler, Keyes, & Hasin, 2009; Hatzenbeuhler, McLaughlin, Keyes, & Hasin, 2010; Hatzenbuehler et al., 2014), although the consequences for HIV/AIDS have been less examined. Further exploration of the structural pathways through which sexual stigma and inequality impact HIV risk for black SMM requires further exploration.

CONCLUSION

While this study contributes to the literature on HIV risk among black SMM through conceptually describing one area of inquiry, this study also has clear limitations. Notably, it focuses on but one of many circulating hypotheses regarding sexual risk, rather than the literature as a whole, which may be contain more variation. Despite this important limitation, this study addresses issues that are critical to future conceptual development regarding racial and sexual stigma and inequality in relationship to HIV risk among black SMM.

Our finding that the literature describes racial and sexual inequalities as interpersonal phenomena occurring primarily within the LGBT and black communities suggests that we need to take a more comprehensive and structural approach. Rather than focusing primarily on individual acts of discrimination within LGBT and black communities, we need to better understand the multiple contexts in which black SMM experience racial and sexual inequalities. This finding is consistent with qualitative data suggesting that black SMM experience stigma and inequality in multiple settings, beyond the LGBT and black communities (Haile et al., 2011).

Also, our finding that racial and sexual inequalities tend to be described in an additive fashion suggests that we need more qualitative work to better understand the multiple ways in which racial and sexual identities intersect in the lives of black SMM. It is also vital that we understand how their identities and experiences intersect within the context of state-sanctioned inequalities in areas including employment and housing. A better comprehension of these ubiquitous experiences may help practitioners devise more effective ways to promote black SMM's well-being and sexual health and to improve the quality of care they receive in screening and treatment centers. Such efforts should be informed by an understanding of the constant, overarching, and intersectional impact of racial and sexual stigma and inequalities. Instead of only increasing levels of tolerance within specific communities for example, the further development of social policies that prohibit discrimination will likely bring us closer to effectively addressing the structural roots of discrimination.

NOTE

1. Readers can contact the corresponding author for a list of included articles.

REFERENCES

Battle, J., Cohen, C., Warren, D., Fergerson, G., & Audam, S. (2002). *Say it loud: I'm Black and I'm proud, Black pride survey 2000.* New York, NY: The Policy Institute of the National Gay and Lesbian Task Force.

Bernstein, K., Liu, K., Begier, E., Koblin, B., Karpati, A., & Murrill, C. (2008). Same-sex attraction disclosure to health care providers among New York City men who have sex with men: Implications for HIV testing approaches. *Archives of Internal Medicine, 168*(13), 1458–1464.

Bornstein, L., & Bench, M. (2016). Married on Friday, fired on Sunday: Approaches to federal LGBT civil rights protections. *William and Mary Journal of Women and the Law, 22*(1), 31–71.

Bowleg, L. (2008). When Black + lesbian + woman ≠ Black lesbian woman: The methodological challenges of qualitative and quantitative intersectionality research. *Sex Roles, 59*(5), 312–325.

Centers for Disease Control and Prevention. (2003). HIV/STD risks in young men who have sex with men who do not disclose their sexual orientation—Six U.S. cities, 1994–2000. *Morbidity and Mortality Weekly Report, 139,* 820–821.

Centers for Disease Control and Prevention. (2008). Trends in HIV/AIDS diagnoses among men who have sex with men – 33 states, 2001–2006. *Morbidity and Mortality Weekly Report, 57,* 681–86.

Centers for Disease Control and Prevention. (2014a). Diagnoses of HIV infection in the United States and dependent areas, 2014. *HIV Surveillance Report, 26.*

Centers for Disease Control and Prevention. (2014b). Monitoring selected national HIV prevention and care objectives by using HIV surveillance data— United States and 6 Dependent Areas—2012. *HIV Surveillance Supplemental Report 2014, 19*(3). Retrieved from http://www.cdc.gov/hiv/library/reports/surveillance/

Centers for Disease Control and Prevention. (2016). HIV among African American gay and bisexual men. Retrieved from http://www.cdc.gov/hiv/group/msm/bmsm.html

Chng, C., & Geliga-Vargas, J. (2000). Ethnic identity, gay identity, sexual sensation seeking and HIV risk taking among multiethnic men who have sex with men. *AIDS Education & Prevention, 12*(4), 326–339.

Chu, S., Peterman, T., Doll, L., Buehler, J., & Curran, J. (1992). AIDS in bisexual men in the United States: Epidemiology and transmission to women. *American Journal of Public Health, 82*(2), 220–224.

Cohen, C. (1997). Punks, bulldaggers, and welfare queens: The radical potential of queer politics? *GLQ: A Journal of Lesbian and Gay Studies, 3*(4), 437–465.

Crawford, I., Allison, K., Zamboni, B., & Soto, T. (2002). The influence of dual-identity development on the psychosocial functioning of African-American gay and bisexual men. *Journal of Sex Research, 39*(3), 179–189.

Dang, A., & Frazer, S. (2005). Black same-sex couple households in the 2000 U.S. Census: Implications in the debate over same-sex marriage. *Western Journal of Black Studies, 29*(1), 521–530.

Diaz, R., Ayala, E., Bein, J., Henne, J., & Marin, B. (2001). The impact of homophobia, poverty, and racism on the mental health of gay and bisexual Latino men: Findings from 3 US cities. *American Journal of Public Health, 91,* 927–32.

Dodge, B., Jeffries, W., & Sandfort, T. (2008). Beyond the down low: Sexual risk, protection, and disclosure among at-risk Black men who have sex with both men and women. *Archives of Sexual Behavior, 37*(5), 683–696.

Doll, L., Peterson, L., White, C., Johnson, E., Ward, J., & the Blood Donor Study Group. (1992). Homosexually and nonhomosexually identified men who have sex with men: A behavioral comparison. *Journal of Sex Research, 29*(1), 1–14.

Duggan, L. (2001). Making it perfectly queer. In A. Herrmann & A. Stewart (Eds.), *Theorizing feminism: Parallel trends in the humanities and social sciences* (pp. 215–231). Boulder, CO: Westview Press.

————. (2002). The new homonormativity: The sexual politics of neoliberalism. In R. Castronovo, & D. Nelson (Eds.), *Materializing democracy: Toward a revitalized cultural politics* (pp. 175–194). Durham, NC: Duke University Press.

Essien, E., Ross, M., Fernandez-Esquer, M., & Williams, M. (2005). Reported condom use and condom use difficulties in street outreach samples of men of four racial and ethnic backgrounds. *International Journal of STDs and AIDS, 16*(11), 739–743.

Ferguson, R. (2004). *Aberrations in Black: Toward a queer of color critique*. Minneapolis, MI: University of Minnesota Press.

Flores, S., Mansergh, G., Marks, G., Guzman, R., & Colfax, G. (2009). Gay identity-related factors and sexual risk among men who have sex with men in San Francisco. *AIDS Education and Prevention, 21*(2), 91–103.

Goffman, E. (1963). *Stigma: Notes on the management of spoiled identity*. New York, NY: Prentice Hall.

Goldbaum, G., Perdue, T., Wolitski, R., Rietmeijer, C., Hedrich, A., Wood, R., ... AIDS Community Demonstration Projects. (1998). Differences in risk behavior and sources of AIDS information among gay, bisexual, and straight-identified men who have sex with men. *AIDS and Behavior, 2*(1), 13–21.

Haile, R., Padilla, M., & Parker, E. (2011). "Stuck in the quagmire of an HIV ghetto": The meaning of stigma in the lives of older Black gay and bisexual men living in New York City. *Culture, Health & Sexuality, 13*(4), 429–442.

Halkitis, P., & Jerome, R. (2008). A comparative analysis of methamphetamine use: Black gay and bisexual men in relation to men of other races. *Addictive Behaviors, 33*(1), 83–93.

Hall, H., Byers, R., Ling, Q., & Espinoza, L. (2007). Racial/ethnic and age disparities in HIV prevalence and disease progression among men who have sex with men in the United States. *American Journal of Public Health, 97,* 1060–1066.

Hart, T., & Peterson, J. (2004). Predictors of risky sexual behavior among young African American men who have sex with men. *American Journal of Public Health, 94*(7), 1122–1124.

Hatzenbuehler, M., Keyes, K., & Hasin, D. (2009). State-level policies and psychiatric morbidity in lesbian, gay, and bisexual populations. *American Journal of Public Health, 99*(12), 2275–2281.

Hatzenbuehler, M., McLaughlin, K., Keyes, K, & Hasin, D. (2010). The impact of institutional discrimination on psychiatric disorders in lesbian, gay, and bisexual populations: A prospective study. *American Journal of Public Health, 100*(3), 452–459.

Hatzenbuehler, M., Bellatorre, A., Lee, Y., Finch, B., Muennig, P., & Fiscella, K. (2014). Structural stigma and all-cause mortality in sexual minority populations. *Social Science & Medicine, 103,* 33–41.

Heckman, T. (1999). HIV risk differences between African-American and white men who have sex with men. *Journal of the National Medical Association, 2*(91), 92–100.

Herek, G., Chopp, R., & Strohl, D. (2007). Sexual stigma: Putting sexual minority health issues in context. In I. Meyer & M. Northridge (Eds.), *The health of sexual* minorities: *Public health perspectives on lesbian, gay, bisexual, and transgender populations* (pp. 171–208). New York, NY: Springer.

Kennamer, J., Honnold, J., Bradford, J., & Hendricks M. (2000). Differences in disclosure of sexuality among African American and white gay/bisexual men: Implications for HIV/AIDS prevention. *AIDS Education & Prevention, 12*(6), 519–531.

Magnus, M., Kuo, I., Phillips, G., Shelley, K., Rawls, A., Montanez, L. ... Greenberg, A. (2010). Elevated HIV prevalence despite lower rates of sexual risk behaviors among Black men in the District of Columbia who have sex with men. *AIDS Patient Care and STDS, 24*(10), 615–622.

Manalansan, M. (2005). Race, violence, and neoliberal spatial politics in the global city. *Social Text, 23*(3–4), 141–155.

Martinez, J., & Hosek, S. (2005). An exploration of the down-low identity: Nongay-identified young African-American men who have sex with men. *Journal of the National Medical Association, 97*(8), 1103–1112.

Mason, H., Simoni, J., Marks, G., Johnson, C., & Richardson, J. (1997). Missed opportunities? Disclosure of HIV infection and support seeking among HIV+ African-American and European American men. *AIDS and Behavior, 1*(3), 155–162.

McKirnan, D., Stokes, J., Doll, L., & Burzette, R. (1995). Bisexually active men–Social characteristics and sexual-behavior. *Journal of Sex Research, 32*(1), 65–76.

McKirnan, D., Vanable, P., Ostrow, D, & Hope B. (2001). Expectancies of sexual "escape" and sexual risk among drug and alcohol-involved gay and bisexual men. *Journal of Substance Abuse, 13*(1–2), 137–154.

Millett, G., Peterson, J., Wolitski, R., & Stall, R. (2006). Greater risk for HIV infection of Black men who have sex with men: A critical literature review. *American Journal of Public Health, 96*(6), 1007–1019.

Montgomery, J., Mokotoff, E., Gentry, A., & Blair, J. (2003). The extent of bisexual behaviour in HIV-infected men and implications for transmission to their female sex partners. *AIDS Care, 15*(6), 829–837.

Mutchler, M., Bogart, L., Elliott, M., McKay, T., Suttorp, M., & Schuster, M. (2008). Psychosocial correlates of unprotected sex without disclosure of HIV-positivity among African American, Latino, and White men who have sex with men and women. *Archives of Sexual Behavior, 37*(5), 736–747.

Ostrow, D., Whitaker, R., Frasier, K., Cohen, C., Wan, J, Frank, C., & Fisher, E. (1991). Racial differences in social support and mental health in men with HIV infection: A pilot study. *AIDS Care, 3*(1), 55–62.

Padilla, M., Castellanos, D., Guilamo-Ramos, V., Reyes, A. M., Sanchez Marte, L., & Soriano, M. (2008). Stigma, social inequality, and HIV risk disclosure among Dominican male sex workers. *Social Science & Medicine, 67*, 380–388.

Parker, R. G., & Aggleton, P. (2003). HIV and AIDS-related stigma and discrimination: A conceptual framework and implications for action. *Social Science & Medicine, 57*, 13–24.

Pathela, P., Hajat, A., Schillinger, J., Blank, S., Sell, R., & Mostashari, F. (2006). Discordance between sexual behavior and self-reported sexual identity: A population-based survey of New York City men. *Annals of Internal Medicine, 145*(6), 416–425.

Peterson, J., Coates, T., Catania, J., Middleton, L., Hilliard, B., & Hearst, N. (1992). High-risk sexual behavior and condom use among gay and bisexual African-American men. *American Journal of Public Health, 82*(11), 1490–1494.

Purcell, D., Moss, S., Remien, R., Woods, W., & Parsons, J. (2005). Illicit substance use, sexual risk, and HIV-positive gay and bisexual men: Differences by serostatus of casual partners. *AIDS, 19* Suppl 1, S37–47.

Rhodes, S., Yee, L., & Hergenrather, K. (2006). A community-based rapid assessment of HIV behavioural risk disparities within a large sample of gay men in southeastern USA: A comparison of African American, Latino and white men. *AIDS Care: Psychological and Sociomedical Aspects of AIDS/HIV, 18*(8), 1018–1024.

Rietmeijer, C., Wolitski, R., Fishbein, M., Corby, N., & Cohn, D. (1998). Sex hustling, injection drug use, and non-gay identification by men who have sex with men: Associations with high-risk sexual behaviors and condom use. *Sexually Transmitted Diseases. 25*(7), 353–360.

Rosario, M., Schrimshaw, E., & Hunter, J. (2004). Ethnic/racial differences in the coming-out process of lesbian, gay, and bisexual youths: A comparison of sexual identity development over time. *Cultural Diversity and Ethnic Minority Psychology, 10*(3), 215–228.

Ross, M., Essien, E., Williams, M., & Fernandez-Esquer, M. (2003). Concordance between sexual behavior and sexual identity in street outreach samples of four racial/ethnic groups. *Sexually Transmitted Diseases, 30*(2), 110–113.

Siegel, K., Schrimshaw, E., Lekas, H., & Parsons, J. (2008). Sexual behaviors of non-gay identified non-disclosing men who have sex with men and women. *Archives of Sexual Behavior, 37*(5), 720–735.

Simoni, J., Mason, H., & Marks, G., (1997). Disclosing HIV status and sexual orientation to employers. *AIDS Care, 9*(5), 589–599.

Singh, S., Hu, X., Wheeler, W., & Hall, H. (2015). HIV diagnoses among men who have sex with men and women—United States and 6 dependent areas, 2008–2011. *American Journal of Public Health, 104*(9), 1700–1706.

Stokes, J. P., & Peterson, J. L. (1998). Homophobia, self-esteem, and risk for HIV among African American men who have sex with men. *AIDS Education & Prevention, 10*(3), 278–292.

Stuber, J., Meyer, I., & Link, B. (2008). Stigma, prejudice, discrimination and health. *Social Science & Medicine, 67*, 351–357.

Sullivan, P., Peterson, J., Rosenberg, E., Kelley, C., Cooper H, Vaughan A... Sanchez, T. (2014). Understanding racial HIV/STI disparities in Black and White men who have sex with men: a multilevel approach. *PloS one, 9*(3), 1–10.

Taylor, B., Chiasson, M., Scheinmann, R., Hirshfield, S., Humberstone, M., Remien, R. ... Wong, T. (2012). Results from two online surveys comparing sexual risk behaviors in Hispanic, Black, and White men who have sex with men. *AIDS and Behavior, 16*, 644–652.

Torian, L., Makki, H., Menzies, I., Murrill, C., & Weisfuse, I. (2002). HIV infection in men who have sex with men, New York City department of health sexually transmitted disease clinics,1990–1999: A decade of serosurveillance finds that racial disparities and associations between HIV and gonorrhea persist. *Sexually Transmitted Diseases, 29*(2), 73–78.

Vaid, U. (2008). *Race, sex and power: Observations in 2008.* Talk presented at *the Race, Sex and Power Conference at the University of Illinois, Chicago.* Retrieved from http://test.urvashivaid.net/wp/texts-speeches/race-sex-and-power-conference-2009/

Vaid, U. (2013). Now you get what you want, do you want more? *New York University Review of Law & Social Change, 37*(1), 101–111.

Warren, J., Fernandez, M., Harper, G., Hidalgo, M., Jamil, O., & Torres, R. (2008). Predictors of unprotected sex among young sexually active African American, Hispanic, and white MSM: The importance of ethnicity and culture. *AIDS & Behavior, 12*(3), 459–468.

Wheeler, D., Lauby, J., Liu, K., Van Sluytman, L., & Murrill, C. (2008). A comparative Analysis of sexual risk characteristics of Black men who have sex with men or with men and women. *Archives of Sexual Behavior, 37*(5), 697–707.

White, J., Mimiaga, M., Reisner, S., & Mayer, K. (2012). HIV sexual risk behavior among Black men who meet other men on the internet for sex. *Journal of Urban Health, 90*(3), 464–481.

Williams, J., Wyatt, G., Rivkin, I., Ramamurthi, H., Li, X., & Liu, H. (2008). Risk reduction for HIV-positive African American and Latino men with histories of childhood sexual abuse, *Archives of Sexual Behavior, 37*(5), 763–772.

Wilson, P., & Yoshikawa, H. (2004). Experiences of and responses to social discrimination among Asian and Pacific Islander gay men: Their relationship to HIV risk. *AIDS Education and Prevention, 16*(1), 68–83.

Wohl, A., Johnson, D., Lu, S., Jordan, W., Beall, G., Currier, J., & Simon, P. (2002). HIV risk behaviors among African American men in Los Angeles County who self-identify as heterosexual. *Journal of Acquired Immune Deficiency Syndrome, 31*(3), 354–360.

Wolitski R., Jones, K., Wasserman, J., Smith, J. (2006). Self-identification as "down low" among men who have sex with men (MSM) from 12 US cities. *AIDS & Behavior, 10*(5), 519–529.

Chapter 10

Shades of Black

A Psychotherapy Group for Black Men Who Have Sex with Men

Tfawa T. Haynes and Sannisha K. Dale

While there is an established body of literature about the health disparities and risk factors facing Black men who have sex with men (BMSM) in the United States, there is a dearth of information about group psychotherapy topics that are important to help BMSM thrive in the face of multiple adversities. BMSM face high rates of psychosocial, physical health, and mental health challenges including racism, discrimination, HIV/STI infections, depression, and substance abuse (Dale et al., 2015, Dyer, 2013). For social workers and psychologists, there is a mandate to provide culturally and linguistically appropriate services (American Psychological Association [APA], 2002; Mizrahi et al., 2001), while in medicine and public health there are mandates to reduce behavioral and social risk factors for the transmission of HIV/STIs among BMSM (American Public Health Association, 2015; Graham et al., 2011; Smedley et al., 2002). Each field demands that these interventions be cost-effective and require little financial or administrative resources to deliver. Group psychotherapy is a cost-effective intervention that may promote improvement in the psychosocial health of BMSM. Group therapy minimizes experiences of isolation by promoting mutual aid between members and provides a safe space where members are challenged to work toward healthy behavioral change (Gitterman & Shulman, 2005; Malekoff, 2016; Steinberg, 2014; Yalom & Leszcz, 2005). Group members can share their individual experiences, listen to the experiences of other group members, and both give and receive feedback that may be beneficial in making change.

This chapter describes *Shades of Black,* an open, integrative psychotherapy group for BMSM that is intended to foster resilience. The group is designed to help members integrate their social identities (racial, ethnic, cultural, religious, gender, and sexual); increase their self-esteem and self-acceptance; and reduce social isolation and the internalization of negative messages about their identities. The group offers a safe environment for BMSM to share their experiences in the local LGBT community and their communities of origin. The group shifts clinical work with BMSM from a limited focus on sexual health risks (Millett, Peterson, Wolitski, & Stall, 2006; Wilson et al., 2015) to a broadened lens of the BMSM experience.

This chapter is designed to be a resource for students, scholars, and practitioners seeking to deliver behavioral health services to BMSM by providing: (a) a model and rationale for clinical group work with BMSM; (b) an understanding of core topics for a clinical group for BMSM; (c) a discussion about group processes and dynamics unique to BMSM; and (d) an explanation of how to navigate boundaries and the professional use of self for Black therapists providing care to BMSM clients. Readers will have an opportunity to consider their approach and may use this model to improve social and behavioral interventions.

MAKING A CASE FOR GROUP PSYCHOTHERAPY WITH BLACK MSM

There is a dearth of literature on the group therapy needs of BMSM beyond the needs of the therapist to consider issues that arise from cultural overlaps (Green, 1997, 2000; Ritter & Terndrup, 2002). Yalom and Leszcz (2005) liken the role of the group facilitator to that of a "mechanic" (p. 117), one who is engaged in maintaining the group culture, supporting the creation and maintenance of group cohesion through mutual aid, and keeping the group focused on things happening in the "here-and-now" (p. 142). The facilitator must convey the group's purpose, which is agreed upon by the facilitator and the group members. The intention in clarifying the purpose of the group is to provide a basis upon which mutual aid will develop (Kurland & Salmon, 1999; Malekoff, 2016; Steinberg, 2014). The purpose may evolve with the group's and members' needs over time (Malekoff, 2016; Steinberg, 2014).

There is a strong need for both a sense of sameness and diversity within the group (Gitterman & Shulman, 2005). According to Steinberg (2014), groups foster a sense of "we-ness" (p.16) where members develop a sense of cohesion when the facilitator highlights similarities in shared identities, while attending to individual needs (Gitterman & Shulman, 2005; Malekoff, 2016). Beyond the tenets of mutual aid, scholars emphasize additional aspects for marginalized individuals. Schiller (2007) discusses the need for (a) members of a marginalized experience to establish safety before trusting and engaging in group process based on the sociocultural experience of oppression of these individuals; and (b) a facilitator to be vigilant of his own cultural lens, societal norms, and oppression that may permeate the group.

Group treatment may have an additional benefit over individual therapy as it allows the individual and the group to assume the role of the expert in their experiences. However, there is nothing in the published literature regarding the outcomes or benefits of group versus individual therapy for BMSM. In addition, the level of isolation that many BMSM experience as a result of homonegativity, heterosexism, and racism might be counteracted by the experience of being with other BMSM (Bowleg, 2013). A group may hold the complex and complete identities of BMSM and challenge the notion that individuals are isolated in their experiences, while also providing opportunities for members to support each other. Group work provides each member with an opportunity for personal change and growth, relieves isolation, and enhances skills to build community with other BMSM that carries into the real world.

Many therapists with caseloads consisting of men who are BMSM might welcome an opportunity to have these men in the same room (Goode-Cross, 2011; Goode-Cross & Grim, 2016). The wish stems from the possibility that once in a group, these individuals could hear their experiences reinforced by peers. The opportunity to have ones' reality validated while also being exposed to new perspectives can bring a profound sense of relief, healing, and provide new social skills (Goode-Cross, 2011; Goode-Cross & Grim, 2016).

THERAPEUTIC USE OF SELF AND SELF DISCLOSURE IN GROUP WORK WITH BMSM

In combination with group members' validation of one another, the group facilitator may also enhance the group environment through *self-disclosure* and the *therapeutic use of self*. *Self-disclosure* is defined as the intentional acknowledgment of the facilitator's and the group members' shared identities in order to normalize the clients' experience. *Therapeutic use of self* is defined as the facilitator's intentional use of his own experience to support a client by normalizing, validating, and challenging the client's experience. When used effectively, the facilitator's disclosure of personal struggles can allow the facilitator to further engage and connect with members (Aponte & Kissil, 2014). However, the facilitator must maintain an awareness of the similarities and differences of his experience in relation to the members as well as his role as a facilitator, not succumbing to temptation to be "one of the gang" (Aponte & Kissil, 2014; Malekoff, 2016).

Although the *use of self* and *self-disclosure* are useful tools to engage with clients, there are gaps in the professional literature regarding psychotherapy with Black clients. What is known is that there is a lack of clinical training for Black clinicians working in dyad and group therapy settings with Black clients

(Goode-Cross, 2011; Goode-Cross & Grim, 2016). Most training focuses on general awareness of diversity and multiculturalism for students of all racial/ethnic backgrounds (Goode-Cross & Grim, 2016). In many instances, there is no formal training focused on multicultural issues for Black clinicians working with Black clients, forcing these clinicians to gain this experience "on the job" (Goode-Cross, 2011; Goode-Cross & Grim, 2016). The shared racial experience between client and therapist offers an opportunity for the client to have authentic conversations with their provider with an assumption that the racialized experience will be understood and valued (Cabral & Smith, 2011; Goode-Cross & Grim, 2016). The client's fear of rejection and nullification around experiences of racism is diminished, providing an opportunity for a deeper level of therapeutic connection than may otherwise occur were the therapist of a different race (Goode-Cross & Grim, 2016; Townes, Chavez-Korell, & Cunningham, 2009). However, the therapist needs to be mindful of issues of transference and countertransference as well as continued access to support in the form of supervision and mentorship (Goode-Cross, 2011; Goode-Cross & Grim, 2016). In addition, while there can be a shared connection based on skin tone and/or ethnoracial background, Black therapists and their Black clients may vary on many other aspects of identity.

SUGGESTED TOPICS TO BE ADDRESSED IN GROUP WORK WITH BMSM

BMSM Identity and Intersectionality

Intersectionality has historically been focused on the experiences of Black women, centering their experiences of their identities as women generally and Black women specifically (Bowleg, 2013; Crenshaw, 1991; Warner & Shields, 2013). When applying intersectionality to the experiences of BMSM, it is important to look at the interplay between race, ability, male identity and privilege, expected gender role presentation, socioeconomic status, sexual identity, and sexual behavior (Bowleg, 2013). BMSM are men, Black, Black men, men who have sex with other men, and Black men who have sex with other men (Warner & Shields, 2013).

BMSM may utilize similar coping strategies to challenge gender norms (e.g., self-advocacy) that they have used to cope with racism and homonegative behaviors (Bowleg, 2013; Icard, Gripton, & Valentich, 1986). BMSM have coped with a long-standing history of systematic racism and oppression (Bowleg, 2013; George et al., 2012) through advocacy, creating house/ball communities (Phillips et al., 2010), queering language as a form of resistance and subversion (Butler, 1997; Johnson, 2011), and deploying a passive-aggressive communication style to deflect intrusive comments or unwanted questions from others (Johnson, 2011; Sue, 1990). Given the multiple experiences of racism, homonegative behaviors, and prescribed gender roles, clinicians have to be mindful of the clients' whole experience and the interchange between their identities when engaging in identity work with them (Bowleg, 2013; Shields & Shields, 2013). According to Smith (1987), minorities are made to experience their identities as worlds that they are unable to fully experience. The experience of seeing one's self through the lens of one component, without the interplay of one's intersecting identities, results in a perpetuation of marginalization of a minority group. BMSM might engage in personal "identity ranking" where they affirm their Black identity first, and at the same time view their identities as Black along with sexual orientation as integrated (Bowleg, 2013).

Community

In the social science and popular culture literature, there is the overarching theme of straddling two worlds in the lives of BMSM (Bowleg, 2013; George et al., 2012; Goode-Cross & Good, 2008). Some BMSM are both insiders and outsiders in their ethnoracial community due to others' feelings about their sexual orientation. They may feel like outsiders in the LGBT community based on systematic racism and racialized gender role expectations for Black men (Barnes & Meyer, 2012; Bowleg, 2013; George et al., 2012). Some BMSM have been shunned and disconnected from the dominant White gay community and Black community along lines of racism and homonegativity (George et al., 2012; Icard et al., 1986). Many BMSM experience loneliness and isolation while in gay-identified spaces (Cohen, 1996; hooks, 1989) because these settings are dominated by and cater to White gay men. An example is going to local gay clubs where there are few if any BMSM in the room. In these clubs they are not engaged by non-Black patrons, and when engaged, they feel objectified by the interaction. BMSM seek environments where they are not the only BMSM and where they have commonalities with other BMSM.

BMSM cope with life stressors by engaging in varying levels of outness and connection (e.g., participation or lack thereof in gay community events) with the gay community as well as the Black community (George et al., 2012; Icard et al., 1986). Many BMSM tend to be selective in disclosing their sexual orientation due to prior knowledge or experiences of homonegativity and racism within the two communities they navigate. Many BMSM are selective about their friendships, sexual partnering, and other emotional supports because they seek connections with individuals who are supportive and understanding of their experiences (Goode-Cross & Good, 2008). In their selectiveness there is a need to conceal their identities for the sake of safety while navigating the Black and gay communities (Goode-Cross & Good, 2008; Greene, 1994).

Religion

Religiosity is a widely used coping strategy within Black communities and the church is considered a cornerstone within the community (George et al., 2012). However, BMSM congregants are exposed to homonegative messages within some religious denominations (Lassiter, 2014; Pitt, 2010a, 2010b). For some BMSM, strong Black and religious community connections relate to a positive sense of self, which correlates with improved health outcomes, sexual health behavior, HIV care adherence, and mental well-being (George et al., 2012). BMSM therefore have both "affirming" (e.g., love and support) and "non-affirming" (e.g., homonegative messages and heterosexist) religious experiences (Barnes & Meyer, 2012). Many BMSM have reported coping with anti-gay messages by forming connections with members who challenge the veracity of homonegative religious messages (Barnes & Meyer, 2012; Pitt, 2010a).

Sex and Dating

Literature focused on stigma and race-based stereotyping for BMSM is intertwined with the literature on HIV/AIDS, internalized homonegativity, and selective partnering based on race and culture (Grov et al., 2015; Meyer, 2010; Wilson et al., 2009). BMSM struggle within the MSM and Black heterosexual communities when viewed as undesirable sexual partners due to wide-spread acceptance of negative stereotypes about them (Boone et al., 2016; Wilson et al., 2009). Many BMSM turn to Internet sites and mobile applications in search of sexual partners (Liau, Millett, & Marks, 2006; Paul, Ayala, & Choi, 2010). The listing of physical characteristics and racial identities perpetuates the selection of partners based on a narrow standard of beauty that privileges young White MSM (Wilson et al., 2009).

White MSM are viewed as the gold standard of masculinity, and their sexuality has been presented as the norm for comparisons (Connell, & Messerschmidt, 2005; Han, 2007). Black men are stigmatized as sexual aggressors or objectified based on negative stereotypes about the Black male body (Fields et al., 2012). They are viewed as a sexual curiosity that some would like to "try," much like sampling an exotic delicacy (Gilman, 1985; Taylor, 2000). The rich complexities of BMSM are boiled down to fantasy, limiting them to the size of their penis and curiosity around what it would be like to be with them (Collins, 2004; Pinar, 2001).

SHADES OF BLACK: A GROUP THERAPY MODEL FOR BMSM

Shades of Black was born out of the facilitator's own need to find a place where he could explore his identities (Black, gay, Jamaican immigrant) and develop a sense of community in a space where he felt lost and disconnected. As a trained mental health professional, the facilitator aimed to develop a group for BMSM that decentralized the facilitator's role and emphasized mutual aid. Schiller's (1997) model guided the decision-making process to select interventions that best suited a group for BMSM.

This model suggests developing a relational base before delving deeper in the work of exploring members' intersecting identities in relation to racism, homonegativity, and developing a sense of community and belonging (Schiller, 1997). *Shades of Black* has been in existence for over four years and during this period, there have been ongoing development and maintenance of the relational base as members have joined and left the group. Though membership has changed over time, the group has a strong foundation based on mutual aid and support, and a good rapport between the members and the facilitator.

Below is a summary of the key components covered in *Shades of Black* based on the perspective of the group founder and facilitator. Data was not collected on or from group members in order to uphold confidentiality. Key components of the group, including the facilitator, an initial intake appointment, and core group discussion topics are based on the rationale provided. Topics are covered in non-sequential order as best suited to the needs of the group.

Intake

Members are referred to the group by mental health practictioners and medical care providers in the community, or are self-referred. The group facilitator is employed by the host healthcare clinic and assessed each client's readiness to engage in the group based on their identity development and openness to having conversations about their racial, gender, and sexual identities in their daily lives. The facilitator accomplished this by: (a) describing the goal of the group as a space for conversations about BMSM's intersecting identities; (b) engaging the individual in a brief conversation around multiple identities; and (c) discussing the limits of confidentiality in a group setting. Participants are evaluated on their engagement around the topic of their interconnecting identities and their desire for a place where they can connect with other BMSM. Potential participants were excluded from the group if the facilitator judged that engaging in the group would present an undue burden for them or if they are unwilling or unable to engage in conversations related to the outlined topics. Participants are deemed appropriate for treatment if they articulate a struggle with or are contemplating the impact of their racial and sexual identities on their life experiences.

During the intake session, past engagement in group treatment, readiness to engage in group treatment, and goals for participating in group treatment are assessed. Potential group members' expectations for confidentiality are explored. The facilitator highlights the limitations to confidentiality in group therapy (i.e., disclosure of intent to harm self or others; the possibility that fellow group members may disclose specifics about the group and its members to others outside the group) and explores participants' thoughts about maintaining a confidential and safe environment. All group members sign a confidentiality agreement. This allows for the group members to share the responsibility of maintaining a safe and confidential space rather than making confidentiality a rule created by the facilitator. The group takes ownership for the maintenance of a confidential environment and consequences if this rule is broken.

GROUP TOPICS AND PROCESSES

The name of the group, *Shades of Black*, refers to the varying hues of skin tones that are encompassed in the Black community. The topics for the group—identity, community, religion and spirituality, sex and dating, and sexuality—were all selected based on the lead author's work with BMSM. This section provides a glimpse into *Shades of Black*.

Session Topic: Who Am I?

Table 10.1 Issues Addressed in Session Topic: Who Am I?

Key issues addressed:	Skills to develop in this session:
• What does it mean to be a MSM? • What does it mean to be a Black man? • What does it mean to be a BMSM?	• Identify differences in others' expectations and perceptions of them as "gay," "bisexual," "Black," and "man." • Identify stereotypes based on racial, gender, and sexual norms that affect their life. • Identify differences in personal gender norms and sexual norms related to their roles as a Black man and as an MSM. • Identify specific things that make them proud of their identities. • Identify personal strengths they associate with their identity.

A common theme in this group is experiencing one's sexual identity as being centered on sexual behavior, that is, related to same-gender "sex." As a result, some in this group of BMSM question their sexuality, wondering whether they are *gay* (a label ascribed on sexual behavior, not their identities) if they do not engage in a particular sexual act or behavior. Having one's identity limited to sexual behavior limits the expression and diversity of BMSM. BMSM struggle to find examples of Black same gender loving love, intimacy, kinship, mentorship, education, and visible social representations that reflect their experiences (Applewhite & Littlefield, 2016; Battle et al., 2006; Gwadz et al., 2006; Wilson et al., 2015). Having the word gay be synonymous with sex denies individuals the opportunity to assert a sense of self that is diverse and challenges stereotypes. In the "Who Am I?" session, some group members assert their conviction around being a person first, challenging the expectation to disclose sexual behaviors.

Group members grapple with the discord between internalized homonegativity, experiences of racism and stigma, and gender stereotypes for BMSM. The group is often the only place for participants to verbalize their experience. They take significant risks in opening up to each other and naming things that they never had the opportunity to share with others. They provide insight into how they navigate communities filled with landmines that challenge them to be flexible and require quick thinking. In these topics, there is a tendency for participants to gloss over their traumatic or distressing experiences, presenting challenges as matter-of-fact and happenstance. In these instances, the facilitator deepens the conversation by asking members to delve deeper into their processes. For instance, "I am noticing a theme of not having a role model when you were growing up. I would like to invite you all to think back to a time where you felt you needed the most support being a BMSM. Suppose you were able to speak to that part of yourself in this moment, what would you say to him? How would he respond?" This type of intervention elicits self-reflection, self-recognition, and self-love.

Session Topic: Finding Community

Table 10.2 Issues Addressed in Session Topic: Finding Community

Key issues addressed:	Skills to develop in this session include:
• Balancing expectations of different communities • Negotiating and managing disclosures of their sexuality and sexual behavior • Managing racism in the local environment	• Identify social norms in the Black community regarding secrecy. • Identify the role of microaggressions, stigma, and shame associated with "spoiled" identities.

(cont. . .)

Table 10.2   Issues Addressed in Session Topic: Finding Community *(cont. . .)*

• Managing feelings of invisibility in the multiple communities to which they belong	• Describe their personal reasons (or needs) for secrecy and develop a personal threat assessment for discussing any need for secrecy they have with others.
• Coping with growing up in a community where they are made to feel they are not good enough	
• Dealing with the competing social values and norms of the various communities to which they belong	• Discuss various positive social norms and values they uphold from the gay/bisexual community and the Black community.
	• Describe the benefits they experience from belonging to a community.

Finding community as BMSMs is daunting as they navigate multiple conflicting identities. Members expressed that they seek settings where they can be whole without checking parts of themselves at the door because it feels safer. BMSM in the group speak of an invisible armor, one that helps to protect them as they navigate the world. This armor is built on past experiences, a positive sense of self and connection to positive community experiences, internalized messages about self-worth, and personal assessments to inform how much of themselves they share (Fries-Britt & Turner, 2002).

The armor is an effective coping tool, yet it burdens BMSM. Having to be "on" at all times is a burden that leads to overgeneralized mistrust (Garcia et al., 2015). Hypervigilance and thinking steps ahead to prepare for the unexpected becomes a constant mental exercise that creates an obstacle to meaningful connections for BMSM (Garcia et al., 2015). While navigating communities, they anticipate racist encounters, microaggressions, and homo-negativity. Yet, they are not aware of the impact this has on their mind and body (Fries-Britt & Turner, 2002; Garcia et al., 2015; Goode-Cross & Good, 2008; Paul, Ayala, & Choi, 2010). In the group, members have the opportunity to explore automatic responses they engage in to cope with the experiences they have in their various communities and are encouraged to bring mindfulness and intentionality to their coping. Common questions that group participants ask during a session on finding community include: "How can the Black community support me when I experience racism, but shun me as a BMSM?" and "How can the gay community discriminate against me based on skin color when we all have experiences of being marginalized?"

An ongoing conversation in the group is the frustration of some of the members that they are unable to take the relationships developed in the group out of the group and into their lives. Members have spoken of the challenges in identifying a Black gay community in the local community. They highlight this by pointing out the lack of spaces dedicated for Black LGBT individuals, stating that when they are in social settings they are often one of a few BMSM present. BMSM need a support system of individuals with whom they share core identities. The shared connection and community allows for support around coping experiences of racism and homonegativity in the Black community and White dominated LGBT community (Goode-Cross & Good, 2008).

Session Topic: Finding Religion

Table 10.3   Issues Addressed in Session Topic: Finding Religion

Key issues addressed:	Skills to develop in this session include:
• Cultural norms and traditions associated with Black churches and faith communities • Balancing positive self-worth and religious identity • Valuing oneself as a sexual and spiritual person	• Identify strengths associated with religious traditions in the Black community. • Discuss religious norms and messages about homosexuality held by their faith community. • Describe open and affirming experiences with religion and spirituality. • Evaluate the costs and benefits of attending or participating in religious services. • Apply rules of healthy personal relationships to their relationships with institutions. • Develop a personal code of conduct for faith, ethics, and morals.

Over the course of the group's existence, members have expressed varying levels of engagement with the church, from those in high leadership roles down to those who stepped away from a homonegative church. For members who remain in church, they speak of the church as the ideal place to connect with other BMSM, naming the church one of the few places where they gather and connect with other Black-identified individuals. Participants speak of the church as a fertile ground to meet other Black men who share their experience of seeking community and connection, but also where they have to cope with homonegative beliefs and behaviors. Members report that the drive to build community and make connections motivated them to seek out like-minded BMSM within the church.

Session Topic: Sex and Dating

Table 10.4   Issues Addressed in Session Topic: Sex and Dating

Key issues addressed:	Skills to develop in this session include:
• Sexual expectations ascribed to being a BMSM • Sexual fetishization and being seen as an object to be conquered	• Identify personal boundaries appropriate to dating and sexual encounters. • Analyze sexual stereotypes ascribed to gay/bisexual men.

(cont. . .)

Table 10.4   Issues Addressed in Session Topic: Sex and Dating *(cont. . .)*

• Issues that arise in interracial dating and sexual relationships	• Analyze personal decision-making processes for partner selection in sexual encounters and dating.
• Differences between and motivations for "hooking up" and "dating"	• Evaluate the costs and benefits of discriminate partnering and interracial partnering.
• Qualities and values that affect partner selection in "hooking up" and "dating"	• Create a personal set of expectations for partner's conduct that they discuss with others.

In the *Shades of Black* group, curiosity about the race of members' intimate partners is common. Within the group, curiosity about the individual's race is linked to underlying thoughts about interracial dating. While many BMSM sexually experiment with Whites at points in their lives, many report engaging exclusively with BMSM (Berry et al., 2007; Bingham et al., 2003; Millett et al., 2006; Mimiaga et al., 2009). Experiences of racism and objectification in the larger gay community informs some members' decisions to exclusively partner with other BMSM, while for others it is a matter of preference (Callander, Newman, & Holt, 2015; Paul, Ayala, & Choi, 2010; Teunis, 2007; Wilson et al., 2009).

ROLE OF THE FACILITATOR

As stated by Yalom and Leszcz (2005), the facilitator has an intimate relationship with the group. He ebbs between delving deep into the inner working of the group while stepping back and being objectively attentive to the functioning of the group. The facilitator has his eye on the needs of the individual members as well as the needs of the group. The facilitator of the group has a dynamic role and serves as a conduit to bridge conversations and create room for mutual aid to flourish (Gitterman & Shulman, 2005; Steinberg, 2014). Engaging in group work that addresses issues faced by BMSM provides opportunities for individual growth for the facilitator and macro level work for the BMSM community (e.g., policy advocacy, community engagement, integrating multiple minority perspectives). Understanding systematic racism and homonegativity and its impact on the thoughts and behaviors of BMSM further empowers that facilitator to engage in effective work within and outside the group.

There are benefits to having shared identities with group members with respect to building group trust, alliance, and a common purpose (Humble, Lewis, Scott, & Herzog, 2013). However, shared identities presents challenges of *transference* (projecting one's feelings for a person toward another) and *countertransference* (the emotional reaction the facilitator has toward a group member's projected emotions; Gitterman & Shulman, 2005; Yalom & Leszcz, 2005). The facilitator may be idealized and assumed to have "figured it out" and the power and privilege in his role as a group facilitator may lead participants to believe that he is immune from racism and homonegativity. The facilitator validates some of the group members' perceptions of him while challenging their assumptions that occupying a professional role with power and privilege removes the racism and homonegativity that BMSM face.

CONCLUSION

The vast majority of research about BMSM focuses on HIV/AIDS (Bowleg, 2013; Follins et al., 2014; Wilson et al., 2009), and less on the strengths of BMSM and clinical approaches that benefit them. Capitalizing on the innate strengths and resilience of BMSM, *Shades of Black* provides BMSM with a chance to support each other through mutual aid, discuss their identities and experiences, as well as enhance their adaptive coping skills. In fostering a system of mutual aid, the facilitator taps into the strengths and protective factors manifested by BMSM through navigating systems of oppression (Association for the Advancement of Social Work with Groups, 2010; Bowleg, 2013; Humble et al., 2013; Malekoff, 2016; Steinberge, 2014). While research is necessary to evaluate the efficacy of *Shades of Black*, it can be a useful model for students, scholars, and clinical practitioners who are striving to provide culturally and gender-appropriate behavioral health services for BMSM.

REFERENCES

American Public Health Association (2015). *Better health through equity: Case studies in reframing public health work.* Retrieved from https://www.apha.org/~/media/files/pdf/topics/equity/equity_stories.ashx

American Psychological Association. (2003). Guidelines on multicultural education, training, research, practice, and organizational change for psychologists. *The American Psychologist, 58*(5), 377–402. doi: 10.1037/0003–066X.58.5.377

Aponte, H. J., & Kissil, K. (2014). 'If I can grapple with this I can truly be of use in the therapy room': Using the therapist's own emotional struggles to facilitate effective therapy. *Journal of Marital & Family Therapy, 40*(2), 152–164. doi:10.1111/jmft.12011

Applewhite, S., & Littlefield, M. B. (2016). The role of resilience and anti-resilience behaviors in the romantic lives of Black same gender loving (sgl) men. *Journal of Black Sexuality and Relationships 2*(2), 1–38.

Association for the Advancement of Social Work with Groups. (2010). *Standards for social work practice with groups* (2nd ed.). Alexandria, VA: Author.

Barnes, D., & Meyer, I. (2012). Religious affiliation, internalized homophobia, and mental health in lesbians, gay men, and bisexuals. *American Journal of Orthopsychiatry, 82*(4), 505–515. doi:10.1111/j.1939–0025.2012.01185.x

Battle, J. J., Bennett, M., & Lemelle Jr, A. J. (Eds.). (2006). *Free at last?: Black America in the twenty-first century*. New York, NY: Transaction.

Bingham, T. A., Harawa, N. T., Johnson, D. F., Secura, G. M., MacKellar, D. A., & Valleroy, L. A. (2003). The effect of partner characteristics on HIV infection among African American men who have sex with men in the young men's survey, Los Angeles, 1999–2000. *AIDS Education & Prevention, 15*39, 39–52.

Boone, M. R., Cook, S. H., & Wilson, P. A. (2016). Sexual identity and HIV status influence the relationship between internalized stigma and psychological distress in Black gay and bisexual men. *AIDS Care, 28*(6), 764–770. doi:10.1080/09540121.2016.1164801

Bowleg, L. (2013). 'Once you've blended the cake, you can't take the parts back to the main ingredients': Black gay and bisexual men's descriptions and experiences of intersectionality. *Sex Roles, 68*(11/12), 754–767. doi:10.1007/s11199–012–0152–4

Butler, J. (1997). Gender is burning: Questions of appropriation and subversion. In McClintock, A., Mufti, A., & Shohat, E., (Eds.), *Dangerous liaisons: Gender, nation and postcolonial perspectives* (pp. 380–395). Minneapolis, MN: University of Minnesota Press.

Cabral, R. R., & Smith, T. B. (2011). Racial/ethnic matching of clients and therapists in mental health services: A meta-analytic review of preferences, perceptions, and outcomes. *Journal of Counseling Psychology, 58*(4), 537–554. doi: 10.1037/a0025266

Callander, D., Newman, C. E., & Holt, M. (2015). Is sexual racism really racism? Distinguishing attitudes toward sexual racism and generic racism among gay and bisexual men. *Archives of Sexual Behavior, 44*(7), 1991–2000.

Cohen, C. J. (1996). Contested membership: Black gay identities and the politics of AIDS. In S. Seidman (Ed.), *Queer Theory/Sociology* (pp. 362–394). Blackwell.

Collins, P. (2004). *Black sexual politics: African Americans, gender, and the new racism*. New York, NY: Routledge.

Connell, R. W., & Messerschmidt, J. W. (2005). Hegemonic masculinity rethinking the concept. *Gender & Society, 19*(6), 829–859.

Crenshaw, K. (1991). Mapping the margins: Intersectionality, identity politics, and violence against women of color. *Stanford Law Review*, 1241–1299.

Dale, S. K., Bogart, L. M., Wagner, G. J., Galvan, F. H., Pantalone, D. W., & Klein, D. J. (2015). Discrimination and hate crimes in the context of neighborhood poverty and stressors among HIV-positive African-American men who have sex with men. *Journal of Community Health, 41*(3), 574–583. doi: 10.1007/s10900–015–0132–z

Dyer, T. P., Regan, R., Wilton, L., Harawa, N. T., Wang, L., & Shoptaw, S. (2013). Differences in substance use, psychosocial characteristics and HIV-related sexual risk behavior between Black men who have sex with men only (bmsmo) and Black men who have sex with men and women (bmsmw) in six US cities. *Journal of Urban Health, 90*(6), 1181–1193. doi: 10.1007/s11524–013–981–1

Fields, E. L., Bogart, L. M., Smith, K. C., Malebranche, D. J., Ellen, J., & Schuster, M. A. (2012). HIV risk and perceptions of masculinity among young Black msm. *The Journal of Adolescent Health, 50*(3), 296–303. http://doi.org/10.1016/j. jadohealth.2011.07.007

Follins, L. D., Walker, J. J., & Lewis, M. K. (2014). Resilience in Black lesbian, gay, bisexual, and transgender individuals: A critical review of the literature. *Journal of Gay & Lesbian Mental Health, 18*(2), 190–212. doi:10.1080/19359705.2013.8 28343

Fries-Britt, S., & Turner, B. (2002). Uneven stories: Successful Black collegians at a Black and a white campus. *The Review of Higher Education, 25*(3), 315–330. doi:10.1353/rhe.2002.0012

Garcia, J., Parker, C., Parker, R. G., Wilson, P. A., Philbin, M. M., & Hirsch, J. S. (2015). "You're really gonna kick us all out?" Sustaining safe spaces for community-based HIV prevention and control among Black men who have sex with men. *PloS ONE, 10*(10), e0141326.

George, C., Adam, B. A., Read, S. E., Husbands, W. C., Remis, R. S., Makoroka, L., & Rourke, S. B. (2012). The mabwana Black men's study: Community and belonging in the lives of African, Caribbean and other black gay men in Toronto. *Culture, Health & Sexuality, 14*(5), 549–562. doi:10.1080/13691058.2012.674158

Gilman, S. L. (1985). *Difference and pathology: Stereotypes of sexuality, race, and madness.* Ithaca, NY: Cornell University Press.

Gitterman, A., & Shulman, L. (2005). *Mutual aid groups, vulnerable and resilient populations, and the life cycle.* New York, NY: Columbia University Press.

Goode-Cross, D. T. (2011). Same difference: Black therapists' experience of same-race therapeutic dyads. *Professional Psychology: Research and Practice, 42*(5), 368–374. doi:10.1037/a0025520

Goode-Cross, D. T., & Good, G. E. (2008). African American men who have sex with men: Creating safe spaces through relationships. *Psychology of Men & Masculinity, 9*(4), 221–234. doi:10.1037/a0013428

Goode-Cross, D. T., & Grim, K. A. (2016). "An unspoken level of comfort." *Journal of Black Psychology, 42*(1), 29–53. doi:10.1177/0095798414552103

Greene, B. (1994). Ethnic-minority lesbians and gay men: Mental health and treatment issues. *Journal of Consulting & Clinical Psychology, 62*(2), 243–251. doi:10.1037/0022–006X.62.2.243

Grov, C., Saleh, L. D., Lassiter, J. M., & Parsons, J. T. (2015). Challenging race-based stereotypes about gay and bisexual men's sexual behavior and perceived penis size and size satisfaction. *Sexuality Research and Social Policy, 12*(3), 224–235.

Gwadz, M. V., Clatts, M. C., Yi, H., Leonard, N. R., Goldsamt, L., & Lankenau, S. (2006). Resilience among young men who have sex with men in New York City. *Sexuality Research and Social Policy, 3*(1), 13–21.

Han, C. (2007). They don't want to cruise your type: Gay men of color and the racial politics of exclusion. *Social Identities, 13*(1), 51–67. doi:10.1080/13504630601163379 hooks, b. (1989). *Talking back: Thinking feminist, thinking Black.* Boston, MA: South End Press.

Humble, M. N., Lewis, M. L., Scott, D. L., & Herzog, J. R. (2013). Challenges in rural social work practice: When support groups contain your neighbors, church members, and the pta. *Social Work with Groups, 36*(2–3), 249–258 10p. doi:10.1080/01609513.2012.753807

Hutson, D. J. (2010). Standing out/fitting in: Identity, appearance, and authenticity in gay and lesbian communities. *Symbolic Interaction, 33*(2), 213–233. doi: 10.1525/si.2010.33.2.213

Icard, L., Gripton, J., & Valentich, M. (1986). Black gay men and conflicting social identities: Sexual orientation versus racial identity. *Social Work Practice in Sexual Problems, 4*(1/2), 83.

Institute of Medicine (2011). The health of lesbian, gay, bisexual, and transgender people: Building a foundation for better understanding. Washington, DC: Author. doi:10.17226/13128

Jackson, B. (2012). Black identity development: Influences of culture and social oppression. In C. Wijeyesinghe & B. Jackson (Eds.), *New perspectives on racial identity development: Integrating emerging frameworks,* 2nd ed. (pp. 33–50). New York, NY: New York University Press.

Johnson, E. P. (2011). *Sweet tea: Black gay men of the south.* Chapel Hill, NC: University of North Carolina Press.

Kurland, R., & Salmon, R. (1999). Purpose: A misunderstood and misused keystone of group work practice. *Social Work with Groups, 21*(3), 5–17.

Lassiter, J. (2014). Extracting dirt from water: A strengths-based approach to religion for African American same-gender-loving men. *Journal of Religion & Health, 53*(1), 178–89. doi: 10.1007/s10943–012–9668–8

Liau, A., Millett, G., & Marks, G. (2006). Meta-analytic examination of online sex-seeking and sexual risk behavior among men who have sex with men. *Sexually Transmitted Diseases, 33*(9), 576–584.

Malekoff, A. (2016). *Group work with adolescents: Principles and practice.* 3rd ed. New York, NY: Guilford Press.

Meyer, I. H. (2010). Identity, stress, and resilience in lesbians, gay men, and bisexuals of color. *The Counseling Psychologist,* (3), 442–454. doi: 10.1177/0011000009351601

Millett, G. A., Peterson, J. L., Wolitski, R. J., & Stall, R. (2006). Greater risk for HIV infection of Black men who have sex with men: A critical literature review. *American Journal of Public Health, 96*(6), 1007–1019.

Mimiaga, M. J., Reisner, S. L., Cranston, K., Isenberg, D., Bright, D., Daffin, G., ... & Mayer, K. H. (2009). Sexual mixing patterns and partner characteristics of Black msm in Massachusetts at increased risk for HIV infection and transmission. *Journal of Urban Health, 86*(4), 602–623.

National Association of Social Workers. (2001). *National association of social workers (NASW) standards for cultural competence in social work practice.* Washington DC: Author.

Paul, J. P., Ayala, G., & Choi, K. (2010). Internet sex ads for msm and partner selection criteria: The potency of race/ethnicity online. *Journal of Sex Research, 47*(6), 528–538. doi:10.1080/00224490903244575

Phillips, G., Peterson, J., Binson, D., Hidalgo, J., Magnus, M., & YMSM of Color SPNS Initiative Study Group. (2011). House/ball culture and adolescent African-American transgender persons and men who have sex with men: A synthesis of the literature. *AIDS Care, 23*(4), 515–520. doi:10.1080/09540121.2010.516334

Pinar, W. F. (2001). Black men: You don't even know who I am. *Counterpoints, 163*, 855–938.

Pitt, R. N. (2010a). "Killing the messenger": Religious Black gay men's neutralization of anti-gay religious messages. *Journal for the Scientific Study of Religion, 49*(1), 56–72. doi:10.1111/j.1468–5906.2009.01492.x

———. (2010b). "Still looking for my Jonathan": Gay Black men's management of religious and sexual identity conflicts. *Journal of Homosexuality, 57*(1), 39–53. doi:10.1080/00918360903285566

Ritter, K., & Terndrup, A. I. (2002). *Handbook of affirmative psychotherapy with lesbians and gay men.* New York, NY: Guilford Press.

Schiller, L. Y. (1997). Rethinking stages of development in women's groups: Implications for practice. *Social Work with Groups*, (3), 3–19. doi: 10.1300/J009v20n03_02

Schiller, L. Y. (2007). Not for women only: Applying the relational model of group development with vulnerable populations. *Social Work with Groups*, (2), 11–26.

Smith, D. E. (1987). *The everyday world as problematic: A feminist sociology.* Boston, MA: Northeastern University Press.

Smedley, B. D., Stith, A. Y., & Nelson, A. R. (2002). *Unequal treatment: Confronting racial and ethnic disparities in health care.* Washington DC: Institute of Medicine. doi: 10.17226/10260

Steinberg, D. M. (2014). *A mutual-aid model for social work with groups.* Abingdon, UK: Routledge.

Sue, D. W. (1990). Culture-specific strategies in counseling: A conceptual framework. *Professional Psychology: Research and Practice, 21*(6), 424–433. doi: 10.1037/0735–7028.21.6.424

Taylor, J. S. (2000). Tourism and "embodied" commodities: Sex tourism in the Caribbean. In S. Clift and S. Carter (Eds.), *Tourism and sex: Culture, commerce and coercion* (pp. 41–53). London, UK: Wellington House.

Teunis, N. (2007). Sexual objectification and the construction of whiteness in the gay male community. *Culture, Health, & Sexuality*, (3), 263–275. doi: 10.1080/13691050601035597

Townes, D. L., Chavez-Korell, S., & Cunningham, N. J. (2009). Reexamining the relationships between racial identity, cultural mistrust, help-seeking attitudes, and preference for a Black counselor. *Journal of Counseling Psychology, 56*(2), 330–336. doi: 10.1037/a0015449

Warner, L., & Shields, S. (2013). The intersections of sexuality, gender, and race: Identity research at the crossroads. *Sex Roles, 68*(11/12), 803–810. doi:10.1007/s11199–013–0281–4

Wilson, P. A., Valera, P., Ventuneac, A., Balan, I., Rowe, M., & Carballo-Dieguez, A. (2009). Race-based sexual stereotyping and sexual partnering among men who use the internet to identify other men for bareback sex. *Journal of Sex Research,* *46*(5), 399–413. doi:10.1080/00224490902846479

Wilson, P. A., Valera, P., Martos, A. J., Wittlin, N. M., Muñoz-Laboy, M. A., & Parker, R. G. (2015). Contributions of qualitative research in informing HIV/ AIDS interventions targeting Black msm in the United States. *The Journal of Sex Research,* 1–13. doi: 10.1080/00224499.2015.1016139

Yalom, I. D., & Leszcz, M. (2005). *The theory and practice of group psychotherapy.* New York, NY: Basic Books.

Chapter 11

Effective Strategies Used by African American Same Gender Loving Men in Promoting Health and Well-Being

Lawrence O. Bryant

Institutional oppression in the form of homophobia and racism presents significant challenges for African American same gender loving (SGL) men in their quest to live a healthy, meaningful and fulfilled life. These forms of discrimination can have deleterious effects on their physical and mental well-being (Battle, 2004; Bryant, 2008; Lassiter, 2014). This chapter positions health and wellness as a primary concern for African American SGL men. Through a critique of social, political, and environmental factors, this chapter analyzes the intersectionality of oppressive social systems as they impact the daily lives of African American SGL men. It will also describe coping mechanisms identified by African American SGL men in a research study that sought to understand the experiences and associated coping strategies of a population that often struggles with the impacts of homophobia, heterosexism, and racism in their daily lives. Specifically, the questions that guided this study were:

• How have African American SGL men experienced homophobia and racism?
• How have African American SGL men coped with homophobia and racism?
• How did African American SGL men learn coping strategies to manage homophobia and racism?

NEXUS OF OPPRESSION

Oppression is so ingrained into the social, political, economic, religious, and educational systems in this country, that it is often is unrecognizable (Boykin, 1996; Bryant, 2008). Many SGL men must navigate multiple interlocking systems of oppressions (e.g., racism, homophobia, heterosexism) at once

(Collins, 2006; Lorde, 1992). Collins (2000) puts this phenomenon into perspective, she eloquently states:

> As opposed to examining gender, sexuality, race, class, and nation as separate systems of oppression, the construct of intersectionality references how these systems mutually construct one another. Intersectional paradigms suggest that certain ideas and/or practices surface repeatedly across multiple systems of oppression. Serving as focal points for intersecting systems of oppression, these ideas and practices may be central to how gender, sexuality, race, class, and nation mutually construct one another. (p. 48)

Andersen and Collins (2006) refer to the above conceptualization of oppression as the *matrix of domination*. This concept also includes *cultural hegemony* which refers to the idea that the supremacy of a social group is manifested through domination in both epistemological and moral domains of social life. When it comes to African American SGL men, various social systems, knowledge and values are promulgated that center the lives of white, heterosexual males at the expense of the "other" (Collins, 2004). African American SGL men often occupy the space of the "other." The experiences of African American SGL men can best be understood from a dominant cultural perspective that is grounded in hegemonic power relations situated within systems of patriarchy, racism, and heterosexism. It is the interlocking nature of these systems that shapes the lives of African American SGL men (Collins, 2004).

The current debate in America about the role and place of SGL men in American society is symptomatic of the deep-seated anxieties and fears that characterize the attitude of many Americans toward gays. Contentious political and social debates over SGL men's rights in the United States, including religion-based homophobia and the violence recently seen in the Orlando massacre are but a couple of ways in which the understanding of SGL life is at odds with mainstream culture (Griffin, 2006). To then talk about African American male masculinity further complicates and distorts this debate, because African American sexuality has traditionally been a taboo subject (Bryant, 2008; Constantine-Simms, 2001; Griffin, 2006). As West (1993) observes, African American sexuality has played a key role in the racial demonization of African American people. The historic characterization of heterosexual African American men's masculinity as voracious, deviant, and primitive created conditions that led to white sanctions on African American sexuality and produced self-loathing among African Americans and the demeaning of African American bodies (Bryant, 2008; Malebranche, Fields, Bryant, & Harper, 2007).

Additionally, African American masculinity is an especially ambiguous and misunderstood subject in the African American community, especially as it relates to gender role conflict (Malebranche et al., 2007). Behavioral and social scientists have pointed to America's historical legacy of slavery as the culprit, with its identification of African American masculinity with physical labor, breeding, servitude, and physical endowment (all African American men have large penises) (Malebranche et al., 2007). Nevertheless, these factors contribute to stigmatization and oppression within the African American SGL community.

HETERONORMATIVITY, HETEROSEXISM, AND THEIR INTERPLAY WITH RELIGION AND SPIRITUALITY

Heteronormativity and Heterosexism

The term *heteronormative* reflects the widespread notion that heterosexuality is normal and everything else is somehow deviant (hooks, 1994). Writings by postmodern feminists such as bell hooks, Patricia Hill Collins, and Marlon Riggs challenge the patriarchal standards of heterosexuality as normal, and reject the double standard that rebukes women for the same behaviors for which men are equally culpable, yet unsanctioned (Collins, 2004; hooks, 1989, 2004). Interestingly, African American SGL men have complained that these same sexual mores deny them the right to participate in and be fully accepted by institutions in the African American community such as family, church, health care, and institutions of higher education (Boykin, 1996; Bryant, 2008; hooks 2004; Collins, 2004; Constantine-Simms, 2001; Lorde, 1992). Much of the exclusion of SGL men from the African American mainstream comes in the form of heterosexism. Burn, Kadlec, and Rexer (2005) defined *heterosexism* as prejudice against those persons who are not heterosexual. For many African American SGL men, heterosexism comes from the one institution within the African American community that is supposed to nurture and help protect them—African American religious institutions (Johnson & Henderson, 2005; Lassiter, 2014; Woodard, 2000).

African American SGL Men and Christianity

According to Lassiter (2014), the term "African American church" includes the following denominations: African Methodist Episcopal, African Methodist Episcopal Zion, Christian Methodist Episcopal, National Baptist Convention, USA, Inc., National Baptist Convention of America, Southern Baptist Convention, Progressive National Baptist Convention, and Church of God in Christ. These Protestant denominations constitute the African American church, and will be used for the remainder of this chapter when referring to "the African American church" or "African American churches." African American churches are multidimensional and for many, represent a place of solace, refuge and empowerment. However, while some churches are tolerant of same sex relationships, many others oppose homosexuality (Griffin, 2006; Lassiter, 2014). Woodard (2000) argues that "the literature reflects no sustained effort to support church-going SGL men" (p. 452). Many African American Christians believe homosexuality is immoral, unnatural, and an abomination in the sight of God (Bryant, 2008). Further adding to this quandary is African American Christians' intolerance of any type of romantic or sexual relationship outside of traditional heterosexual marriage, a party to which African American SGL men have only recently been reluctantly invited. In spite of the open hostility by some African American Christians, African American SGL are active participants in the body of Christ (Lassiter, 2014; Lemelle & Battle, 2004; Woodard, 2000).

Because of anti-gay sentiment within African American communities and racism within mainstream American culture, African American SGL men may face additional barriers to integrating their sexual and racial identities when compared with their white counterparts. Many other indigenous institutions within the African American community, such as African American fraternities and sororities and mainstream African American political organizations either explicitly or implicitly espouse strong antipathy toward African American SGL people (Boykin, 1996). While some African American organizations are slowly beginning to moderate their stances toward SGL issues, many African American SGL men still feel rejected and condemned by these institutions, which are sites of critical support for African American communities.

Even while confronting the effects of homophobia, many African American SGL men struggle with their sexuality and even actively seek to conceal their sexual orientation (King, 2004). In response to these sometimes combative societal forces, African American SGL struggle to find ways to cope with racism and homophobia and to develop useful strategies to confront these oppressive realities. Since many African American SGL men are victimized by religious dogma, progressive leading scholars on the subject suggest that these men become more aware of the difference between pathological and healthy belief systems, and choose belief systems which empower them in their lives rather than those which tear them down (Bryant, 2008; Pitt, 2010).

African American SGL Men's Spirituality

This author was personally impacted by the writings of John McNeal, through his book *"Taking a Chance on God"* I first became aware that there were other ways of interpreting scripture that was affirming of homosexuality. This concept was absolutely radical for me, being raised in a Church of God in Christ.

McNeal (1988), a white theologian and leading scholar on homosexuality and the Bible, wrote from the premise that "There are questions that gay people ask regarding their relationship with God, that differ from heterosexual questions, and that there is thus a distinct contribution to be made to theology and spirituality from a gay perspective" (p. xi). For example, how do I love and accept myself just as I am in a homophobic and racist society? He further states, "When pathological belief systems and feelings become deeply rooted in the unconscious of gay people, the result can be resistance to healthy self-acceptance, pathological religious teachings can also result in destruction of one's psychological health and spiritual development" (1988, p. 16).

Recent work done by African American scholars affirm some of these assertions as they relate to the experiences of SGL men and their contribution to the African American church. For example, work by Lassiter (2014) and Woodard (2000) examines SGL men's contribution and involvement in the African American church. They note that SGL men are represented in the pulpits, deacon boards, trustee boards, usher boards, and numerous committees and auxiliaries. It is not atypical to have a choir full of SGL men bringing the saints to a fever pitch come Sunday morning, only to be followed by a homophobic sermon that relegated SGL men to the pits of hell and placed in categories with prostitutes, cheaters, and drug addicts. Lassiter (2014) posits that "this spiritual genocide is the psychological damaging of SGL men as they are separated from their higher power and the strength such a connection engenders within them" (p. 180). This chapter presents qualitative data from a recent study (Bryant, 2008) which explored the positive psychological factors associated with health and well-being among a selected group of African American SGL men.

METHODS

This project received approval from the University of Georgia's Institutional Review Board (IRB). This study utilized a qualitative methodology utilizing one-on-one, face-to-face semi-structured interviews. Research that focuses on understanding the perspectives and experiences of those being studied offer the greatest chance of making contributions to the field of public health (Creswell, 2014). Using a phenomenological approach, ten participants were interviewed. Prior to conducting the interview, the author verbally reviewed a consent form describing the study's procedures, goals, risks and benefits.

Procedures and Participants

The participants ranged in age from twenty-one to fifty-five years, with an average age of thirty (see Table 11.1). Most participants were single

(70 percent), and had at least some college education (40 percent had bachelor's degrees). Their identification with religious institutions ranged from non-denominational to Baptist. Participants were recruited through flyer distribution (with author contact information) at targeted community venues such as SGL men's bars and parks where African American SGL men were known to frequent. Participants could express interest in the study by sending an e-mail, or leaving a voicemail message on the author's office phone. On initial contact, participants were evaluated for eligibility. The inclusion criteria were as follows: (1) self-identify as same gender loving or gay, (2) Black or African American, (3) between twenty-one and fifty-five years, participants were then enrolled in the study if inclusion criteria were met. A mutually agreed upon time and place was determined to conduct the interviews.

The interview guide included questions relevant to African American SGL men in their social environment and included the following topical areas: (1) experiences with homophobia and racism; (2) coping strategies; (3) how they learned their coping strategies; (4) issues related to sexual orientation; (5) their upbringing; and (6) the African American community and homosexuality. Each interview was tape-recorded, transcribed verbatim, and the transcripts were corrected for any errors.

Data Analysis

Analysis of data was conducted using comparative content analysis to identify, code, and categorize themes and patterns in the data (Creswell, 2014; Patton, 1990). Data analysis focused on three interrelated questions: experience of homophobia and racism, means of coping with homophobia and racism, and learning processes related to developing coping strategies. Major thematic findings related to each question are presented and discussed in the next section.

RESULTS

Eight themes were extracted from the data: (1) homophobia within the African American community, (2) racism within the gay community, (3) struggling with initial same sex attraction, (4) challenging homophobia and racism, (5) using social networks, (6) embracing teachable moments, (7) trusting one's Higher Power, and (8) defining one's own idea of masculine identity. The names used in this chapter are pseudonyms and are used in order to protect the anonymity and confidentiality of the participants.

Table 11.1   Relevant Themes

Research Questions	Theme	% Endorsed Theme	Sub-Themes
How have AA SGL men experienced homophobia and racism?	Facing homophobia within the African American community.	90	Discrimination by church leaders Different moral standards for SGL men Living with racism within the gay community
	Struggling with the initial realization of same sex attraction	60	SGL men have varied behavioral characteristics
How have AA SGL men coped with homophobia and racism?	Challenging homophobia and racism	60	
	Using social networks	70	Relationships based on acceptance and trust, not sexual identity
How did AA SGL men learn coping strategies?	Embracing teachable moments	60	
	Trusting in one's Higher Power	70	
	Defining one's own idea of masculine identity	55	

Facing Homophobia within the African American Community

Ninety percent of SGL men in this study believed that homophobic attitudes exist in the African American community. Many participants reported that many people in the African American community perpetuated homophobic oppression toward them that in a way similar to whites enact racial oppression against African Americans. Jack (age thirty-two) gives a poignant example:

Within the African American community, we readily discriminate against people for being gay. It's one of our pet peeves; I always said that people who were oppressed become the best oppressors, because they know how to do it. As people, as African Americans, we were put down, relegated as being second class citizens. Because you are African American, knowing how that felt, being a recipient of it, all of a sudden now you have been told, 'Okay, you are as good as everybody else'. Well the one thing that they were waiting for, the opportunity to do, how do I know I am as good as everybody else, because I can put somebody else down. That's what people on top do, that's how, you know, they are on top, they put other people down.

One participant (George, aged forty-five) even posed the question: "How could a people who experienced dehumanizing conditions under both chattel slavery and the institutionalized discrimination of Jim Crow perpetrate this behavior on others—especially their own ethnic group?" George (age forty-five), who has also been in a monogamous relationship with the same person for the last eighteen years, thinks he has one possible explanation for the African American community's stance on homosexuality.

> The problem is that it's easy for people to hate something that they can't put a face to. So a lot of times when our community has this adamant hatred, or this shut down mode of not accepting homosexuality, a lot of it is based on the fact that they don't have a real depiction of what it looks like. But if we could get every brother and sister that is same gender loving to come out of the closet and to be who they are, we would wipe out homophobia in our community overnight.

There was a widespread feeling among participants that if more heterosexuals personally got to know African American SGL men who were open about their sexual orientation identity, there would be fewer negative attitudes and discrimination toward them. Realizing that African American SGL men are their neighbors, their doctors, their lawyers, and even their ministers, some of the stereotypes associated with them might be dispelled.

Living with Racism within the Gay Community

Several participants expressed shock and disappointment that other white gay men would also treat them with disrespect, disdain, and contempt. Participants expressed a sense of violation and betrayal because of their experiences with white gay men who, they reported, discriminated against them because of their race.

Fred (age forty-four) noted that he faced discrimination when attempting to gain entrance into mostly white gay social clubs. Most gay clubs normally ask for some form of identification ("ID") as a standard procedure; however, in an effort to minimize the number of African Americans that enter their establishment, the doormen in many white establishments ask African Americans for multiple forms of identification (Bryant, 2008). Fred shared:

> I remember going to white gay bars and being asked for, you know, five pieces of ID. I need five picture IDs, you know, to get in, and to me that was clearly racist, you know, because they weren't asking the white patrons for five pieces of ID, you know to get in.

Adam (age thirty-six) affirmed that this practice occurs:

You know, if I only had one ID, they would ask for two, or when I am standing in line to get into a club, you know. They will let the white ones in before they will let a African American in. That is pretty much it; I don't hang around a lot of people who don't like me. I hang around with my own race a lot.

Struggling with the Initial Realization of Same Sex Attraction

Most men in this study realized their same sex attraction early in life. This recognition is not a single event or experience, but is a process that occurred over time (Bryant, 2008; Woodard, 2000). These experiences involve physical sexual encounters with other boys and men, coming out to family, and internal conflict related to same sex feelings. The conflict and confusion that some participants experienced surrounding the morality of homosexuality was mostly the of result of religious and family teachings. However, over time most (60 percent) participants became more comfortable with and accepting of their same sex attraction. For example, Adam asserted:

> I have been taught that it was [a sinful lifestyle], but as I have gotten older, I don't believe it, so it's sort of a catch 22. I would say no, I do not believe, the core of my belief systems I would say no; I do not believe that it is a sin.

George (age forty-five) had similar experiences and his initial conflict about his sexuality was a result of religious teachings about homosexuality. He realized his same sex attraction at the age of six. He engaged in the traditional sports-related activities expected of him by his family and community. He came to grips with his sexuality and finally accepted these same sex attractions at the age of fourteen after disclosing his sexual identity to his mother. He stated:

> Well for me my experience, I actually came out to my mom when I was fourteen and for me, I felt that that was probably the catalyst for the person I am today. I grew up in a very religious, church going home, where the belief system was that, of course, homosexuality was wrong. But I discovered at the age of six that I had an attraction for the same gender . . .

For other participants in the study, the only seemingly viable solution to the homophobia problem was to keep their sexuality and sexual desires a secret from others.

Challenging Homophobia and Racism

Participants described different ways they cope with the daily challenges of living in a homophobic and racist society (60 percent). Fred stated that he copes by challenging the forces of homophobia and racism. He says he is very vocal about the subject: "I tend to be very vocal, you know, I will express my displeasure, you know, and whether that's sending a letter or calling the management, or you know, I follow-up on those things, I don't let them just go." Adam, on the other hand, becomes defensive in coping with the stress of oppression. He states:

> Well like I said, I get very defensive; if it is brought up I defend my sexuality and the sexuality of others if they are gay. Like I said, if the word faggot is used, I approach the person and I ask them, you know, if they would not use that around me. I am very sensitive about it and people who don't accept me, you know, I just, I don't judge them, but I look at them as being ignorant, you know. So I guess how I deal with homophobia and people who discriminate against homosexuals I tend to just, block them out.

Adam's and Fred's comments captured the overall sentiments expressed by the majority of the participants regarding how they cope with homophobia and racism. While others may choose to deal with oppression by becoming hostile or physically violent, these men choose a more diplomatic approach in coping with these issues. The most inspiring element of their coping strategy is that they have decided to fight to maintain their dignity instead of just accepting what is dealt to them. Participants reported utilizing a variety of other strategies to cope with homophobia and racism, especially talking with friends and family.

Using Social Networks

Participants discussed having networks of friends that help them cope with sometimes antagonistic environments. The men in this study identified qualities important to them when choosing people to be part of their networks. These qualities include individuals they can trust, people that help them maintain balance, people who are honest, and those that are totally accepting of their sexual orientation. Acceptance was an integral ingredient in the relationships that these men developed within their networks.

The majority of participants (70 percent) said the most important factor is having friends that they can depend on and trust. They asserted that, although they value their gay friends, their relationships are not based solely on sexual orientation or race. Jack shared the following:

> My close friends are level, they have balance, and they keep me grounded. They let me know when I have not been accessible; they let me know when I am too accessible, you know, if I am on track or off track, most friends provide that for me. I have gay friends and straight friends and both sides, I have close friends that come into both categories. I appreciate my straight friends a little more,

not more, but I appreciate them because that friendship is not based on sex, not necessarily sex with that person, it is not based on who I go to bed with.

Mike (age thirty-five) agreed that in selecting his support network, sexual orientation is not the deciding factor. He stated that he values honesty in his friends regardless of their sexual orientation. He remarked:

> I have some good, meaningful relationships with some people and some people I don't, just like anything else in life. I think you know the criteria in which you establish friendship is not based on someone's sexuality. It's about truth and honesty, you know, and I would rather have a relationship with someone friendly who is an honest person and supportive, if he is heterosexual or if he's gay and dishonest and don't really give a damn about who I am, or my principals, or will reach out to do anything for me.

This statement underscores the quality and importance of these relationships for many of the men in this study. Participants used words like honesty, trust, dependence, forthrightness, and loving to describe characteristics they admire in their friends. Participants have learned to celebrate their lives and relationships as meaningful and to accept themselves and their sexual orientation unconditionally.

Additionally, these men engage in non-formal learning through personal and community activities that help them cope with their daily struggles. Some of these activities include: (1) educating themselves and others about homophobia and racism, (2) attending community workshops and support groups, (3) consulting with those in their social networks for support, (4) attending same sex affirming churches or spiritual venues, and (5) reading materials that help them better understand sexuality and sexual orientation.

Embracing Teachable Moments

Sixty percent of participants described how they learned to utilize principles such as acceptance, love, and spirituality to educate others about homophobia and racism. For example, Jack described what he calls "teachable moments":

> I think we have some very teachable moments, and I think a lot of times people will engage in racist acts and not even be aware of it. I think that it has been so engrained that this is the status quo as to how things happen, that they will do things or say things, and not even realize that it was offensive or inappropriate. At that point, you know you take it upon yourself to say this is a very teachable moment. This is not a spot where I can get revenge and fix you and hurt you, but this is a spot where I can teach you a better way of being in this environment, a better way of being in our society today.

Fred supported Jack's position; he said that he has learned how important it is to always be prepared to deal with these issues by educating people:

> It would be a beautiful world if it wasn't there. But it is there and, you know, expect it. But also be able, you know, not only when you expect it to be there, always put yourself in a position where you are able to teach, should that situation arise. I think nothing is worse than for a situation to arise and you are not equipped to deal with it. Where you find yourself just having to resort to some form of violence, because you can't deal with what was presented. So if we are aware that someone is going to approach you, someone is going to say something, somebody is going to do something, that is inappropriate, that is discriminatory, what do you have? What have you armed yourself with? How can you teach this person?

Jack has learned that there are personal benefits in coping with homophobia and racism in a positive manner; he posits that in the process of teaching others, he enhances his own spirituality and well-being.

Trusting in One's Higher Power

Although participants described church as a site where they often experienced homophobia and identified the church as a primary source in perpetuating discrimination, 70 percent nevertheless spoke passionately about having a relationship with a higher power in helping them cope with oppression and life. Sam (forty-nine) explained:

> I trust in God, if my mother, my father, puts me down then God lifts me up and a lot of times there is a lot of disagreements when it comes to the Bible and God, and what he said. I don't care, you know, God is real and I think all of us have a tendency of looking at God in one light or another, then we see the need for him. So when things get to a point where others don't treat me, or even if the government or society have different laws with prejudice and police brutality, and all this kind of stuff, I have to say I resort to trusting the Lord God to the best of my ability. That is how I cope, you know, where else can I go, what else can I do?

Sam's comments reinforced the importance of trusting in God because he feels that there is no other alternative. Adam is equally committed to reliance on a higher power as a source of strength; he utilizes prayer as a coping mechanism and strongly asserted:

> I pray, I pray, I ask for forgiveness, if I am doing anything that is not right in God's eyes, because you know what, I don't know how God sees homosexuality. God, my God, I believe, and I believe this deeply, he looks at my heart not at my actions.

Defining Their Own Ideas of Masculine Identity

Fifty-five percent of participants in this study overwhelmingly agreed that the most important lesson learned in coping with issues related to masculinity is that masculinity and manhood are much more than just having sexual relationships. Although many participants in this study mentioned that they are often stereotyped as hypersexual and promiscuous, they see a direct link between their manhood and values (e.g., acceptance of others' differences, philanthropy, personal responsibility, giving to others, valuing friendships, loving one's self, and spirituality). George (age forty-five) noted that, although subjective, being masculine is a desirable trait:

> I think being a real man can be defined in many ways now. I mean, I can't always say that I have felt this way. But I think being a real man is about being loving, caring, being considerate, those things define a real man, you know.

Jack has learned to question societal norms and expectations of masculinity, although he's not clear on a specific definition of masculinity. He declared:

> We mimic what the heterosexual communities display as masculinity. So if they say masculine men walk around with their pants sagging off and one leg rolled up, then even the gay men, you know, they want to demonstrate, display masculinity, they will do the same thing. They are going to mimic their heterosexual counterpart. Now that's a surface level masculinity, yeah, it's such a subjective term as you know; we look at them, and say real masculinity, what is that? I don't know exactly. Is that because you pay your bills? Is that because you don't disrespect women? Take care of your kids? I mean there are so many different ways of people describing what masculinity is, but I do know that it's considered a desirable trait.

Participants eloquently described how they have learned to define and articulate their own construct of masculinity based on their reality and personal experiences. In the face of what seems like insurmountable obstacles, these men are proud of who they are and their contribution to the betterment of society.

DISCUSSION

The purpose of this chapter was to examine African American SGL men's experiences with homophobia and racism. The research questions that guided this study were: 1. How have SGL men experienced homophobia and racism? 2. How have SGL men coped with issues related to homophobia and racism? 3. How have SGL men learned their coping strategies in dealing with homophobia and racism? This study explores the learning and coping experiences of SGL men as they negotiate racist and heterosexist environments. This study supports other relevant literature which affirms that in spite of the many obstacles African American SGL men must contend with, they still manage to maintain pride in their sexuality. Moreover, there is a positive connection between African American SGL spirituality and their sexual orientation (Lassiter, 2014; Pitts, 2010; Woodard, 2000).

A study by Lassiter (2015) examined the methods Black SGL men utilize in resolving conflict between their spirituality and their sexuality. One of the themes was that Black SGL men reported physically distancing themselves from their childhood family and church, that is, in early adulthood participants began questioning their childhood religious and family teachings and understandings regarding sexuality. This initial moving away was in response to their perceptions of hypocrisy, sexism, heterosexism, and lack of personal or cultural support. These experiences are consistent with findings in this research study and in Bowman and Bryant's autoethnographical study (2010), where participants' perspective on various aspects of their childhood religious beliefs, particularly around sexuality changed over time.

These findings suggest that African American SGL men look beyond the traditional religious rhetoric in exploring their faith and the meaning of their existence (Pitt, 2010). A study by Lassiter (2014) suggests that religion can actually be a source of strength for African American SGL men in navigating racism and homophobic experiences. This study has attempted to address some of the social and psychological issues that African American SGL men face during a time when SGL people in particular, and African American men overall are struggling. Although this subject remains sparsely investigated in the literature, I hope that this research will stimulate more studies that examine issues specific to African American SGL men. Many questions remain regarding masculinity, internalized homophobia, and racism among African American males in our society. Answering these questions will take a comprehensive research agenda that starts with placing an emphasis on querying those who best understand the lives of African American SGL men—themselves. Qualitative inquiry will continue to play an increasingly critical role in addressing these deeply nuanced questions.

Learning in the service of fighting oppression has been a topic of significant work in adult education. However, a cautionary note should be sounded inasmuch as the suggestion could be made that the men in this study had "overcome" oppression. In fact, that was not the case. Fighting oppression is an ongoing process. It involves engaging in social networks and creating meaningful and generative relationships. One limitation of this study was the small numbers of interviews conducted, this was because of the limited time and resources afforded the author in completing the dissertation; future studies can very well expand this number. Learning in the face of powerful forces should not be understood as a finite process; instead, as the participants in this study made clear, it is an ongoing process that focuses primarily on the well-being of the individuals engaged in struggle. That is what permits these men to live reasonably fulfilling lives with meaningful relationships.

REFERENCES

Anderson, M. L., & Collins, P. H. (2006). *Race, class, and gender: An anthology.* Belmont, CA: Wadsworth Press.

Bowman, L., & Bryant L. (2010). *Black gay men at midlife: Learning self-acceptance.* Paper session presented at the Adult Education Research Conference, Sacramento State University, Sacramento, CA.

Boykin, K. (1996). *One more river to cross: Black and gay in America.* New York, NY: Random House.

Bryant, L. (2008). *How Black men who have sex with men learn to cope with homophobia and racism.* (Unpublished doctoral dissertation). University of Georgia, Athens, GA.

Burn, S., Kadlec, K., & Rexer, R. (2005). Effects of heterosexism on gays, lesbians, bisexuals. *Journal of Homosexuality, 49*(2), 23–38.

Collins, P. H. (1998). *It's all in the family: Intersections of gender, race and nation. Hypatia, 13*(3), 62–82.

———. (2000). Gender, Black feminism, and Black political economy. *Annals of the American Academy of Political and Social Science, 568,* 41–53.

———. (2004). *Black sexual politics.* New York, NY: Routledge.

Constantine-Simms, D. (2001). Is homosexuality the greatest taboo? In D. Constantine-Simms (Ed.), *The greatest taboo: Homosexuality in the Black community* (pp. 76–87). Los Angeles, CA: Alyson Books.

Creswell, J. W. (2014). *Research design: Qualitative, quantitative, and mixed methods approaches* (4th ed.). Thousand Oaks, CA: Sage.

Grace, A. P. & Hill, R. J. (2001). Using queer knowledge to build inclusion pedagogy in adult education. *Proceedings of the 42*nd *Annual Adult Education Research Conference* (pp. 145–150). Michigan State University, Lansing, MI.

Griffin, H. (2006). *Their own receive them not: African American lesbians and gays in Black churches.* Cleveland, OH: Pilgrim Press.

Hemphill, E. (2001). Does your mama know about me? In R. P. Byrd. & B. Guy-Sheftall (Eds.), *Traps: African American men on gender and sexuality* (pp. 297–300). Bloomington, IN: Indiana University Press.

hooks, b. (1989). *Talking back: Thinking feminist, thinking Black.* Boston, MA: South End Press.

———. (1994). *Sexism and misogyny: Who takes the rap?* Retrieved from http://race.eserver.org/misogyny.html

————. (2004). *The will to change: Men, masculinity, and love.* New York, NY: Atria Books.

Johnson, E., & Henderson, M. (2005). *Black queer studies.* Durham, NC: Duke University Press.

King, J. (2004). *On the down low: A journey into the lives of "straight" Black men who sleep with men.* New York, NY: Broadway Books.

Lemelle, A. J., & Battle, J. (2004). Black masculinity matters in attitudes toward gay males. *Journal of Homosexuality, 47,* 39–51.

Lassiter, J. M. (2014). Extracting dirt from water: A strengths-based approach to religion for African American same-gender-loving men. *Journal of Religious Health, 53,* 178–189.

————. (2015). Reconciling sexual orientation and Christianity: Black same-gender loving men's experiences. *Mental Health, Religion & Culture, 18*(5), 342–353.

Lincoln, C., & Mamiya, L. (1990). *The Black church in the African-American experience.* Durham, NC: Duke University Press.

Lorde, A. (1992). Women redefining difference. In M. Anderson & P. H. Collins (Eds.), *Age, race, class, and sex* (pp. 495–502). Belmont, CA: Wadsworth Press.

Malebranche, D., Fields. L., Bryant, L., & Harper, S. (2007). Cool pose revisited: The social context of masculinity and sexual risk among Black men who have sex with men. *Men and Masculinities.* Retrieved from http://jmm.sagepub.com/cgi/rapidpdf/1097184X07309504v1

Manago, C. (1989). Mission and history. *SGL BMX Washington DC Chapter.* Retrieved from http://bmxdc.org/who-we-are/mission-and-history/

McBride, D. A. (2001). Can the queen speak? Racial essentialism, sexuality, and the problem of authority. In D. Constantine-Simms (Ed.), *The greatest taboo: Homosexuality in the Black community* (pp. 76–87). Los Angeles, CA: Alyson Books.

McNeal, J. J. (1998). *Taking a chance on God.* Boston, MA: Beacon Press.

Parks, C. (2001). African-American same-gender-loving youths and families in urban schools. *Journal of Gay & Lesbian Social Services, 13,* 41–56. doi:10.1300/J041v13n03_03

Pitt, R. N. (2010). "Killing the messenger": Religious Black gay men's neutralization of anti-gay religious messages. *Journal for the Scientific Study of Religion, 49*(1), 56–72.

Patton M. (1990). *Qualitative evaluation and research methods.* Newbury Park, CA: Sage.

Tisdell, E. (1998). Poststructural feminist pedagogies: The possibilities and limitations of a feminist emancipatory adult learning theory and practice. *Adult Education Quarterly, 48*(3), 139–156.

West, C. (1993). *Race matters.* Boston, MA: Beacon Press.

————. (2001). Black sexuality: The taboo subject. In R. P. Byrd. & B. Guy-Sheftall (Eds.). *Traps: African American men on gender and sexuality* (pp. 301–307). Bloomington, IN: Indiana University Press.

Woodard, J., Peterson, L., Stokes, J., & Joseph, P. (2000). Let us go into the house of the Lord: Participation in African American churches among young African American men who have sex with men. *Journal of Pastoral Care, 54*(4), 451–460.

Chapter 12

Perceptions of Health

Self-Rated Health among Black LGB People

Kasim Ortiz, Angelique Harris,
Kenneth Maurice Pass, and Devon Tyrone Wade

One of the primary objectives of Healthy People 2020 is to eliminate health disparities facing racial and sexual minorities (U.S. Department of Health and Human Services, 2010). The 2011 Institute of Medicine's report on lesbian, gay, bisexual, and transgender (LGBT) health identified a need for more research highlighting the intersectional perspectives of those that have multiple stigmatized identities (e.g., racial + sexual minority statuses), particularly because members of these populations grapple with extensive and persistent health disparities that disproportionately impact them (Institute of Medicine, 2011). Several studies have identified adverse health outcomes among sexual minorities when compared to their heterosexual counterparts, which includes but is not limited to: mental health outcomes (Cochran, Mays, Alegria, Ortega, & Takeuchi, 2007; Duncan & Hatzenbuehler, 2013; Hatzenbuehler & Keyes, 2013; McLaughlin, Hatzenbuehler, Xuan, & Conron, 2012), physical health outcomes (Cochran & Mays, 2007), and tobacco and other substance use and abuse (Cochran, Bandiera, & Mays, 2013; Cochran, Grella, & Mays, 2012; Duncan, Hatzenbuehler, & Johnson, 2013; Ortiz-Hernandez, Gomez-Tello, & Valdes, 2009). As the number of sexual minorities continues to grow and their sociodemographic compositions continue to vary greatly, research agendas evaluating greater population level health indicators are needed.

Self-rated health (SRH) as an indicator of population level health has been used by public health researchers for over thirty years, particularly after the validation of its psychometric properties. As a measurement, SRH has consistently shown strong predictive validity, demonstrating its usefulness in accurately predicting several diseases. Sarkin et al. (2013) demonstrated that racial differences in SRH might be decelerating although racial minorities consistently report worse SRH among the general population (i.e., no stratifying by sexual orientation, identity, or behavior). Moreover, racial differences

185

in SRH are partially explained by social status, healthcare services, and health behavior measures (Lo, Howell, & Cheng, 2013). In the United States, racial minorities are less likely to report excellent SRH than their white counterparts and are more likely to report fair or poor health; this substantiates the significance of race in predicting reported appraisals of health statuses (Borrell & Dallo, 2008; Borrell, Kiefe, Williams, Diez-Roux, & Gordon-Larsen, 2006; Hudson, Puterman, Bibbins-Domingo, Matthews, & Adler, 2013; Lo et al., 2013).

SRH has also been used to understand differences in sexual minority status in comparison to heterosexual status (Cochran & Mays, 2007; Thomeer, 2013). Such studies have shown that some sexual minorities have worse SRH compared to their heterosexual counterparts, while other studies have found no difference. Researchers have found that men in same-sex couples were more likely to report excellent or very good health than men in different-sex couples (Heck et al., 2006; Tjepkema, 2008), while an inverse relationship between SRH and sexual minority status has been discovered among women. Thomeer (2013) discovered that respondents who were only behaviorally heterosexual and same-sex people reported similar levels of health. In addition, very little research has considered racial differences in SRH, particularly between Black sexual minorities and their white counterparts. However, no studies have explored within-group heterogeneity to determine whether race is statistically significant in explaining SRH and how sociodemographic characteristics interact with race to explain SRH among racially diverse sexual minority populations. Furthermore, no studies have assessed within group heterogeneity among Black sexual minorities in specifically.

The current study employs data from a 2010 study that examined SRH among Black sexual minorities (Social Justice Sexuality Project, "SJS Project"). The SJS Project is one of the largest community-based national surveys of Black, Latina/o, and Asian Pacific Islander, and multiracial sexual minorities aged 18 and older. Black sexual minorities occupy several different social statuses that are important in understanding how health is shaped among sexual minority populations. Thus, we utilize an intersectional approach by recognizing that sexual minority populations are not homogenous and that assessing the role of race in explaining SRH is a step toward understanding the heterogeneity among sexual minorities. Furthermore, contextualizing the experience of Black sexual minorities requires specific identification of divergent lived experiences, which can be achieved quantitatively by exploring heterogeneity within Black sexual minority populations. The rationale for focusing attention on the SRH of Black sexual minorities include, but are not limited to: (1) the health of Black sexual minorities has largely been viewed within public health through the lens of sexual health and sexual risk behaviors (e.g., HIV) in recent years, fueling continued fixation on Black sexuality as a means for social control; (2) sociodemographic variations among Black sexual minorities has been largely an overlooked area of investigation; (3) understanding variations in SRH can produce a baseline measurement of how Black sexual minorities view their own health, outside of medicalized approaches. Thus, this could assist in producing person-centered knowledge in which Black sexual minorities can facilitate the development of targeted efforts to improve their own health; and (4) research on sexual minority populations has increasingly emphasized the need to apply nuanced research approaches that shed light on sociodemographic variation among sexual minorities, which is vital for achieving health equity among sexual minorities (Gates, 2013; Institute of Medicine, 2011; Kertzner, Meyer, Frost, & Stirratt, 2009; Wong, Schrager, Holloway, Meyer, & Kipke, 2013). The remainder of this chapter includes justification for the application of intersectionality theory to this secondary data analysis, a description of the methods used and the findings of this study, a discussion of the results, and suggestions for future health disparities research.

INTERSECTIONALITY THEORY

Rooted in the histories of Black women in the United States, Black feminist scholars and activists have complicated notions of single identity issues (e.g., gender, race, sexuality, and class) that white feminists often employed, emphasizing that there is no hierarchy of identity and oppression (hooks, 1982; Lorde, 1984). It was Sojourner Truth who reportedly asked, "Ain't I a Woman" at the 1851 Ohio Women's Rights Convention where she challenged notions of single identity oppression and discussed her experiences as not just a Black *person* or a *woman*, but a *Black woman.* Over 100 years later, the women of the Combahee River Collective highlighted sexual and class oppression (Combahee River Collective, 1977). In 1989, Kimberle Crenshaw called this notion of power, identity, and oppression, "intersectionality." Harris and Bartlow (2015) explain that intersectionality refers to how "race, class, gender, sexual orientation, age, religion, and other locations of social group membership impact lived experiences and social relations. The term emphasizes the mobility of social group identities and locations, not simply of their appearances in individual bodies" (p. 261).

Intersectionality is not just a theoretical framework that improves comprehension of intersecting identities, it is also a methodology that helps the researcher take these identities into account during data collection and analysis. This is particularly the case in examining the experiences of Black lesbian, gay, bisexual, and transgender people of color, who often experience multiple and simultaneous forms of marginalization. Some Black LGBT individuals experience not only racism within LGBT communities and homophobia and transphobia within communities of color, but some lesbians and other same-gender-loving women of color experience racism, homophobia, sexism, transphobia, and misogyny. Furthermore, some Black elderly LGBT experience age discrimination within both LGBT and Black communities. Using an intersectional approach to research aids in understanding the experiences of Blacks who have socially stigmatized identities such as racial minority and sexual minority.

Recent research utilizing an intersectional framework notes the resilience that Black LGBT often have developed as a result of their experiences with different group memberships. Fredriksen-Goldsen's (2011) research on resiliency and discrimination among elderly LGBT adults showed that racial minorities, particularly Black elderly LGBT folks, expressed unique forms of resiliency. Meyer (2010) found that LGB people of color have positive racial, ethnic, and sexual identities which could potentially explain why primary group membership (i.e., the group members in which one is primarily socialized and integrates within society) matters. Further research notes that often for Black LGBT individuals, community connectedness and sociopolitical involvement within communities are more likely to be dependent on their experiences within LGBT communities than their experiences within Black communities (Harris & Battle, 2013; Harris, Battle, Pastrana, & Daniels, 2013, 2015). However, this research begs the following question: Does primary group membership for one's racial identity matter more than one's sexual identity? While it is important to recognize that identities can change considerably across the life-course, typically one can easily identify a group membership for which they first experienced discrimination. Consequently, examining identity through an intersectional lens can facilitate understanding the contextual drivers that shape Black LGBT individuals' appraisal of their health.

The goal of this study was to understand SRH among Black sexual minorities across the nation. Since very little published research exists about racial differences or SRH among Black sexual minority populations, the following analyses are exploratory in nature. We center Black sexual minorities by comparing other racial/ethnic groups to Black sexual minorities in terms of SRH. Additionally, we conduct gender-stratified analyses illuminating an intersectional perspective on the gendered and racial/ethnic dynamics of SRH within sexual minority populations.

METHODS

Sample and Procedures

The current study did not have to obtain IRB approval because this study involves secondary data analysis of de-identifiable respondents. This secondary data analysis used data from the 2010 Social Justice Sexuality Project (SJS Project). The purpose of the SJS project was to collect data on the experiences of sexual minorities of color in the following five areas: racial and sexual identity, physical and mental health, family, religion and spirituality, and sociopolitical involvement. Data collection efforts were employed to create a dataset that included an oversample of racial minorities. Data were collected from over 5,500 respondents throughout the United States (including Washington, DC, and Puerto Rico) from January 2010 to December 2010. The survey was administered in both English and Spanish. Several data collection strategies were used including venue-based sampling, snowball sampling, the Internet, and partnerships with community-based organizations, activists and opinion leaders. The dataset does not permit stratification by venue type and therefore, we did not do so in our analyses. The venues were primarily LGBT people of color Pride marches, parades, religious gatherings, festivals, senior events, and small house parties across the nation. The total sample consists of 4,953 valid surveys. We focused our analyses on both spectrums of SRH, as other researchers using SRH as a population level indicator have done previously. SRH is a 5-point Likert scale in which most researchers focus on either excellent or fair/poor reports of SRH. The current analyses specifically focus on a subsample of respondents who had complete data for the outcome variables of fair/poor or excellent SRH respectively yielding an analytic sample N = 2,167. This categorization follows standard approaches for studying SRH. If individuals did not report excellent SRH they were coded as 0 and excellent SRH was coded as 1; and the same was done for fair/poor SRH. Subsequent sensitivity analyses comparing our analytic sample to the entire sample of respondents indicated no statistically significant differences between those having complete information on our outcome measures compared to individuals that were missing data.

MEASURES

Dependent Variable

Self-Rated Health

For self-reported health status, respondents rated their health on a 5-point Likert scale from poor to excellent based on a single question: "In general, would you say your health is . . .?" Respondents could choose from: excellent, very good, good, fair, and poor. Consistent with previous research, we combined fair and poor for all racial groups, given that the number of respondents in each was relatively low (Frankenberg & Jones, 2004; Idler & Benyamini, 1997; Thomeer, 2013). SRH as a health indicator has usefulness for clinical, practice, and public health policy for its predictive ability among various sociodemographic groups.

Independent Variable

Race

Race was assessed using the question, "Which of the following racial groups comes closest to which you identify (choose all that apply)?" Respondents had the choice of responding to the following categories: Black, Latino/Hispanic, Asian Pacific Islander, Multiracial, Native Americans, white, and other. In our first model approach, we exclusively focus on the Black subsample, particularly Black women. Other models explicitly focus on comparing Blacks to other racial/ethnic groups (e.g., Latinos, Asian Americans, whites).

Covariates

Sex

Sex was assessed by the question, "What was the sex reported on your original birth certificate?" Respondents were able to choose from: male, female, unsure (not included in our analyses), which was coded accordingly as: male = 0 and female = 1.

Educational Attainment

Educational attainment was measured by the question, "What is the highest level of schooling you have completed?" Respondents were given the following response choices: less than high school; high school diploma or GED; some college, no degree; associates degree; bachelor's degree; some graduate/professional school; or graduate/professional degree. We sorted educational attainment into three categories: high school diploma/GED or less = 0; some college = 1; and bachelor's degree or higher = 2.

Health Insurance

Health insurance status was evaluated by the question, "Do you currently have health insurance?" This item was dichotomized as yes = 1 and no = 0.

Relationship Status

Relationship status was gauged by the question, "What is your current relationship status?" Respondents could choose from the following categories: not partnered; partnered with someone of the same sex; partnered with someone of a different sex; married to a same-sex partner, including civil union and/or domestic partnership; married to a different sex partner, including civil union and/or domestic partnership; and other. This item was dichotomized as single = 1 and partnered = 0.

Income

Household income was assessed by the question, "Including all income sources, what do you estimate was your household income last year?" Respondents could choose from one of 12 categories. We took the log of income to reflect income's curvilinear association with health (Ecob & Davey Smith, 1999).

Age

Age was reported in years and treated as continuous. Respondents ranged in age from eighteen to ninety-one years old.

Analytic Approach

We first calculated descriptive statistics for each variable, stratified by respondents' racial identification (Table 12.1). We then calculated simple bivariate analyses between study measures, in which we conducted x^2 tests for categorical variables and t tests for continuous variables comparing racial minority groups to Whites (Gee, Ryan, Laflamme, & Holt, 2006). Then, we fit two series of regression models. The first series of regression models assessed reporting of excellent SRH. Three models were included in each series of regressions: (1) all respondents; (2) only male respondents; and (3) only female respondents. Log Poisson regression models were conducted, which allowed us to produce prevalence ratios (PR) with corresponding 95% confidence intervals. In our case, there were more than 20 percent of respondents reporting both excellent and fair or poor SRH; thus, substantiating our decision to utilize PRs. STATA 13.0 was utilized for all analyses in which we employed STATA's GLM package (for the binomial family with unbiased standard error estimates) for all logistic regression models (StataCorp, 2013).

RESULTS

Table 12.1 displays characteristics of the study sample as well as results from bivariate analyses. For study measures, the distribution of respondents was roughly similar between racial groups. Bivariate analyses revealed SRH, income and age to be strongly significant among all racial minority groups (P < 0.001 respectively). Table 12.2 provides analyses exploring sociodemographic contributions to SRH among the Black subsample solely. Among sociodemographic characteristics, in Model 1 women were statistically less likely to rate their health as excellent (PR= 0.66, 95% CI [0.53, 0.83]; those with some college were statistically more likely to report excellent SRH

Table 12.1 Descriptive Statistics of Participants by Race: Social Justice Sexuality Project, 2010 (N = 4091)

	White (n = 914)	Black (n = 1445)		Latino/Hispanic (n = 619)		Asian American/Pacific Islander (n = 250)		Native American (n = 75)		Multiracial (n = 508)		Other (n = 280)	
	No. or Mean (SD)	No. or Mean (SD)	t Value or x^2 Statistic	No. or Mean (SD)	t Value or x^2 Statistic	No. or Mean (SD)	t Value or x^2 Statistic	No. or Mean (SD)	t Value or x^2 Statistic	No. or Mean (SD)	t Value or x^2 Statistic	No. or Mean (SD)	t Value or x^2 Statistic
Self-Rated Health			$x^2 =$ 560.00***		$x^2 =$ 250.00***		$x^2 =$ 100.00***		$x^2 =$ 300.00***		$x^2 =$ 200.00***		$x^2 =$ 100.00***
Excellent	130	302		132		55		21		113		56	
Very Good	368	510		228		82		24		166		92	
Good	304	450		207		82		21		180		97	
Fair/Poor	92	132		52		31		9		49		25	
Sex			$x^2 =$ 20.74***		$x^2 =$ 15.27***		$x^2 =$ 11.24*		$x^2 =$ 3.11		$x^2 =$ 13.65**		$x^2 =$ 8.74
Male	448	766		324		127		41		231		139	
Female	446	628		295		123		34		277		141	
Educational Attainment			$x^2 =$ 21.77**		$x^2 =$ 16.41*		$x^2 =$ 13.69		$x^2 =$ 7.78		$x^2 =$ 13.12		$x^2 =$ 7.59
>High School Diploma/GED	321	545		284		91		37		232		120	
Some college/Associates Degree	260	440		198		94		20		146		89	
<Bachelor's Degree	313	409		137		65		18		130		71	
Health Insurance			$x^2 =$ 4.51		$x^2 =$ 9.31		$x^2 =$ 3.10		$x^2 =$ 5.59		$x^2 =$ 10.09*		$x^2 =$ 7.96*
Yes	714	1 135		450		211		53		381		220	
No	180	259		169		39		22		127		60	
Relationship Status			$x^2 =$ 16.54**		$x^2 =$ 1.91		$x^2 =$ 7.85		$x^2 =$ 4.39		$x^2 =$ 2.29		$x^2 =$ 2.03
Single	340	698		265		127		37		231		108	
Partnered	554	696		354		123		38		277		172	
Log Income, $	1.94 (0.76)	1.94 (0.76)	t = 95.64***	1.76 (0.88)	t = 49.60***	1.84 (0.82)	t = 35.03***	1.87 (0.71)	t = 22.31***	1.82 (0.85)	t = 47.61***	1.92 (0.72)	t = 43.60***
Age, y	38.48 (14.40)	38.19 (12.49)	t = 114.44***	33.20 (10.50)	t = 79.25***	30.74 (10.28)	t = 46.98***	37.79 (14.72)	t = 21.77***	33.18 (11.95)	t = 61.94***	34.80 (12.50)	t = 46.23***

Note: Descriptive Statistics are for respondents answering the self-rated health question.
*P < 0.05; **P < 0.01; ***P < 0.001; significance tests between racial/ethnic groups comparing to Whites for each measure separately.

Table 12.2 Log Poisson Regression Models Predicting Excellent and Fair/Poor Self-Rated Health (Black subsample): Social Justice Sexuality Project, 2010

	(1) Black Excellent Self-Rated Health	(2) Black Men Excellent Self-Rated Health	(3) Black Women Excellent Self-Rated Health	(4) Black Fair/Poor Self-Rated Health	(5) Black Women Fair/Poor Self-Rated Health	(6) Black Men Fair/Poor Self-Rated Health
Gender						
Male (ref)	—	—	—	—	—	—
Female	0.67*** (0.532–0.836)			1.24 (0.880–1.756)		
Health Provider						
Yes (ref)	—	—	—	—	—	—
No	0.72 (0.522–1.003)	0.89 (0.609–1.309)	0.49* (0.272–0.884)	1.25 (0.734–2.128)	1.07 (0.510–2.242)	1.53 (0.731–3.208)
Educational Attainment						
< High School (ref)						
Some College	1.34* (1.057–1.693)	1.50** (1.120–2.000)	1.12 (0.745–1.685)	0.66 (0.432–1.020)	0.49* (0.265–0.924)	0.88 (0.492–1.589)
College Graduate	1.09 (0.831–1.424)	1.28 (0.920–1.793)	0.84 (0.527–1.329)	0.92 (0.619–1.354)	0.90 (0.526–1.542)	0.94 (0.536–1.663)
Age (in years)	0.98*** (0.968–0.987)	0.97*** (0.961–0.984)	0.99 (0.972–1.002)	1.03*** (1.018–1.045)	1.03** (1.011–1.052)	1.03*** (1.016–1.052)
Health Insurance						
Yes (ref)	—	—	—	—	—	—
No	1.05 (0.774–1.418)	0.87 (0.593–1.284)	1.40 (0.885–2.213)	1.34 (0.811–2.204)	1.60 (0.823–3.093)	1.10 (0.531–2.286)
Relationship Status						
Partnered (ref)						
Single	1.21 (0.974–1.499)	1.07 (0.829–1.383)	1.48* (1.032–2.113)	1.32 (0.933–1.853)	1.29 (0.801–2.086)	1.37 (0.828–2.252)
Current Smoking Status						
No (ref)	—	—	—	—	—	—
Yes	0.79 (0.605–1.038)	0.86 (0.626–1.176)	0.67 (0.412–1.087)	1.19 (0.810–1.749)	0.68 (0.373–1.240)	1.96** (1.192–3.219)
Constant	0.51** (0.341–0.763)	0.60* (0.371–0.971)	0.26*** (0.140–0.495)	0.02*** (0.011–0.042)	0.03*** (0.012–0.086)	0.01*** (0.006–0.037)
Observations	1,322	722	600	1,335	607	728

***p<0.001, **p<0.01, *p<0.05

(PR= 1.33, 95% CI [1.05, 1.69]) compared to their counterparts who had up to high school; and younger age was associated with a lower prevalence of reporting excellent SRH (PR= 0.97, 95% CI [0.96, 0.98]). In Model 2, there were two measures that were statistically significant: some college education and age. Model 3 revealed that not having a health provider and being single were the only significant measures for Black women's excellent SRH. Model 4 revealed that age was statistically significant in predicting fair/poor SRH among Black respondents. Model 5, assessing Black men's SRH, revealed that older respondents were at increased risk of identifying fair/poor SRH and current smokers were more likely to endorse fair/poor SRH. Model 6, assessing Black women's SRH, identified that having some college education decreased prevalence of identifying fair/poor SRH compared to their counterparts having only a high school diploma or less of educational attainment. Also older Black women had an increased prevalence of identifying fair/poor SRH than younger Black women.

When controlling for sociodemographic variables, we see that there are no significant racial differences in SRH between Black people and white Americans (Table 12.3) and Latina/o people (Table 12.4). However, there were significant differences in SRH between Black people and Asian Americans (Table 12.5). Specifically, Asian Americans had a higher prevalence of fair/poor SRH than Black Americans overall. Subgroup analyses revealed that significant differences in SRH varied by gender. Asian American men were more than 2 times more likely to report fair/poor SRH than Black men. There were no significant differences in SRH among Black and Asian American women.

DISCUSSION

Although multiple studies have examined differences in SRH with respect to sexual minority status in comparison to heterosexual individuals (Buchmueller & Carpenter, 2010; Heck, Sell, & Gorin, 2006; Liu, Reczek, & Brown, 2013; Ortiz-Hernández et al., 2009; Thomeer, 2013; Tjepkema, 2008), very few studies have explicitly examined the influence of race in predicting SRH among sexual minorities. This study is an effort to address this gap in the literature. Within group analyses among the Black subsample demonstrated that some sociodemographic characteristics are extremely salient when considering SRH. Particularly having at least some college education, age, and then specifically among Black women having a health provider and being single. Our findings indicate that Blacks do not have a higher prevalence of identifying fair/poor SRH and decreased prevalence of identifying excellent SRH for the most part. Interestingly analyses comparing Asian Americans to

Table 12.3 Log Poisson Regression Models Predicting Excellent and Fair/Poor Self-Rated Health (White/Black Analyses): Social Justice Sexuality Project, 2010

	(1) All Excellent Self-Rated Health	(2) Men Excellent Self-Rated Health	(3) Women Excellent Self-Rated Health	(1) All Fair/Poor Self-Rated Health	(2) Men Fair/Poor Self-Rated Health	(3) Women Fair/Poor Self-Rated Health
Race						
Black (ref)	—	—	—	—	—	—
White	1.04 (0.879–1.222)	0.99 (0.811–1.217)	1.11 (0.842–1.458)	1.04 (0.803–1.354)	0.97 (0.644–1.450)	1.11 (0.786–1.575)
Gender						
Male (ref)	—			—		
Female	0.66*** (0.556–0.786)			1.30 (0.995–1.700)		
Health Provider						
Yes (ref)	—	—	—	—	—	—
No	0.70** (0.540–0.904)	0.75 (0.542–1.024)	0.62* (0.403–0.953)	1.10 (0.731–1.658)	1.64 (0.886–3.031)	0.79 (0.464–1.349)
Educational Attainment						
< High School (ref)	—	—	—	—	—	—
Some College	1.38*** (1.143–1.659)	1.52*** (1.208–1.912)	1.15 (0.833–1.587)	0.58** (0.412–0.809)	0.69 (0.427–1.120)	0.51** (0.317–0.819)
College Graduate or above	1.26* (1.019–1.546)	1.39* (1.072–1.812)	1.10 (0.783–1.551)	0.87 (0.634–1.182)	0.84 (0.526–1.343)	0.90 (0.589–1.367)
Age (in years)	0.98*** (0.974–0.988)	0.97*** (0.961–0.980)	1.00 (0.985–1.008)	1.02*** (1.011–1.031)	1.03*** (1.018–1.045)	1.01 (0.999–1.028)
Health Insurance						
Yes (ref)	—	—	—	—	—	—
No	0.97 (0.761–1.225)	0.83 (0.612–1.123)	1.23 (0.848–1.799)	1.38 (0.944–2.020)	1.20 (0.665–2.153)	1.58 (0.980–2.549)
Relationship Status						
Partnered (ref)	—	—	—	—	—	—
Single	1.11 (0.940–1.306)	1.00 (0.826–1.222)	1.29 (0.981–1.692)	1.34* (1.027–1.755)	1.30 (0.871–1.954)	1.39 (0.975–1.995)
Current Smoking Status						
No (ref)	—	—	—	—	—	—
Yes	0.93 (0.776–1.125)	0.94 (0.748–1.176)	0.90 (0.658–1.233)	1.34* (1.014–1.763)	1.64* (1.086–2.467)	1.16 (0.799–1.689)

*** p<0.001, ** p<0.01, * p<0.05

Table 12.4　Log Poisson Regression Models Predicting Excellent and Fair/Poor Self-Rated Health (Asian/Black Analyses): Social Justice Sexuality Project, 2010

	(1) Asian Excellent Self-Rated Health	(2) Asian Men Excellent Self-Rated Health	(3) Asian Women Excellent Self-Rated Health	(1) Asian Women Fair/Poor Self-Rated Health	(2) Asian Fair/Poor Self-Rated Health	(3) Asian Men Fair/Poor Self-Rated Health
Race						
Black (ref)	—	—	—	—	—	—
Asian	0.87	0.84	0.90	1.14	1.68**	2.23**
	(0.661–1.140)	(0.594–1.179)	(0.574–1.420)	(0.620–2.083)	(1.153–2.433)	(1.376–3.621)
Gender						
Male (ref)						
Female	0.66***	—	—	—	1.08	—
	(0.536–0.812)				(0.794–1.461)	
Health Provider						
Yes (ref)						
No	0.69*	0.84	0.47*	1.43	1.50	1.54
	(0.511–0.938)	(0.590–1.199)	(0.264–0.835)	(0.751–2.714)	(0.965–2.331)	(0.847–2.794)
Educational Attainment						
< High School (ref)						
Some College	1.35**	1.48**	1.21	0.48*	0.60**	0.71
	(1.088–1.685)	(1.127–1.939)	(0.828–1.762)	(0.267–0.850)	(0.409–0.884)	(0.415–1.205)
College Graduate	1.14	1.29	0.97	0.87	0.91	0.95
	(0.888–1.471)	(0.939–1.760)	(0.631–1.485)	(0.533–1.432)	(0.641–1.299)	(0.578–1.569)
Age (in years)	0.98***	0.98***	0.99*	1.03**	1.03***	1.03**
	(0.971–0.988)	(0.965–0.987)	(0.971–1.000)	(1.009–1.047)	(1.014–1.039)	(1.010–1.043)
Health Insurance						
Yes (ref)						
No	1.04	0.94	1.24	1.53	1.23	1.01
	(0.785–1.390)	(0.661–1.346)	(0.786–1.961)	(0.816–2.888)	(0.784–1.927)	(0.537–1.886)
Relationship Status						
Partnered (ref)						
Single	1.16	1.06	1.36	1.20	1.33	1.51
	(0.955–1.417)	(0.837–1.345)	(0.977–1.884)	(0.769–1.858)	(0.983–1.799)	(0.970–2.344)
Current Smoking Status						
No (ref)						
Yes	0.81	0.90	0.67	0.70	1.13	1.70*
	(0.633–1.037)	(0.670–1.201)	(0.433–1.041)	(0.407–1.201)	(0.802–1.587)	(1.092–2.631)
Constant	0.48***	0.52**	0.28***	0.04***	0.03***	0.02***
	(0.330–0.709)	(0.329–0.838)	(0.155–0.498)	(0.015–0.088)	(0.015–0.051)	(0.009–0.047)
Observations	1,560	843	717	727	1,576	849

*** p<0.001, ** p<0.01, * p<0.05

Table 12.5 Log Poisson Regression Models Predicting Excellent and Fair/Poor Self-Rated Health (Latino/Black Analyses): Social Justice Sexuality Project, 2010

	(1) Latino Excellent Self-Rated Health	(2) Latino Men Excellent Self-Rated Health	(3) Latina Women Excellent Self-Rated Health	(1) Latina Women Fair/Poor Self-Rated Health	(2) Latino Fair/Poor Self-Rated Health	(3) Latino Men Fair/Poor Self-Rated Health
Race						
Black (ref)	—	—	—	—	—	—
Latino	1.00 (0.829–1.214)	1.01 (0.805–1.272)	0.99 (0.707–1.381)	1.21 (0.793–1.833)	0.95 (0.690–1.295)	0.70 (0.438–1.128)
Gender						
Male (ref)	—	—	—	—	—	—
Female	0 64*** (0.531–0.777)	—	—	—	1.38* (1.033–1.838)	—
Health Provider						
Yes (ref)	—	—	—	—	—	—
No	0.73* (0.554–0.961)	0.81 (0.580–1.135)	0.61* (0.381–0.971)	0.86 (0.476–1.552)	1.23 (0.825–1.844)	1.74* (1.017–2.986)
Educational Attainment						
< High School (ref)						
Some College	1.35** (1.103–1.655)	1.51** (1.175–1.934)	1.12 (0.788–1.581)	0.64 (0.399–1.013)	0.68* (0.479–0.958)	0.74 (0.442–1.236)
College Graduate	1.24 (0.990–1.554)	1.45** (1.103–1.918)	0.96 (0.652–1.424)	0.79 (0.495–1.268)	0.82 (0.585–1.163)	0.86 (0.518–1.421)
Age (in years)	0.98*** (0.976–0.992)	0.98*** (0.968–0.987)	0.99 (0.981–1.007)	1.02 (1.000–1.034)	1.02*** (1.011–1.036)	1.03*** (1.015–1.049)
Health Insurance						
Yes (ref)	—	—	—	—	—	—
No	1.00 (0.775–1.302)	0.87 (0.626–1.210)	1.26 (0.836–1.893)	1.64 (0.957–2.817)	1.39 (0.940–2.043)	1.21 (0.705–2.075)
Relationship Status						
Partnered (ref)	—	—	—	—	—	—
Single	1.14 (0.951–1.360)	0.96 (0.781–1.180)	1.53* (1.131–2.063)	1.28 (0.865–1.888)	1.35* (1.015–1.794)	1.52 (0.980–2.370)
Current Smoking Status						
No (ref)	—	—	—	—	—	—
Yes	0.82 (0.660–1.013)	0.82 (0.629–1.059)	0.79 (0.552–1.141)	0.62* (0.387–0.988)	1.14 (0.834–1.553)	2.10*** (1.389–3.183)
Constant	0.40*** (0.281–0.582)	0.52** (0.343–0.794)	0.18*** (0.102–0.331)	0.06*** (0.028–0.124)	0.03*** (0.016–0.050)	0.02*** (0.007–0.035)
Observations	1,913	1,030	883	892	1,932	1,040

*** p<0.001, ** p<0.01, * p<0.05

their Black counterparts, revealed that both Asian American men and women were more likely to report fair/poor SRH compared to their Black counterparts. This novel finding could be explained by many factors. For example, future research should assess immigration processes such as country of origin and variations in acculturation processes once in the United States; especially in terms of length of time in the United States. It is well documented that racial/ethnic immigrant populations experience American society differently than non-immigrant populations (e.g., varying experiences of interpersonal and institutional discrimination) and thus this could be extremely salient when comparing Asian Americans to their Black counterparts. Interestingly, sociodemographic characteristics in our regression models revealed patterns which mirrored those previously found in the literature, namely, age and educational attainment.

These results raise important directions for future research, including identifying mechanisms through which other societal influences may mediate the relationship between race and SRH which will provide greater insight into the heterogeneity among sexual minorities. As it has been identified that SRH is only partially explained by healthcare related factors (Lo et al., 2013), it is important to consider other social issues that may explain SRH more precisely than race alone. Recent research examining the important role by which stigma and discrimination can negatively impact the health of sexual minorities is one such direction (Doyle & Molix, 2015; Earnshaw, Rosenthal, & Lang, 2016; Gattis & Larson, 2016). Black sexual minorities may be at increased risk of psychological impairment and physical health by virtue of simultaneously occupying multiple marginalized social positions, such as facing discrimination within sexual minority communities and within their racial primary group membership. It has been postulated (Nieblas, Hughes, Andrews, & Relf, 2015) that this in turn, may result in internalized racism and homophobia, although this has not been assessed in terms of SRH among Black sexual minorities. It is also possible that there are underlying mechanisms at play, such as resiliency, which can help researchers, community members, and policy makers understand these counterintuitive findings.

A resilience perspective counteracts the narrative of Black sexual minorities being at increased risk for *double jeopardy* (the state of having multiple marginalized identities resulting in increased stress that manifests in riskier health behaviors; Herrick, Stall, Goldhammer, Egan, & Mayer, 2014). Some of this work has suggested that there might be other factors impacting one's appraisal of one's health in relation to other pressing issues (Herrick et al., 2014). It is also important to recognize that resiliency may manifest differently depending on contextual factors and while our study includes a large sample, our findings are not generalizable. The SJS Project did not ask many questions about sexual health and since Black sexual minorities are disproportionately burdened with negative health outcomes relative to sexual health (e.g., HIV and other STIs), it could be surmised that if such questions were included along with SRH then the results might differ. Nonetheless, within the public health literature, resilience is a relatively nascent area of inquiry in sexual minority health (Herrick et al., 2014), and unfortunately the SJS Project did not collect information on resiliency constructs previously used within the literature.

Future research is needed not only in terms of resilience and SRH in general, but also to determine if there are specific elements of resilience among Black sexual minority communities that can inform the general population (e.g., non-sexual minority population). Moreover, in applying concepts of resilience it is extremely important to approach such discussions with appropriate cultural sensitivity and structural competency, so as to not perpetuate pathologizing ideas concerning racial minorities (e.g., racialized notions of survival of the fittest). For example, historically, scientists suggested that Blacks have extra bones which contributed to athletic prowess. Such negative racialized suggestions could be used if work seeking to integrate resilience are not applied with cultural specificity and structural competency. Future research should explore other influences such as nativity and length of time in the United States among Black sexual minorities to assess whether this impacts appraisal of health; these influences have been shown to be important among the general population (Huh, Prause, & Dooley, 2008). The acculturation processes of Black foreign-born sexual minorities may impact their appraisal of their health differentially than those born in the United States (Todorova et al., 2013). Additionally, research should assess how income and age moderate the relationship between SRH among racial sexual minorities in which not only merely stratifying by race is considered by the interaction between race and these factors. The findings demonstrated that there is variability within Black sexual minority populations. Furthermore, they highlight differences between Blacks and other racial groups in terms of SRH. Contextualizing among sexual minority populations can produce the knowledge necessary for developing specified targeted interventions aimed at decreasing disparities within Black sexual minority populations.

REFERENCES

Borrell, L., & Dallo, F. (2008). Self-rated health and race among Hispanic and Non-Hispanic adults. *Journal of Immigrant and Minority Health, 10*(3), 229–238. doi:10.1007/s10903–007–9074–6

Borrell, L. N., Kiefe, C. I., Williams, D. R., Diez-Roux, A., & Gordon-Larsen, P. (2006). Self-reported health, perceived racial discrimination, and skin color in

African Americans in the CARDIA study. *Social Science & Medicine, 63*(6), 1415–1427. doi:10.1016/j.socscimed.2006.04.008

Buchmueller, T., & Carpenter, C. S. (2010). Disparities in health insurance coverage, access, and outcomes for individuals in same-sex versus different-sex relationships, 2000–2007. *American Journal of Public Health, 100*(3), 489–495. doi:10.2105/AJPH.2009.160804

Cochran, S. D., Bandiera, F. C., & Mays, V. M. (2013). Sexual orientation–related differences in tobacco use and secondhand smoke exposure among US adults aged 20 to 59 Years: 2003–2010 National Health and Nutrition Examination Surveys. *American Journal of Public Health, 103*(10), 1837–1844. doi:10.2105/AJPH.2013.301423

Cochran, S. D., Grella, C. E., & Mays, V. M. (2012). Do substance use norms and perceived drug availability mediate sexual orientation differences in patterns of substance use? Results from the California quality of life survey II. *Journal of Studies on Alcohol & Drugs, 73*(4), 675–685.

Cochran, S. D., & Mays, V. M. (2007). Physical health complaints among lesbians, gay men, and bisexual and homosexually experienced heterosexual individuals: Results from the California quality of life survey. *American Journal of Public Health, 97*(11), 2048–2055. doi:10.2105/AJPH.2006.087254

Cochran, S. D., Mays, V. M., Alegria, M., Ortega, A. N., & Takeuchi, D. (2007). Mental health and substance use disorders among Latino and Asian American lesbian, gay, and bisexual adults. *Journal of Consulting and Clinical Psychology, 75*(5), 785–794. doi:10.1037/0022–006X.75.5.785

Combahee River Collective. (1977). *The combahee river collective statement.* Retrieved from http://circuitous.org/scraps/combahee.html

Doyle, D. M., & Molix, L. (2015). Perceived discrimination and social relationship functioning among sexual minorities: Structural stigma as a moderating factor. *Analyses of Social Issues and Public Policy, 15*(1), 357–381. doi:10.1111/asap.12098

Duncan, D., Wolin, K., Scharoun-Lee, M., Ding, E., Warner, E., & Bennett, G. (2011). Does perception equal reality? Weight misperception in relation to weight-related attitudes and behaviors among overweight and obese US adults. *International Journal of Behavioral Nutrition and Physical Activity, 8*(1), 20.

Duncan, D. T., & Hatzenbuehler, M. L. (2013). Lesbian, gay, bisexual, and transgender hate crimes and suicidality among a population-based sample of sexual-minority adolescents in Boston. *American Journal of Public Health*, e1–e7. doi:10.2105/AJPH.2013.301424

Duncan, D. T., Hatzenbuehler, M. L., & Johnson, R. M. (2013). Neighborhood-level LGBT hate crimes and current illicit drug use among sexual minority youth. *Drug and Alcohol Dependence, Article in Press.* doi:10.1016/j.drugalcdep.2013.11.001

Earnshaw, V. A., Rosenthal, L., & Lang, S. M. (2016). Stigma, activism, and well-being among people living with HIV. *AIDS Care, 28*(6), 717–721. doi:10.1080/09540121.2015.1124978

Ecob, R., & Davey Smith, G. (1999). Income and health: What is the nature of the relationship? *Social Science & Medicine, 48*(5), 693–705. doi:10.1016/S0277–9536(98)00385–2

Frankenberg, E., & Jones, N. R. (2004). Self-rated health and mortality: Does the relationship extend to a low income setting? *Journal of Health and Social Behavior, 45*(4), 441–452. doi:10.1177/002214650404500406

Gates, G. (2013). Demographics and LGBT health. *Journal of Health and Social Behavior, 54*(1), 72–74. doi:10.1177/0022146512474429

Gattis, M. N., & Larson, A. (2016). Perceived racial, sexual identity, and homeless status-related discrimination among Black adolescents and young adults experiencing homelessness: Relations with depressive symptoms and suicidality. *American Journal of Orthopsychiatry, 86*(1), 79–90. doi:10.1037/ort0000096

Gee, G. C., Ryan, A., Laflamme, D. J., & Holt, J. (2006). Self-reported discrimination and mental health status among African descendants, Mexican Americans, and other Latinos in the New Hampshire REACH 2010 initiative: The added dimension of immigration. *American Journal of Public Health, 96*(10), 1821–1828. doi:10.2105/AJPH.2005.080085

Harris, A., & Battle, J. (2013). Unpacking civic engagement: The sociopolitical involvement of same-gender loving Black women. *Journal of Lesbian Studies, 17*(2), 195–207. doi:10.1080/10894160.2012.711679

Harris, A., Battle, J., Pastrana, A., & Daniels, J. (2013). The sociopolitical involvement of Black, Latino, and Asian/Pacific Islander gay and bisexual men. *The Journal of Men's Studies, 21*(3), 236–254. doi:10.3149/jms.2103.236

———. (2015). Feelings of belonging: An exploratory analysis of the sociopolitical involvement of Black, Latina, and Asian/Pacific Islander sexual minority women. *Journal of Homosexuality, 62*(10), 1374–1397. doi:10.1080/00918369.2015.1061360

Hatzenbuehler, M. L., & Keyes, K. M. (2013). Inclusive anti-bullying policies and reduced risk of suicide attempts in lesbian and gay youth. *Journal of Adolescent Health, 53*(1, Supplement), S21–S26. doi:10.1016/j.jadohealth.2012.08.010

Heck, J. E., Sell, R. L., & Gorin, S. S. (2006). Health care access among individuals involved in same-sex relationships. *American Journal of Public Health, 96*(6), 1111–1118. doi:10.2105/AJPH.2005.062661

Herrick, A., Stall, R., Goldhammer, H., Egan, J., & Mayer, K. (2014). Resilience as a research framework and as a cornerstone of prevention research for gay and bisexual men: Theory and evidence. *AIDS and Behavior, 18*(1), 1–9. doi:10.1007/s10461-012-0384-x

hooks, b. (1982). *Ain't I a woman: Black women and feminism*. Boston, MA: South End Press.

Hudson, D., Puterman, E., Bibbins-Domingo, K., Matthews, K. A., & Adler, N. E. (2013). Race, life course socioeconomic position, racial discrimination, depressive symptoms and self-rated health. *Social Science & Medicine, 97*(0), 7–14. doi:10.1016/j.socscimed.2013.07.031

Huh, J., Prause, J., & Dooley, C. D. (2008). The impact of nativity on chronic diseases, self-rated health and comorbidity status of Asian and Hispanic immigrants. *Journal of Immigrant and Minority Health, 10*(2), 103–118. doi:10.1007/s10903-007-9065-7

Idler, E. L., & Benyamini, Y. (1997). Self-rated health and mortality: A review of twenty-seven community studies. *Journal of Health and Social Behavior, 38*(1), 21–37.

Institute of Medicine. (2011). *The health of lesbian, gay, bisexual, and transgender people: Building a foundation for better understanding*: Washington, DC: The National Academies Press.

Kertzner, R. M., Meyer, I. H., Frost, D. M., & Stirratt, M. J. (2009). Social and psychological well-being in lesbians, gay men, and bisexuals: The effects of race, gender, age, and sexual identity. *American Journal of Orthopsychiatry, 79*(4), 500–510. doi:10.1037/a0016848

Liu, H., Reczek, C., & Brown, D. (2013). Same-sex cohabitors and health: The role of race-ethnicity, gender, and socioeconomic status. *Journal of Health and Social Behavior, 54*(1), 25–45. doi:10.1177/0022146512468280

Lo, C., Howell, R., & Cheng, T. (2013). Disparities in Whites' versus Blacks' self-rated health: Social status, health-care services, and health behaviors. *Journal of Community Health, 38*(4), 727–733. doi:10.1007/s10900-013-9671-3

Lorde, A. (1984). *Sister outsider*. Freedom: CA: The Crossing Press.

McLaughlin, K. A., Hatzenbuehler, M. L., Xuan, Z., & Conron, K. J. (2012). Disproportionate exposure to early-life adversity and sexual orientation disparities in psychiatric morbidity. *Child Abuse & Neglect, 36*(9), 645–655. doi:10.1016/j.chiabu.2012.07.004

Nieblas, R., Hughes, L., Andrews, R., & Relf, M. (2015). Reframing and understanding the HIV epidemic in MSM: Masculinity, racism, and homophobia. *Journal of the Association of Nurses in AIDS Care, 26*(5), 514–519. doi:10.1016/j.jana.2015.04.007

Ortiz-Hernández, L., Gómez Tello, B. L., & Valdés, J. (2009). The association of sexual orientation with self-rated health, and cigarette and alcohol use in Mexican adolescents and youths. *Social Science & Medicine, 69*(1), 85–93. doi:10.1016/j.socscimed.2009.03.028

StataCorp. (2013). Stata Statistical Software (Version Release 13). College Station, Texas: StatCorp LP.

Thomeer, M. B. (2013). Sexual minority status and self-rated health: The importance of socioeconomic status, age, and sex. *American Journal of Public Health, 103*(5), 881–888. doi:10.2105/AJPH.2012.301040

Tjepkema, M. (2008). Health care use among gay, lesbian and bisexual Canadians. *Health Reports, 19*(1), 53.

Todorova, I. L. G., Tucker, K. L., Jimenez, M. P., Lincoln, A. K., Arevalo, S., & Falcón, L. M. (2013). Determinants of self-rated health and the role of acculturation: Implications for health inequalities. *Ethnicity & Health, 18*(6), 563–585. doi: 10.1080/13557858.2013.771147

Wong, C., Schrager, S., Holloway, I., Meyer, I., & Kipke, M. (2013). Minority stress experiences and psychological well-being: The impact of support from and connection to social networks within the Los Angeles house and ball communities. *Prevention Science*, 1–12. doi:10.1007/s11121-012-0348-4

Conclusion

This volume has provided an examination of Black lesbian, gay, bisexual, and transgender (LGBT) people's biopsychosocial-spiritual health. It weaves together quantitative data, qualitative narratives, and theoretical critiques of Black LGBT people's health that are presented from both mainstream and radical perspectives. This volume's scholarship covered a range of topics focused on people who are often overlooked or considered deficient in white-centered scholarship. This work intentionally aimed to challenge the status quo of mainstream research and healthcare solutions that have focused too much on Black LGBT people as pathological or at-risk for disease. The chapters in this volume could be conceptualized as having underscored four main components of Black LGBT people's health: (1) identities and social realities, (2) in-depth insight into Black LGBT people's physical and mental health, (3) interventions and treatment strategies within Western paradigms, and (4) creative modes of resistance to systems of oppression.

IDENTITIES AND SOCIAL REALITIES

Black LGBT people's identity conflict management and social realities were explored. Brooks assessed how Black LBT women managed conflict between their intersecting racial and sexual identities among their families-of-origin, religious communities, and in mental healthcare systems. She found that Black LBT women find peace at the intersections of their identities by forming families-of-choice composed of friends and members of the House ballroom community. Black LBT women also reported rejecting homonegative religious messages, embracing personal spirituality, and working toward becoming healthcare providers themselves so that they could help other Black LBT women be healthier.

Black LGBT people's social experiences in healthcare settings, white gay and Black heterosexual communities, the juvenile justice system, and society at large were examined. Dante' Bryant drew attention to the ways in which US medical practitioners often marginalize Black gay and bisexual men in the process of providing healthcare due to implicit Eurocentric and heterosexist operating praxes that blame Black gay and bisexual men for their own health disparities. He theorized that healthcare transformation may be achieved through a process of *pedagogical displacement* enacted in medical training. It is hypothesized that an alternative pedagogical approach that seeks to displace normative ideas and social categories about race and sexuality will challenge developing healthcare providers to have more holistic conceptions of their future patients as well as equip them with skills to better serve Black gay and bisexual men. Lawrence O. Bryant drew attention to the discriminatory experiences of Black gay and bisexual men. He found that these men struggle with racism in white gay contexts, homonegativity in Black communities, and have difficulties accepting their initial same-sex attractions. Yet, these men eventually began to challenge homonegativity and racism by finding social support that bolstered them as Black gay and bisexual men as well as educating others about prejudice.

Robinson provided detail about the hardships and resiliencies of Black LGBT youth along the continuum of juvenile justice system involvement. She highlighted risk factors for being involved in the juvenile justice system (e.g., being in foster care, homelessness, harsh school punishments) as well as how youth often experience violence and discrimination from fellow inmates and correctional officers once they are incarcerated. She also explained how Black LGBT youth use dance and support groups to sustain themselves during their sentences. Finally, she provided individual, institutional, and structural recommendations that focused on creating culturally sensitive and LGBT-affirming environments for Black LGBT youth, including interventions that involve working with their families-of-origin to prevent them from being incarcerated. She also proposed policy that prevents violence, rape, and hormone medication denial for LGBT youth who are in the juvenile justice system.

Haile and her colleagues critiqued the broader conceptualization of racial and sexual inequalities in HIV scholarly literature focused on Black gay and bisexual men. Their major finding that racial and sexual inequalities are often conceptualized in interpersonal domains while neglecting the ways in which these inequities are perpetuated at the structural level suggests that mainstream LGBT health research and policy have yet to challenge institutional biases and discrimination that contribute to health disparities affecting Black

LGBT people in the United States. Overall, these authors provided clear descriptions and critiques of the social environments of Black LGBT people and how their identities influence and are shaped by these social realities.

BLACK LGBT PEOPLE'S PHYSICAL AND MENTAL HEALTH OUTCOMES

New, cutting-edge research about specific physical and mental health outcomes was also presented in this volume. Ortiz and his colleagues investigated the associations between a Black LGB person's self-rated health and sociodemographic statuses. They found that Black lesbian and bisexual women had lower prevalence of rating their health as excellent compared to Black gay men. For Black women, not having a medical healthcare provider negatively impacted their self-rated health, while being single was related to better health. For Black men, having obtained at least some college education was related to better health, while being older was related to poorer health. Poteat and Follins examined the health and healthcare experiences of Black trans men. They found that many of their participants were coping with chronic illnesses such as recurrent tendonitis, migraine headaches, diabetes, and depression. Many of these trans men reported structural barriers such as lack of health insurance and economic difficulties that kept them from receiving treatment for these chronic conditions. However, Black trans men utilized dancing, prayer, and social support networks to help them manage their health. Lassiter's systematic literature review found that Black bisexual women experienced a range of physical and mental health conditions (e.g., STIs, reproductive coercion, depression, posttraumatic stress disorder) more than their heterosexual counterparts. Many of these women nevertheless remain resilient by engaging in bisexual advocacy and eliminating non-affirming personal relationships. These novel findings about Black LGBT people's specific health outcomes provide a cursory view into the type of medical and psychological issues—beyond HIV—that specifically impact Black LGBT people's lives in the United States. More research is needed to determine the specific courses and treatment possibilities for these conditions.

CULTURALLY SPECIFIC INTERVENTIONS WITHIN WESTERN MODALITIES

A few of the authors in this volume presented detailed accounts of their work with Black LGBT people that blended culturally specific approaches with traditional Western medicine. Haynes and Dale described the development of a psychotherapy group for Black gay and bisexual men. This group was based on the foundations of intersectionality and traditional group therapy principles; it aimed at helping Black gay and bisexual men build resilience. Topics explored in the group included intersecting racial, sexual, and gender identities; community; sex and dating; and religion. This group helped the men develop holistic identity integration and increase their social support. Johnson and McElroy outlined the creation of a group therapy intervention for Black women who were at-risk for or suffering from breast cancer. The group was designed in accordance with womanist theory and public health critical race methodology. It aimed to increase Black women's health literacy for breast cancer, facilitate social support, provide a forum for Black women to discuss their general and health-specific concerns, and offer a context for discussions about the intersection of spiritual and physical health. While utilizing the Western modality of group therapy, these interventions successfully prioritized the culturally relevant aspects of Black LGB people's lives to create culturally comprehensive health initiatives.

CREATIVE MODES OF RESISTANCE TO SYSTEMS OF OPPRESSION

Finally, some authors in this volume went beyond Western paradigms and presented the conception of health outside of the status quo. Williams offered an account of the creation of a sacred sexual space called Black Funk, that occupied both physical and virtual realms (via the Internet). Black Funk served as a maroon society outside of white supremacist, heteropatriarchal norms and allowed Black bisexual men to gather to use their sexual energies to form sacred and sensual connections. These connections helped them grapple with issues of sexual health, overall well-being, and mental decolonization. Mosley and colleagues reported on the ways in which Black bisexual people resist the status quo via defining themselves outside of monosexual frameworks, educating others on the intersection of Blackness and bisexuality, and by holding Black heterosexual people and white LGBT people accountable for their homonegativity and racism, respectively. Black bisexual people's resistance has also taken shape through forming Black bisexual communities and engaging in non-heteronormative romantic relationships. However, Mosley and colleagues emphasized that two of the most revolutionary ways that Black bisexual people resisted systems of oppression was by choosing to prioritize the love of themselves over others' acceptance and approval, while also giving love to deserving others in the face of biphobia. These modes of resistance highlight that Black bisexual people do not belong to solely heterosexual or homosexual worlds and thus create radical alternate spaces that do not adhere to monosexual norms or rigid ways of being defined by oppressive systems.

FINAL THOUGHTS

This volume has highlighted the multifaceted lives of Black LGBT people in the United States, their social circumstances, and how factors intersect at the individual, interpersonal, and structural levels to impact their health. Specifically, the health of bisexual women and men, transgender men, transwomen and women who have sex with women, men who have sex with men, and youth was investigated. A two-pronged approach that acknowledged both risk and resilience was used throughout the book to achieve a fairly balanced assessment of Black LGBT people's health. Overall, this volume illuminated that fact that Black LGBT people in the United States are efficacious human beings who purposefully act in response to and outside of systems of oppression to achieve and maintain their health. It is hoped that researchers, practitioners, policy makers, and lay people will be inspired by the scholarship in this volume to develop, fund, and disseminate health initiatives that center the voices of Black LGBT people and help them live holistic, affirmed lives.

Index

abuse:
  and family rejection, 13, 94;
  and incarceration, 15–16;
  intimate partner violence (IPV),
    29–31, 59;
  reproductive coercion, 29–31, 205;
  sexual, 26, 76–77;
  and trans/gender-nonconforming
    people, 73, 76–77.
  See also sexual assault and rape
Affordable Care Act, 82
Africa, 40–43, 42–44, 52n2, 57
Afrocentric theory:
  and Eurocentrism, 126, 128–31, 204;
  and intersectionality, 121–32;
  and research, 34
AIDS. *See* HIV/AIDS
alcohol abuse. *See* substance abuse
AmASSI Health and Cultural
  Centers, 7n1
American Cancer Society, 104, 107,
  115n4
American Civil Liberties Union
  (ACLU), 15
American Labor Party, 45
American Psychiatric Association, 125
American Psychological Association, 88
anal sex, 31
anarchism, 45

arthritis, 27
Asante, Molefi, 126
Asian American people, 58, 192, 194, 198

Balagoon, Kuwasi, 45–46
Baltimore, Maryland, 74
bathrooms:
  gender neutral, 18, 78;
  North Carolina law, 97
BDSM and kink, 50
Benjamin, Harry, 88–89
biphobia. *See* bisexuality
bisexuality:
  among Black men, 39–52, 58, 60–62,
    65, 121, 137–44, 151–63;
  bi-negativity and biphobia, x, 29,
    52n3, 56–63, 206;
  Bisexual Manifesto, 51n1;
  in Black radical politics, 44–45;
  in college settings, 29;
  diversity of, 55;
  generational differences, 63;
  and homonormativity, 57–59, 64;
  identity development, 29–31, 33–34;
  and intersectionality, 25–26;
  and intimate partner violence, 30, 59;
  lack of information about, x–xi, 25;
  literature on bisexual women's
    health, 25–35;

and mental health, 31, 60;
and monosexism, 63, 65, 206;
in music, 57;
and poverty, 58;
and reproductive health, 30–31;
and role flexibility, 62;
and STI risk, 31–32;
visibility of, 58, 64–65;
and whiteness, 64
biwoc.org, 65
Black Funk, 49–51, 206
Black Gay Research Group, 50
Black Liberation Army, 45
Black Men's Xchange, 7n1
Black Panther Party (BPP), 45
Black sororities and fraternities, 6, 58,
      111, 172
Black Transmen Incorporated, 83n2
Black Women's Health Imperative, 108
Black Women's Health Project, 108
Brazell, Rashawn, 50
Breast Cancer Action, 109
Brotherhood of African Men, 47
Brown, Carlett A., 89
Brown Boi Project, 83n2

California State University, Fullerton, 90
cancer:
   anal, 127;
   breast, ix, 105–8, 206;
   causes, 109;
   colon, 80;
   disparities in mortality rates, ix,
      104–5;
   endometrial, 104–6;
   gynecological, 3, 108;
   kidney, 105;
   leukemia, 105;
   lung, 105;
   non-Hodgkin's lymphoma, 105;
   "pink ribbon" culture, 107–9, 112;
   in queer communities, 103–15;
   research, 113;
   risk factors, 105–6, 108;
   screening for, 109, 112;

spiritual coping strategies, 103;
support groups and organizations,
      107–9;
thyroid, 105;
and trans patients, 80;
and trauma, 3
chemical castration, 125
children and youth:
   adultification, 14;
   bullying, 17–18;
   homelessness, 12–13, 204;
   incarceration, 11–19;
   mentorship programs, 47;
   sexual assault and rape, 15–16,
      19, 204;
   sex work, 13
civil rights organizations, 58, 172
class:
   in academia, 97;
   and Black feminism, 43;
   and Black sexual minority women, 26;
   and cancer survival rates, 105;
   and discrimination, 4;
   and health insurance, 111, 205;
   and intersectionality, x, 2, 43, 95,
      97, 154;
   and mental health, 96;
   middle-class homonormativity, 44;
   pink-collar work, 111, 115n7;
   and "pink ribbon" culture, 112;
   race as proxy for, 139;
   and self-rated health, 185–86;
   and stigma, 2;
   and stress, 97–98;
   and transphobia, 97
Clinton Correctional Institution for
      Women, 45
Colorlines.com, 65
Combahee River Collective, 125, 187
coming out. *See* identity disclosure
Compton's Cafeteria riot, 89
conceptual incarceration, 2–3
condom use. *See* sexual protective
      behaviors
conversion therapy, 19, 88, 93–94, 125

coping strategies:
  altering one's presentation, 62;
  avoidance, 107;
  avoiding same-sex sexual behavior, 62;
  and cancer, 107, 109–10;
  challenging gender norms, 154–55;
  communication styles, 154–55;
  confronting discrimination, 62,
    177–78;
  dance, 2, 16, 103, 204–5;
  drug use, 81;
  identity disclosure, 139–44;
  oppositional consciousness, 42,
    55, 188;
  physical violence, 178;
  prayer, 180, 205;
  psychotherapy. *See* mental health;
  queering language, 154;
  racial/ethnic pride, 2, 41, 62, 188;
  safe spaces, 160–61;
  self-acceptance, 62;
  and self-definition, 99, 181;
  social support networks, 1–2, 41, 62,
    81, 90, 99, 107–9, 178–79, 188,
    204–5;
  spirituality and religion, 1–2, 26,
    61–62, 81, 93, 97, 99, 109–10,
    156, 180–81;
  visual and performing arts, 2, 16, 39,
    204–5
Crenshaw, Kimberlé, 125, 187
cultural competency and diversity
    trainings:
  about Black bisexual women, 33;
  for health care providers, 33, 74,
    128–31, 204;
  at juvenile detention facilities, 17–18;
  for law enforcement, 18;
  for teachers, 18;
  for therapists, 153–54

dance, 2, 16, 81, 103
DC Bisexual Women of Color
    Collaborative, 64–65
Denmark, 89

diabetes:
  among Black trans men, 205;
  and obesity, 27;
  racial disparities, ix, 33, 111;
  and stress, 78
disability and ability:
  in Black cancer support groups, 113;
  and homonormativity, 44;
  and intersectionality, 154;
  as social identity, 43
discrimination:
  and access to health care, 105–6;
  adultification, 14;
  age, 188;
  body size, 27, 113;
  economic, 4, 63;
  in education, 63, 142;
  employment, ix, 58, 76–78, 90,
    98, 144;
  gender, ix, 74;
  in health care, 78, 142;
  and health policy, 4;
  HIV status, 151;
  housing, ix, 76–78, 98, 144;
  institutional, 3;
  at juvenile detention facilities, 18–19;
  mental health effects of, 27;
  race, ix, 151;
  role in sociocultural health, 39,
    142–43;
  sexual orientation. *See*
    homonegativity;
  in social welfare organizations, 142;
  transphobia, 73, 75–78
"down low." *See* identity disclosure
drug abuse. *See* substance abuse
Du Bois, W.E.B., 104

electroshock, 88, 125
employment:
  discrimination in, ix, 58, 76–78, 90,
    98, 144;
  in higher education, 5, 142;
  services and resources, 2.
    See also sex work

Family Acceptance Project, 17–18
family rejection:
    coping strategies, 16, 203;
    economic effects, 13;
    and homelessness, 12–13;
    and media coverage of LGBT issues,
      97–98;
    and mental health, 13, 92–95;
    and religious communities, 92–93;
    services and resources, 17–18
Fanon, Frantz, 47
Farajajé, Shaykh Dr. Ibrahim
    Abdurrahman, 43, 46
feminist theory:
    Black feminism, 43, 125, 187–88;
    and intersectionality, 43, 125,
      187–88;
    and research, 34.
    See also womanist theology
food:
    allergens, 45;
    culturally appropriate resources,
      45, 112;
    diet and cancer, 105, 112;
    food deserts, 45, 112;
    food insecurity, 111;
    pantries and resources, 2
fraternities. *See* Black sororities and
    fraternities
Freire, Paulo, 47

gender norms:
    and binaries, 82;
    childhood messages about, 14, 29;
    masculinity, 154, 170–71, 181;
    and queer Black women, 114;
    and racist systems of domination,
      57, 88;
    resistance to, 1, 63, 82;
    and respectability politics, 57
government:
    Census Bureau, xii;
    child welfare system, 13;
    health departments, 5;
    Healthy People 2020, 185;

    hiring and recruiting Black LGBT
      people, 4–6, 18;
    Institute of Medicine, 185;
    medical experimentation on Black
      people, 124;
    research funding, 3, 5
Gray, Freddie, 74

Harlem ballroom culture, 16
Hawaii Youth Correctional Facility, 15
health care:
    access to, xi, 78–80, 105–6, 109,
      121, 127, 205;
    administrators, 6, 74;
    barriers for trans patients, 73;
    historical treatment of African
      Americans, 123–25;
    ideological underpinnings, 122;
    indigenous healers, 4, 6;
    integration of cultural resources, 6,
      39, 109, 205–6;
    sociocultural, 39, 45–46;
    therapists, 151–63;
    utilization, xi.
    See also health care providers; health
      insurance
health care providers:
    Black LGBT people as, 6, 203–4;
    cultural competency and diversity
      trainings, 33, 128–31, 204;
    education about Black trans health,
      74, 83;
    identity disclosure to, 32, 106;
    ideological assumptions by, 122–23;
    lack of diversity among, 126;
    for LGBT community, 50, 95–96;
    in mental health, 78–79, 151–63;
    negative interactions with, 27, 32–33,
      60, 79–80, 82;
    and queer Black women, 114;
    and trust, 126–27, 162–63;
    use of research, 35
health insurance:
    access to, 73, 205;
    Affordable Care Act, 82;

and cancer, 108;
and class, 111;
Medicaid, 82;
and transphobia, 79
heart disease:
in Black communities, 112;
and obesity, 27;
racial disparities, ix, 33, 111
heterosexism. *See* discrimination
Hill Collins, Patricia, 51, 113, 170–71
HIV/AIDS:
care adherence, 156;
discrimination, 151;
and identity disclosure, 137–44;
prevention programming, 139;
racial disparities, ix, 121, 137–38;
research among Black LGBT people,
x, 121, 137–44, 186–87, 204;
research on trans men, 73;
risk, x, 60, 73, 95, 137–44;
screening for, 144;
sexual disparities, ix;
social epidemiology, 143;
stigma, 137, 139–44;
and substance abuse, 60;
and trans health, 95, 98;
and trauma, 3
Holmesburg Prison Experiments, 124
homelessness, 12–13, 16, 26, 204
homonegativity and homophobia:
in Black communities, 140, 155–56,
172, 175–76, 188;
in Black families, 13, 177;
in Black women's cancer
organizations, 108;
childhood messages about, 29;
and heteronormativity, 57;
at historically Black colleges and
universities, 63;
internalized, 62, 139–40, 156, 182;
and intersectionality, x;
and isolation, 153;
in religious communities, 2, 13, 59,
89, 98–99, 104, 140, 156, 161–62,
170, 203;

research, 29, 169–82;
resistance to, 87;
role in sociocultural health, 39;
and slavery ideology, 87–88.
See also discrimination;
microaggressions
homonormativity, 44, 57–58, 64, 143
hooks, bell, 171
House Ball scene, 97, 154, 203
housing:
discrimination, ix, 76–78, 98, 144;
projects, 47;
rent strikes, 45;
services and resources, 16;
squatting, 45.
See also discrimination; homelessness
Howard Beach, 46
hypertension, 33

identity development, x, 29, 31, 170
identity disclosure:
among Black trans women, 90–100;
in Black churches, 64;
in Black communities, 26, 155–56;
"Don't Ask, Don't Tell," ix, 59, 90;
"down low," 44–45, 58, 65,
138–44, 159;
in families, 26, 177;
to health care providers, 32, 106;
and homonormativity, 44–45;
and identity "ranking," 155;
in religious communities, 26;
in safe spaces, 62;
selective, 62;
and sexual risk behavior, 137–44;
and stigma management, 139–44;
and threat assessment, 158–60
imperialism and colonialism:
in Africa, 40–41;
of the body, 42, 46;
by British, 42–43;
and Christianity, 88;
in cultural competency and diversity
trainings, 130–31;
and decolonization, 39, 46, 50–52, 206;

and homonormativity, 44;
legacy for Black Americans, 56–57;
and slavery ideology, 87–88;
by Spanish, 42
incarceration:
    and adultification, 14;
    of Assata Shakur, 45;
    and bisexuality, 31;
    juvenile detention, 11–19, 204;
    of Kuwasi Balagoon, 45–46;
    in mental institutions, 88, 94, 125;
    probation, 14;
    and racism, 56–57;
    research on, 12;
    school-to-prison pipeline, 13–15;
    sex offender registries, 16;
    and sexual assault, 15–16, 204;
    of transgender/GNC youth, 14
intersectional theory, x
    and ability, 154;
    and Afrocentrism, 121–32;
    and Black feminism, 43, 125, 187;
    and Black queer men's identities,
        154–56;
    and Black trans men, 77, 82–83;
    and coping strategies, 169–82,
        203–4;
    and Critical Race Theory, 110;
    and identity disclosure, 138;
    and imperialism, 39–40;
    and masculinity, 154;
    and research, 34, 125–26, 185,
        187–88;
    and respectability politics, 95;
    and womanist theology, 110–15.
    See also class; racism
intersex people, 51n1
intimacy, 48–49
intimate partner violence (IPV).
    See abuse

Jackson State University, 16
Jamaica, 42–43, 94
Johns Hopkins Bloomberg School of
    Public Health, 74

Koch, Ed, 46–47

Latino/a people, 12, 89, 192, 194
laws:
    antidiscrimination, 4, 74;
    on bathroom use, 97;
    against conversion therapies, 19;
    curfew, 12, 19;
    employment discrimination, ix;
    environmental, 4;
    against gendered spaces, 19;
    against homosexuality, 88;
    housing discrimination, ix;
    marriage, ix, 93, 97, 142;
    Prison Rape Elimination Act, 19;
    trade, 4;
    against unwarranted searches, 19
LGBT Cancer Network, 107
liberation:
    and Afrocentrism, 126;
    from internalized homophobia, 140;
    and psychopolitical wellness, 56;
    and struggle, 39
Linda Creed Breast Cancer
    Foundation, 108
Lorde, Audre, 52n5, 88, 104
Los Angeles, 47, 63
Louisiana Swanson Center
    for Youth, 15
love:
    in chosen families, 65, 203;
    and mental health, 98–99;
    positive examples, 159–60;
    as resistance to discrimination, 65,
        179–80;
    self-love, 62, 65, 206

Manago, Cleo, 7n1
maroons:
    communities, 47–51;
    health paradigms, 40–52, 206;
    historical roots, 39–40, 42–43, 51;
    and identity disclosure, 44–45
Martin Luther King Jr. Day, 65
McNeal, John, 172–73

media, 58, 64–65, 142
mental health:
　among Black trans men, 73;
　anxiety, x, 91–92, 96, 107;
　bipolar disorder, 60, 78;
　and bisexuality, 30;
　depression, x, 13, 27, 31, 60, 78–79,
　　81, 91–92, 94, 96, 151, 205;
　Diagnostic and Statistical Manual
　　(DSM), 88, 95–96;
　disparities, 3, 185;
　eating disorders, 27;
　"gender dysphoria," 95–96, 98;
　homosexuality as disorder, 125;
　individualist orientation of, 45;
　medications, 96;
　mutual aid for, 100, 151–63;
　and obesity, 27;
　pathologization of LGBT people, 88;
　post-traumatic stress disorder
　　(PTSD), 31, 205;
　preventive services, 82;
　psychoanalysis, 88;
　psychotherapy, 93, 95, 100, 125,
　　151–63, 205–6;
　research, 29, 151–63;
　schizophrenia and related disorders,
　　91–92, 95, 124;
　and slavery ideology, 87–88, 124;
　and stress, 78, 92–93;
　suicide, 3, 79, 88, 94, 96, 121;
　and trans/gender-nonconforming
　　people, 78–79, 82;
　and trauma, 3, 31.
　See also stress; trauma
microaggressions, 17–18, 39, 159–60
migraine headaches, 78, 205
Minority Stress Model, 83
Missouri, 110–15
mixed-race identity, 76, 192
music, 49, 57

National Youth/Student Alliance, 47
Native American people, 58, 192
neighborhood composition, 33

neoliberalism, 41–43
New York City, 44, 46–50, 89
Nickerson Housing Project, 47

obesity, 27, 33, 105
oppositional consciousness, 42
Orlando massacre, 170

patriarchy, 2, 39, 57–58
pedagogical displacement, 130–32, 204
Philadelphia, 48, 87, 90
Planned Parenthood, 115n7
Plutonium Experiments, 124
pneumonia, 45
polyamory, 47, 50
polygamy, 87–88
poverty:
　and access to health care, 80, 111;
　among bisexuals, 58;
　and cancer, 111;
　income disparity, ix
Pride events:
　Black dance groups in, 16;
　DC Black Pride, 48;
　exclusion of bisexuals, 59;
　in New York City, 48;
　in Philadelphia, 48, 90;
　racism at, 59;
　research at, 189
psychopolitical wellness, 55–56
public health, 45
　and food, 45;
　and lead exposure, 45;
　public health critical race (PHCR)
　　methodology, 110–15;
　self-rated health (SRH), 185–87,
　　189–94, 205

racial/ethnic pride, as coping strategy, 2:
racism:
　and beauty standards, 156;
　economic consequences, 142;
　environmental, 45;
　and health care providers, 126–27;
　and immigrants, 198;

and intersectionality, x;
Jim Crow segregation, 56–57, 176;
and mass incarceration, 56–57;
mental health effects of, 153,
169–82;
misogynoir, 2, 26;
and "pink ribbon" culture, 112;
and psychotherapy, 153–54;
within queer communities, 2, 44,
59, 99, 114, 140, 155–56, 159,
161–62, 176–77, 188, 204;
in relationships, 65;
in research, 139, 141;
role in sociocultural health, 39,
110–11, 142, 151;
systemic, 81;
and transphobia, 97;
white supremacy, 39, 44, 57.
See also discrimination;
microaggressions; slavery;
stereotypes
Rainey, Ma, 57
religion. *See* spirituality and religion:
reproductive health:
and bisexuality, 30;
pregnancy, 94;
reproductive coercion, 29–31, 205
research:
Black Gay Research Group, 50;
by Black LGBT researchers, xi–xii,
4–5, 75;
on Black sexual minority men,
74–84, 121, 137–44, 186, 188;
demands for health research, 5, 185;
dissemination, 5–6;
ethnography and
autoethnography, 40;
focus on risk narratives, x, 3, 33, 73,
162, 186–87, 204;
gatekeepers, 3;
on HIV/AIDS, 162;
longitudinal, 34;
mixed-methods, 34;
on pedagogical displacement,
131–32;

on positive experiences and
behaviors, 34;
public health critical race (PHCR)
methodology, 110–15;
on queer Black women and cancer,
113, 114n3;
on trans men's health, 73–84
resilience:
among elderly LGBT adults, 188;
of Black bisexuals, 31, 61–63;
of Black LGBTQ/GNC youth, 11,
16–17, 204;
and cancer, 110–15;
of incarcerated people, 16–17;
and psychopolitical wellness, 55–56;
research, ix–xi, 29, 198–99;
and resistance, 41–43, 55–66, 207;
Transconceptual Model of
Empowerment and Resilience
(TMER), 61–63;
and trauma, 41.
See also coping strategies
respectability politics, 57, 59, 95, 140
Revolutionary Armed Task Force, 45
Riggs, Marlon, 171
Ruth Ellis Center, 16–17

San Francisco, 89
schools:
bullying policies, 18;
gender-neutral bathrooms in, 18;
hostility to Black LGBTQ/GNC
youth, 12–13, 204;
school-to-prison pipeline, 13–15.
See also universities
sexism:
and intersectionality, 97;
misogynoir, 2, 26;
resistance among Black sexual
minority women, 26, 87;
role in sociocultural health, 39
sex-negativity, 29, 46
sex parties, 48–50
sexual assault and rape:
and bisexuality, 31;

in juvenile justice system, 15–16,
19, 204;
Prison Rape Elimination Act, 19;
recovery from, 41;
research, 29
sexual harassment, 15–18
sexually transmitted infections (STIs),
31–32, 151, 205
sexual protective behaviors, 29, 31–33,
50, 139, 156
sexual risk behaviors, 29, 31,
137–44, 198
sex work:
religious antipathy toward, 173;
and substance abuse, 94;
"survival sex," 13, 31, 98;
and youth, 13
Shades of Black, 151–63
Shakur, Assata, 45
Sharpton, Al, 46
sickle cell anemia, 33
Sims, J. Marion, 124
Sisters Network Inc., 107–8
slavery, 40, 42–43, 56–57, 87, 124, 171,
175–76
slurs, 15, 177
Smith, Bessie, 57
Social Justice Sexuality Project, 185–86,
189, 192–99
social media, 2–3, 64
social support networks:
and Black bisexual women, 34, 90;
for cancer patients, 107–15;
as coping strategy, 1–2, 81, 99,
178–79, 206;
and ethnic minority
identification, 141;
exclusion of bisexuals, 59–60;
from families, 91;
fraternities and sororities, 81;
for gender transition, 81;
and incarcerated youth, 16–17;
institutional, 58–59;
and mental health, 60;
and parenting, 26;

for parents of queer youth, 18;
social media, 2–3, 64.
See also coping strategies;
spirituality and religion
sororities. *See* Black sororities and
fraternities:
spirituality and religion:
affirming churches, 61–62, 98–99,
156, 162, 179, 203;
among Black bisexual men, 41;
Baptist, 92;
Bible and Christian scripture,
111–12, 115n9;
Black churches, 59, 64, 89, 98–99,
104, 112, 160–61, 171–73;
Catholicism, 92;
as coping strategy, 1–2, 26, 61, 91,
97, 99, 179–80, 182, 203;
and identity disclosure, 26, 64,
139–44;
Kemetic spirituality, 47;
meditation, 47;
Pentecostalism, 92;
prayer, 81, 93, 103;
religious homonegativity, 2, 13, 31,
59, 89, 92–93, 98–99, 104, 140,
156, 161–62, 170, 203;
research, 29;
and resilience, x, 61–62;
ritual, 39;
sacred spaces, 39;
tai chi chuan, 47;
theology, 43, 109–15, 172–73;
Vodou, 103, 113, 114n1;
yoga, 47, 50;
and youth, 13
state violence, 39, 47, 74, 81, 88–89
stereotypes:
of Black men, 82, 122–25, 156,
180, 199;
of Black youth, 14;
effects on health care, 124–25;
ethnosexual mythologies, 25–26,
57–58, 82, 123, 156, 162–63,
170, 199;

of gay men, 159, 162–63, 180;
and slavery ideology, 171
Stonewall Riots, 44, 89
stress:
    and alcohol abuse, ix, 88, 93, 151;
    and cancer survival rates, 105;
    and class, 97–98;
    disparities in, ix;
    "double jeopardy," 198;
    and drug abuse, ix, 81, 151;
    health effects, 78;
    and media coverage of LGBT issues,
        97–98;
    mental health effects of, 92–93;
    Minority Stress Model, 83;
    from religious homonegativity, 89.
    See also mental health
substance abuse:
    alcoholism, 88, 93, 105;
    among bisexuals, 60, 121;
    among Black sexual minority
        women, 26;
    among queer Black men, 151;
    and cancer risk factors, 105;
    as coping strategy, 81, 94;
    disparities in, ix, 26;
    drug arrests and sentencing, 12;
    as HIV risk factor, 60;
    racial disparities, 121;
    religious antipathy toward, 173;
    sexual minority disparities, 185;
    tobacco use, x, 26–27, 93,
        105–6, 185
suicide. *See* mental health
Susan G. Komen for the Cure, 107, 112,
    115n5, 115n6, 115n7

tendonitis, 78, 205
terminology:
    African, 52n2;
    biphobia, 63;
    bisexual, 51n1, 66n1;
    Black churches, 171–72;
    cisgender, 100n1;
    definitional power, 63–65, 127;

disidentification, 52n4;
    expert power, 132n1;
    gender dysphoria, 95–96, 98;
    genderqueer, 51n1;
    heterosexism, 171;
    intersex, 51n1;
    LGB, 7n2;
    LGBT, 7n1;
    monosexism, 52n3;
    queer, 66n2, 114n2;
    resilience, 41;
    same-gender loving (SGL), 7n1, 7n2;
    siblings, 66n3;
    trans sexuality, 88–89
terrorism, 39
Theatre of the Oppressed, 47
therapeutic use of self, 151–63
transgender and gender nonconfirming
        (GNC) people:
    in Baltimore, 74;
    delaying or avoiding health care, 80;
    educational opportunities for, 98;
    employment needs, 98;
    fraternities, 81;
    gender-affirming surgery, 76,
        88–89;
    health care needs of, 6, 19, 73–84,
        95–96, 98, 205;
    housing needs, 98;
    laws protecting, 18–19;
    and mental health, 73, 78–79, 82,
        96–99;
    ostracism among, 99;
    school policies, 18–19;
    transition, 19, 76, 96;
    unwarranted searches of, 19;
    youth incarceration, 14.
    See also transphobia
transphobia:
    among health care providers, 79–80;
    and Black trans men, 73–84;
    and class, 97;
    and HIV/AIDS, 98;
    and intersectionality, x, 2;
    misgendering, 73;

refusal of care, 73;
in religious communities, 98–99;
resistance among Black sexual
  minority women, 87;
violence, 73.
See also discrimination; transgender
  and gender nonconfirming (GNC)
  people
trauma:
  among Black bisexual women,
    31, 33;
  and family rejection, 13;
  and hostile school climates, 14;
  of oppression, 3;
  and PTSD, 31, 205;
  and resilience, 41;
  treatment programs, 18, 159
Truth, Sojourner, 125, 187
Tuskegee Study of Untreated Syphilis
  in the Negro Male, 124

universities, 5–6, 47, 59, 63
University of Georgia, 173
University of Pennsylvania, 96
University of Southern California, 47

Walking in the Spirit, 110–15
Wall, L. L., 124
Washington, DC, 64–65
West, Crissle, 64
West Indian people, 76
white supremacy. *See* racism
Williamson, Lisa, 47
Witness Project, 108
womanist theology, 109–15
World Professional Association for
  Transgender Health, 19

yeast infections, 32

Zumba, 112, 115n10

About the Editors and Contributors

Roberto L. Abreu, MS, Ed. S., is a doctoral candidate in Counseling Psychology at the University of Kentucky. Roberto received a Bachelor in Science Education and a Master in Clinical Mental Health Counseling from Florida International University. As a Latino gay-identified man, Roberto's research interests include the well-being of sexual minority and gender expansive people of color. More specifically, Roberto is interested in Latina/o LGBT youth and parental and community acceptance. Roberto's clinical experience includes working with children and adolescents on the Autism spectrum, LGBT teenagers and young adults, college students, and incarcerated men and women with severe mental illness.

Siobhan Brooks is an assistant professor of African American Studies at Cal State Fullerton. She received her PhD in sociology from New School University. Brooks' work explores the intersections sexuality, race, gender, class, and mental health among LGBT urban identified Black women. She is the author of *Unequal Desires: Race and Erotic Capital in the Stripping Industry* (SUNY Press, 2010), which won the 2008 Queer Studies Prize. Brooks' current research examines the ways inner-city Black LGBT identified women negotiate identity and homophobia within their home communities in Philadelphia, and how Black lesbians in Los Angles view gay marriage.

Dante' D. Bryant is a doctoral student in the School of Social Work at the University of Texas at Arlington (UTA). He serves as an adjunct faculty member at the UTA and the University of North Carolina at Charlotte. Mr. Bryant has worked in mental health for more than ten years and holds graduate degrees in psychometric psychology, theology: western-philosophical pragmatism, and social work. Mr. Bryant's research interests include theoretical development within and the critical social critique of social work practices, cultural competency within helping professions, the persistence of discursive practices within social work education, and structural violence within formal institutions.

Lawrence O. Bryant has over forty years of experience in healthcare and human services. He earned a master's degree in public health from Emory University in 2001 and his doctorate in Lifelong Learning, Administration, and Policy from the University of Georgia, Athens in 2008. He has worked as an instructor, conducted research, evaluated programs, and developed curricula. Dr. Bryant is an expert in the use of technology to enhance instruction and learning. He is currently working at Children's Health Care of Atlanta and DeKalb Medical Center as part-time respiratory therapist.

Candice Crowell earned her PhD from the University of Georgia in 2015. She is an assistant professor at the University of Kentucky. Dr. Crowell's research interests include sexual health broadly, with a specific, although not exclusive, focus on Black sexuality. Her secondary research focus includes cross-cultural education and training issues in psychology (e.g., social justice, cultural competence, and leadership). Candice employs an integrated use of interpersonal process theory (Teyber model) and multicultural focus for her theoretical orientation. She has served as a leader in the American Psychological Association, the American Psychological Association of Graduate Students, and the Society of Counseling Psychology. She is an American Psychological Association Minority Fellow.

Sannisha K. Dale, PhD, Ed.M., is an African American clinical psychologist and researcher at the Massachusetts General Hospital/Harvard Medical School. Her primary research interests are (a) enhancing our understanding of the relationships between resilience, trauma, and health outcomes among individuals with HIV and those at risk, (b) investigating psychosocial (e.g. discrimination) and structural environmental factors (e.g. poverty) that relate to health disparities, and (c) developing prevention and intervention strategies to promote resilience and good health outcomes among survivors of trauma and individuals with or at risk for HIV, especially Blacks/African Americans and men who have sex with men.

Lourdes Dolores Follins, PhD, LCSW, is a clinical social worker and an associate professor at City University of New York. For over twenty-five years, Dr. Follins has worked as a psychotherapist, an organizational consultant, and a behavioral scientist. Her research and clinical interests are resilience in LGBTQ people of color; decision making in young gay men of color;

health disparities facing LGBTQ people of color around the world; and the experiences of historically underrepresented faculty at community colleges.

Rahwa Haile completed her doctoral studies in public health at the University of Michigan. She is currently an assistant professor of public health at SUNY Old Westbury, and also serves as a director of the SUNY Old Westbury Health Disparities Institute. Dr. Haile's areas of interest include the political economy and social determinants of health and illness. Her recent research projects have focused on the role of stigma and social inequalities in facilitating and contributing to racial disparities in HIV/AIDS among sexual minority men in the United States. Dr. Haile is interested in employing both human rights and community based participatory approaches to addressing racial disparities in health.

Angelique Harris is associate professor of sociology in the Department of Social and Cultural Sciences and Director of Center for Gender and Sexualities Studies at Marquette University. Her research and teaching interests include medical sociology, race and ethnicity, gender and sexuality, religion, urban studies, media studies, and social movements. Dr. Harris's research examines social problems and issues within marginalized communities, primarily focusing on the experiences of women, people of color, and LGBTQ+ communities. She has authored the book *AIDS, Sexuality, and the Black Church: Making the Wounded Whole* and co-authored the writing reference book *Writing for Emerging Sociologists.*

Tfawa T. Haynes, MSW, LICSW, is a Jamaican, Black gay, cisgender male clinical social worker and research study therapist at Fenway Health and The Fenway Institute. He also serves as an adjunct professor at Simmons College. He received his MSW from Boston University focusing on group work and trauma. His areas of interest include intersections of race and gender identity among LGBTQs; transgender care; immigration and acculturation; homelessness; and chronic illnesses. Black men who have sex with men (MSM) are a significantly underserved subgroup and to help meet their needs at Fenway Health. Mr. Haynes created and facilitates the *Shades of Black Group.*

LaShaune P. Johnson is an assistant professor in the Master of Public Health program at Creighton University. She is a medical sociologist with an interest in health disparities. She is a two-time cancer survivor who received the Sociologists for Women in Society's Barbara Rosenblum Dissertation Scholarship in 2009. Since 2013, she has been the co-chair of the Omaha Area Metro African American Breast Cancer Task Force, an educational group. She is also interested in the use of faith-based and community-based outreach to improve health disparities and has conducted research in Black churches and Islamic community centers.

Jonathan Mathias Lassiter, PhD, is a twenty-first-century polymath utilizing psychology, writing, and dance to help others heal and thrive. As a clinical psychologist, he specializes in health psychology, spirituality, and multiculturalism. Currently, he is assistant professor of psychology at Muhlenberg College and Resident Choreographer at Psychosomatic Dance.

Jane A. McElroy is an associate professor in the Research Division of the Department of Family and Community Medicine at the University of Missouri. She is an epidemiologist with emphasis on gynecological cancers through exploring etiology through biomarker analysis and patterns of disease incidence and prevalence associated with environmental exposures. Recently she has focused on cadmium exposure and endometrial cancer risk in a case-control study design funded by the American Cancer Society. She has received grant awards from Susan G Komen with the goal of improving breast cancer for underserved women. Many of her papers have reported on female cancer risk.

Della V. Mosley, M.S., Ed. S., is a doctoral candidate in Counseling Psychology at the University of Kentucky (UK) and a scholar-activist in the movement for Black lives. Della received her MS in School Counseling from The John Hopkins University and her Ed. S. in Counseling Psychology from UK. As a Black bisexual cisgender woman, Della's clinical and research interests focus on the processes of oppression (racial-, gender-, and sexuality-based) and liberation, particularly among Black youth. Della also engages in social justice advocacy through managing the website www.blmactivism. com and facilitating healing justice interventions for communities suffering from identity-based traumas. She is an American Psychological Association Minority Fellow.

Kasim Ortiz is a doctoral student in the Department of Sociology at the University of New Mexico (UNM), as well as a Health Policy Fellow with the Center for Health Policy at UNM. His research and teaching centers upon understanding the influences of social determinants on health as a social stratifying mechanism undergirding health inequities; particularly among racialized sexual minorities. More broadly he is interested in discrimination (institutional & interpersonal), mass incarceration and punitive environments, neighborhoods and spatializing processes, and political contexts and social activism. His current research investigates how neighborhood contexts (especially neighborhood disadvantage and residential segregation) impacts health behaviors among racialized sexual minority populations in the United States.

Mark B. Padilla completed his doctoral studies in anthropology at Emory University. He is currently an associate professor in the Department of Global and Sociocultural Studies at Florida International University. He is a medical anthropologist with cross-training and experience in public health both domestically and internationally. Most of his work is located within the productive synergy between anthropology and the more applied concerns of public health. As an anthropologist trained in ethnographic methods, globalization, and critical medical anthropology, he has sought to trouble the terms of discourse and "intervention" in public health, and to bring structural inequalities and material processes into greater focus in public health.

Edith A. Parker completed her doctoral studies at the University of North Carolina School of Public Health, and is currently professor and head of the Department of Community and Behavioral Health at the University of Iowa, where she also serves as director of the Prevention Research Center for Rural Health, and professor within the Public Policy Center. Dr. Parker's research focuses on the design, implementation, and evaluation of community health promotion interventions to improve health and to reduce racial disparities in health. Her work also focuses on translating and disseminating research findings for program and policy change. She has served as an invited member of the US EPA National Advisory Committee for Environmental Policy and Technology and is an expert on community-based participatory research.

Kenneth Maurice Pass is a PhD student at Northwestern University in the Department of Sociology. Kenneth is interested in studying the social stratification of sexualities within marginalized communities through the prism of health. His broad interests are improving the health and lives of Black gay, bisexual and queer (GBQ) men through innovative partnerships and community-based participatory research. He is also interested in applying sociological theory in exploring how structural risks implicate sexual health inequities experienced by Black GBQ men and, moreover, how these individuals and communities organized and respond to those "risks." He works on domestic and global health projects that focus on young Black GBQ men and lesbian and bisexual women.

Tonia C. Poteat, PhD, PA-C, MPH, is an assistant professor in the Department of Epidemiology at Johns Hopkins Bloomberg School of Public Health and a clinician at Johns Hopkins Hospital. Dr. Poteat graduated from

Yale University with a Bachelor's degree in Biology in 1991 and received a Master of Medical Science from Emory University's Physician Assistant (PA) Program in 1995. She earned a Master of Public Health from Rollins School of Public Health in 2007 and completed a PhD in the Social and Behavioral Interventions Program in the Department of International Health at Johns Hopkins School of Public Health in 2012. During her twenty years as a PA, she has devoted her practice to providing medically appropriate and culturally competent care to members of the LGBTQ community as well as people living with HIV. Her research, teaching, and practice focus on HIV and LGBT health with particular attention to transgender health disparities. In 2014, she received the Johns Hopkins Diversity Leadership Award for her work to promote LGBT Health.

Amorie Robinson is a licensed clinical psychologist practicing in and around Detroit. She received her Bachelor's in Psychology at Oberlin College, Master's degree in Educational Psychology, and doctorate in Clinical Psychology at the University of Michigan. She works at the Third Circuit Court of Michigan Family Division's (Juvenile Court) Clinic for Child Study conducting therapy with adjudicated youth and their families. She also conducts psychotherapy at Northland Clinic and teaches at the Michigan School of Professional Psychology. She conducts LGBT/GNC cultural competency trainings for mental health providers and educators. Dr. Robinson is a co-founder of the Ruth Ellis Center, an agency serving at-risk LGBT/GNC youth and is president of the Metro Detroit Association of Black Psychologists.

Devon Tyrone Wade is a PhD candidate in the Department of Sociology at Columbia University. His research and teaching interests include social and racial inequality, perceptions of crime and deviance, social psychology, sociology of education, and social stratification. Devon's primary research examines the organizational structures of schools and their response to students' trauma and mental health concerns.

H. Sharif "Herukhuti" Williams, PhD, MEd, is professor of interdisciplinary studies in the undergraduate programs at Goddard College and adjunct associate professor in the applied theatre master's program at the City University of New York School of Professional Studies. He is founder and chief erotics officer of the Center for Culture, Sexuality, and Spirituality. He serves on the governing board of the Association of Black Sexologists and Clinicians as well as the editorial boards of *Journal of Bisexuality* and *Journal of Black Sexuality and Relationships*. He is a member of the Bisexual Research Collaborative on Health.